The Origins of
Modern Environmental Thought

The Origins of
Modern Environmental Thought

J. Edward de Steiguer

The University of Arizona Press
Tucson

The University of Arizona Press
© 2006 The Arizona Board of Regents
All rights reserved

Library of Congress Cataloging-in-Publication Data
De Steiguer, Joseph Edward.
The origins of modern environmental thought /
J. Edward de Steiguer.
p. cm.
Includes bibliographical references and index.
ISBN-13: 978-0-8165-2461-7 (pbk. : alk. paper)
ISBN-10: 0-8165-2461-0 (pbk. : alk. paper)
1. Environmental sciences—Philosophy. I. Title.
GE40.D48 2006
333.73—dc22
2006006338

Manufactured in the United States of America on
acid-free, archival-quality paper containing a minimum
of 50% post-consumer waste and processed chlorine free.

11 10 09 08 07 06   6 5 4 3 2 1

To Pam, Laura, and Philip, and to Sonny's memory

Contents

and president of Lamar University, Beaumont, Texas, provided me with an appreciation of the historical evolution of ideas. Victor Bilan, professor of forestry at Stephen F. Austin University, Nacogdoches, Texas, taught me about ecology, as well as about the terror of living in Europe during World War II. John McNeely, professor of agricultural economics, Texas A&M University, introduced me to much of the environmental literature contained in my book. Gene Avery, professor of forestry and noted writer about natural resources, first provided me with insights about writing and publishing. Gus Hall and Ernie Watson, in my youth, taught me to pitch a tent, make a campfire, cook a stew, sharpen an axe, sway in the breeze at the top of an eastern Texas pine tree, fish sandy-bottomed Big Cow Creek and, generally, be at home in nature. All of their instruction was at least as valuable as my first four years in college. Finally, at the University of Arizona Press, I want to thank editor Allyson Carter for her faith in this project and Kirsteen Anderson for her excellent copyediting skills.

J. Edward de Steiguer
Tucson, Arizona

The Origins of
Modern Environmental Thought

1

Foundations of Environmental Thought

The state of the environment is one of the most important issues facing society. Public opinion polls indicate that about 50 percent of U.S. adults are concerned about air and water pollution, while more than 75 percent are disturbed about the effects of acid rain, nuclear waste, and global warming; an equal percentage believe that the environmental movement has been beneficial for society.[1] The world's inhabitants likewise share a wide range of environmental concerns, from the toxic effects of agricultural chemicals to the quality of the water they drink. Most elected officials must now treat environmental and natural resource concerns with the same seriousness that was usually afforded more traditional governmental interests such as the economy or national defense.

This high level of public concern has not always been evident, however. Prior to the 1960s, "the environment" was not often mentioned by politicians, the public, or the media. Aside from certain events seemingly isolated in place or time, such as the smog problems of Southern California or the natural resource conservation interest during the presidential administration of Teddy Roosevelt, environmental issues rarely received sustained public attention.

The one event more than any other that at last made environmentalism an enduring social issue was the 1962 publication of Rachel Carson's *Silent Spring*.[2] The impact of this book on public opinion was truly immense. Indeed, it was a singular historical occurrence. *Silent Spring* addressed the risks posed by pesticides. However, the book went far beyond a simple warning about toxic chemicals. It alerted society to the dangers inherent in traditional human attitudes toward the environment. As such, it made an immediate and lasting impression on the public, especially in North America and western Europe. Once people became aware of the possible threats from environmental problems, the issue simply would not vanish from view. From Rachel Carson's

warnings about pesticides to more recent events such as delibera-
tions over global warming, people are now concerned and even ob-
sessed with environmental quality and its impact on present and future
generations.

To say that *Silent Spring* ushered in the era of environmentalism,[3]
however, is not to suggest that *Silent Spring* alone was responsible for
the era. Rachel Carson's book simply confirmed public suspicions and
unleashed pent-up anxieties. Indeed, for most of humanity's time on
this planet, people have had to deal with environmental dilemmas
in one form or another.[4] The original concerns were with the immediate scarcity of hunting lands, food supplies, shelter, and other essentials provided at least in part by nature. From the dawn of human
existence, individual families and tribes of hunter-gatherers almost
certainly faced periodic resource shortages that threatened their existence. But by the late eighteenth century, the western world was beginning to experience rapid population growth and sweeping social
change. Thus, society came to recognize the theoretical possibility of
pervasive scarcities and famines that could threaten the existence of
civilization itself.

Population growth and natural resource scarcity have, therefore,
long been major societal concerns and, as such, major forces shaping
civilization. They have at times brought on terrible social disruptions in the form of war, conquest, illness, and death. Yet, the concern over resource shortages has also spurred humans to make many
achievements in the form of new technologies. From the plow to the
modern miracles of biological engineering, innumerable inventions
have sprung from the human mind for the purpose of extending nature's bounty.

Many would argue that along with its benefits, technology has
brought huge social costs as well. Events such as the Exxon *Valdez*
oil spill in Alaska's Prince William Sound and the Chernobyl nuclear
disaster in the former Soviet Union are unhappy reminders of the price
paid for technological progress. It was this concern about environmental degradation as an unintended side effect of technology that
inspired Rachel Carson to write her book. Thus, with *Silent Spring* a
new problem, environmental degradation, joined with the older concerns of population growth and resource scarcity to form the inter-

related central issues of modern environmentalism. Environmental study now focuses for the most part on these three key issues of human population growth, natural resource scarcity, and environmental degradation.[5]

Where Rachel Carson led, others soon followed. From 1962 to the mid-1970s[6] during the early years of the modern environmental era, numerous philosopher-scholars made pioneering contributions to what would later constitute a classic body of environmental literature. They came from a variety of academic disciplines including biology, history, theology, philosophy, computer science, and economics. Paul Ehrlich, Barry Commoner, Kenneth Boulding, and Garrett Hardin are among the best known and most frequently cited of these early contributors. Also important were scholars such as Roderick Nash, Fritz Schumacher, Stewart Udall, Lynn White, Harold Barnett, Chandler Morse, Ronald Coase, Donella Meadows, Dennis Meadows, Jørgen Randers, Arne Naess, and Herman Daly. A. C. Pigou, who was deceased by the time *Silent Spring* was published, became influential through the rediscovery of his writings.

The post–Rachel Carson environmental philosophers who are the subject of this book sought one common goal: the reform of human attitudes and behavior regarding the environment. Their hopes for achieving this reform ranged from realistic to idealistic; the specific methods they suggested ranged from incentives to punishment. Nevertheless, they all sought as a common goal the reform of human attitudes and behavior. In order to achieve this goal of social reform, they at times selected words and perspectives in order to gain maximum public attention. As a result, some of these authors' works were commercially successful. *Silent Spring*, as already noted, managed to make the best-seller lists. *The Population Bomb* by Paul Ehrlich, *The Closing Circle* by Barry Commoner, and *The Limits to Growth*, by a group of scientists from MIT, are examples of other writings that had widespread appeal. These writers played a valuable role in helping to popularize the environmental movement.[7]

Some of these works, however, were aimed at academic audiences. As such, they stimulated the various academic disciplines to pursue studies of the environment, a legacy that continues today. The impact of environmental interest by academicians has been, in fact, nothing short of remarkable. Collectively, these early literary offerings have over the years encouraged a massive number of books, journal articles, reports, and news articles concerning the environment.[8] Within a very short time, environmentalism grew in the university curriculum from a few meager course offerings to a wide array of academic classes appealing to a great range of student interests. Today, environmental education in the sciences, engineering, ethics, and related fields abounds at universities.

As innovative and pathbreaking as the works of these post–Rachel Carson environmental philosophers were, they were not without intellectual precedents.[9] For several centuries, scholars had been developing a tradition of environmental thought that would eventually serve as the foundation for the modern authors. Indeed, many of the ecological ideas espoused during the 1960s and 1970s were simply contemporary restatements of earlier environmental thought. This rediscovery and modernizing of previous scholarship was a significant contribution of the modern environmental philosophers.

Some have suggested that the early influences on modern environmentalism extend back to the philosophers of antiquity.[10] One of the oldest influences on the post–Rachel Carson literature—and one explicitly mentioned in the writings of Lynn White—was the medieval monk St. Francis of Assisi (1182?–1226). St. Francis, who lived the austere existence of a religious ascetic, is reputed to have held a deep appreciation for animals, plants, and all the things of creation. One of his most treasured acts was the Sermon to the Birds where he demonstrated that humanity, as a part of religious devotion, should concern itself with the welfare of creatures. His empathy for the whole of life was expressed in such moving ways and with such love that some regard him as a model of inspiration and hope for the future ecology of the Earth.[11]

Most of the individuals who provided the intellectual foundations for modern scholars of environmental thought lived much later than St. Francis. In fact, most appeared during and after the Industrial Revolution, which began in England about the middle of the eighteenth century.[12] Great Britain at the time was undergoing dramatic demographic and economic changes due to the Industrial Revolution, changes that caused scholars to formally consider the sustainability of natural resources and the resulting fate of civilization.[13] By 1760, British industrialization had begun a rapid economic expansion that would continue until about 1830. Production of coal and iron, the two key materials of early British industry, was soaring. Steam engines were developed to provide mechanical energy first to pump water from coal mines and then later to drive machines in the rapidly expanding cotton textile industry. Gas derived from the combustion of coal, in turn, provided fuel for lighting, and as a result factories were able to continue producing at night as well as during the day.

The increase in industrial productivity provided Britain with an economic advantage in foreign trade that created even more factories and more jobs. The cost of general consumer goods plummeted while wages paid to laborers increased markedly.[14] Because most manufacturing jobs were located in towns, urban populations boomed as people came in search of employment. And with people increasingly concentrated in the cities, the population grew even more rapidly. Urbanization provided ready access to mates and, despite the Dickensian images of urban squalor and hardship, living conditions improved enough to lower infant mortality rates and lengthen life spans. Indeed, the conditions of the Industrial Revolution initiated a world population explosion that continues even today.

Not surprisingly, the combination of a larger population and a more consumptive lifestyle raised questions about natural resource consumption and the survival of humanity. This social change was also occurring in a more intellectually permissive atmosphere. Scholars were freer to engage in serious and controversial academic inquiry. Thus, from these early studies emerged some of the first important theories regarding the fate of humanity in relation to natural resources and the environment. Following are some of the more important individuals and groups from the time of the Industrial Revolution and later who influenced the modern environmental philosophers.

Thomas Robert Malthus

One of the most influential contributors to modern environmental thought was the classical English economist and clergyman Thomas

Robert Malthus (1766–1834). He is best remembered for his famous 1798 treatise about the dire social consequences of diminishing agricultural production and excessive population growth. Malthus depicted an unhappy world where an expanding population, unable to produce enough food to feed itself, was kept in check only by famine, disease, and war. With this dismal hypothesis, Malthus, an economist, has been credited with triggering the modern environmental debate.[15]

Neo-Malthusians, proponents of the modern version of the Malthusian view, extended the concerns of Malthus to include the problem of environmental degradation due to pollution. Thus, the combination of resource scarcity and environmental pollution was thought to be enough to destroy civilization. The neo-Malthusians attributed environmental degradation and resource scarcity to a variety of causes, such as innate human sexuality, greed, the influence of religion, new technology, energy entropy, and, importantly, free-market economies.

To many neo-Malthusians the free-market economic system is at least part of the problem, if not the principal cause of environmental degradation. The free market is seen as a system whose inescapable end is to exploit the planet. In order to have investment capital, the entrepreneur is forced to generate a profit, and profits come from business growth, which in turn necessitates resource exploitation and, ultimately, resource exhaustion. Thus, with a market economy a vicious cycle is set in motion. To the neo-Malthusian, as to Karl Marx, capitalism is a system that has sown the seeds of its own destruction. However, unlike Marx, the neo-Malthusians see the cause of civilization's demise as population growth and resource exploitation, not the oppression of the working class.

There are differing degrees of pessimism among neo-Malthusian philosophers. At one end of the spectrum, the extreme neo-Malthusians are entirely fatalistic. There is no hope for any corrective action whatsoever; all is doomed. To the less fatalistic neo-Malthusians, remedial measures are possible, but only if they are extreme, even draconian: changing economic and political systems, changing religious orientations, taking direct nonpolitical action, depriving people of personal freedoms, using coercion, implementing mandatory birth control, and changing societal values. There is little faith in the voluntary ability of humans to prevent disaster.

John Stuart Mill

John Stuart Mill (1806–1873) was a utopian socialist philosopher and synthesizer of economic thought who advanced the theory of the stationary state economy in his 1848 book titled *Principles of Political Economy*.[16] His theory formed an intellectual bridge between the pessimism of the classical economists and the coming optimism of the neoclassical economists, and thus it is not difficult to see elements of both schools in his words. To Mill the issues of resource scarcity and environmental degradation were inseparably linked. He, like the Malthusians, recognized the possibility that humankind could destroy any hope for a tranquil existence through excessive population growth and exploitation of natural resources. At the same time, Mill was optimistic that humanity could stave off social demise through its own efforts. He thought that humans had the native capacity to turn away from the self-destructive path of overpopulation and excessive resource consumption.

Mill foresaw that increases in human population and wealth could not continue in perpetuity. At some time a steady—or as he said "stationary"—state would be reached where both population and consumption would stabilize. But he saw no particular advantage in postponing the inevitable; there was no reason why people who were already rich beyond reasonable need should continue to trample, elbow, crush, and tread on each other simply to double their consumption. What was needed in order to improve the human condition, thought Mill, was a stabilization of population, less resource consumption, and a better worldwide distribution of wealth.

In order to achieve the steady state, Mill advocated a simpler existence where people sought fulfillment through a higher-minded, intellectually elevated lifestyle. Thus, the stationary economic state by no means implied to Mill a stationary state of human improvement. There would always be room for improving mental culture, and for moral and social progress. Furthermore, he thought the chances for cultural improvement would be much better if the world would reject excessive wealth and consumption. In his philosophy Mill seemed a kindred spirit with his American literary contemporary Henry David Thoreau, who had also insisted that our lives needed "simplicity, simplicity, simplicity!"[17]

Henry David Thoreau

Henry David Thoreau (1817–1862) was a New England Yankee, poetic nature writer, and social critic who in his lifetime produced a large collection of books and essays. *Walden, or Life in the Woods,* published in 1854, is perhaps his best-known literary work and certainly the one that had the greatest impact on modern environmentalism. The basis for the book was his two-year stay in a snug, sparsely furnished cabin on the edge of Walden Pond near Concord, Massachusetts. During his time there, Thoreau talked with friends, swam and fished in the pond, cultivated a garden, read books, played the flute, walked a great deal, and observed nature. His study of nature was not as a scientist but rather as a poet who enjoyed a close personal relationship with what he saw. Thoreau's sojourn at Walden Pond, thus, has come to represent an idyllic life where the complexity and materialism of modern industrial society were rejected in favor of bare essentials and a closer relationship with the natural world.

The works of Thoreau, along with those of his mentor Ralph Waldo Emerson, are representative of the philosophical and literary tradition known as nineteenth-century American transcendentalism. Transcendentalism rejected science and objective experience as the basis for developing knowledge in favor of that derived from intuitive thought processes. The transcendentalists, in principle, rejected urban life in favor of nature in all its wildness. Transcendentalist writing expressed a romanticized vision of creation with an appreciation for sunshine, clean air, sparkling rivers, grand mountains, and the opportunity to be alone with nature.[18]

In his personal philosophy, Thoreau regarded all creatures as fellows and neighbors, members of the community of nature.[19] Every creature, he felt, was better alive than dead. Nature merited respect and reverence in its own right, regardless of the uses to which humanity might put it. He is remembered for his simple yet profound statement, "In wildness is the preservation of the world."[20] During his lifetime, Thoreau was virtually alone in his ideas, which were then unique in American literature and philosophy.[21] Henry David Thoreau is today regarded as an originator of ecosystem-centered thought and, as such, an important influence on modern environmental philosophy.[22]

George Perkins Marsh

George Perkins Marsh (1801–1882) was an American diplomat, scholar, and conservationist who in 1864 wrote *Man and Nature, or Physical Geography as Modified by Human Action.* This book significantly changed the way that society viewed its relationship to the environment. Marsh was educated at Dartmouth College and then practiced law for a time. However, his brilliant and inquisitive intellect led him also to study literature, the applied sciences, and foreign languages—of which he could speak twenty. He dedicated most of his life to public service, first as a congressman and later as a diplomat. His amazing career brought him in contact with such important personages as John Quincy Adams, Teddy Roosevelt, Zachary Taylor, and Abraham Lincoln.

While in the diplomatic service, Marsh served in Turkey and Italy, where he took the opportunity to study the geography and agriculture of the Middle East and the Mediterranean region. Through his studies, Marsh observed repeated patterns of human abuse of the natural environment, particularly through deforestation, throughout history. His accumulated knowledge on the destructive impacts of civilization on the environment was eventually summarized in *Man and Nature.* The work not only contained his own views and observations, it was also a grand synthesis of collected knowledge regarding the natural sciences. Marsh's concern was that expanding human populations would one day impoverish the planet.[23] He was comfortable with the idea of human dominion over nature provided that it was both careful and farsighted; however, he was also aware that humankind had been neither.[24] Marsh believed that although the proper care of the Earth's resources would ultimately have to be resolved through political processes, the problem was at its roots a moral issue. An early proponent of world ecology, Marsh has therefore been called the first environmentalist.[25]

Neoclassical Economists

The neoclassical school of economic thought followed the thinking of a late nineteenth-century group of revisionary English economists informally headed by Alfred Marshall (1842–1924). His neoclassical economics followed Malthus' treatise on population by one hundred years and Mill's work in political economy by some fifty years. Whereas the classicists had derived their theories from the philosophy of natural law—that is, the discerning by reason of a naturally endowed set of principles that order human life—the neoclassicists turned to models of markets and human behavior expressed in the form of graphs, mathematics, and differential calculus. This was to be the economics that students would one day endure in college classrooms, the economics of supply and demand curves, and of market equilibria prices and quantities. All told, it was a sharp theoretical departure from the classical economics school.

Natural resources and environmental quality became key issues for the neoclassicists. In contrast to neo-Malthusians, the neoclassicists did not think that the market system was the cause of natural resource depletion and environmental degradation. Indeed, the well-functioning market was the solution. Eliminating scarcity and environmental damage involved an assortment of market-based remedies that seem rather tame when compared to those suggested by the neo-Malthusians. Instead of draconian solutions, they suggested fixes such as taxes, subsidies, assignment of property rights, and negotiated settlements to readjust the market. The neoclassicists seemed to revel in human genius and adaptability, if only one could obtain the proper signals to guide one's corrective actions. Information from a well-functioning market was all that society needed to produce new technologies, a cleaner environment, and a bountiful future.

Modern neoclassicists see both environmental degradation and resource scarcity as problems, but environmental degradation is regarded as the more threatening to civilization. However, to the neoclassicists, both scarcity and degradation can be eliminated under the proper conditions. The existence of both is attributable not to sinister human intentions motivated by acquisitiveness and greed as one might suspect, but rather to a malfunctioning free-market system. If only the market system could be made to work correctly, it would send the proper signals to society. Technological adjustments and changes in consumption could then alleviate resource shortages and eliminate environmental damages.

John Muir and Gifford Pinchot

It is appropriate to examine the contributions of John Muir and Gifford Pinchot together. Once friends but later antagonists on environmental matters, they are frequently contrasted because of their differing views regarding the proper role of society in the care of wilderness and natural resources. John Muir (1838–1914) was a Scottish-born American naturalist, explorer, conservationist, writer, and founder of the Sierra Club. Gifford Pinchot (1865–1946) was twice governor of Pennsylvania, a professional forester, and the first chief of the U.S. Forest Service. Both men played pivotal roles in natural resource politics, especially at the end of the nineteenth and the beginning of the twentieth centuries. This was the era of the conservation movement (1890–1920), a time when the United States first began to cope in earnest with its passage from a frontier with freely available resources to a developing nation with finite natural resources. Muir advocated protection of the country's natural resources from human consumption, whereas Pinchot favored sustained human use and management of resources.

Muir's lifelong dedication to the preservation of wilderness began as a result of Civil War draft dodging. In 1864, when he was twenty-six years of age, Muir fled his Wisconsin home for the Canadian wilderness north of Lake Huron. In 1867, he again had an opportunity to observe the natural world while making a thousand-mile walk to the Gulf of Mexico. He later spent many years wandering the Yosemite Valley and the high sierra of California. His experiences with the natural environment led him to believe that nature existed foremost for its creator and that humankind must not value itself above the rest of creation. The basis of his respect for nature was his recognition that all creatures, including humans, were part of a single, interdependent community. This interconnectedness of nature prompted him to remark, "When we try to pick out anything by itself, we find it hitched to everything else in the universe."[26] Although Muir thought that all things had an inherent right to exist, he also believed in the preservation of natural beauty for the benefit of future human generations, making him a champion of the establishment of national parks and of saving the vanishing wilderness.

Gifford Pinchot, born to a wealthy family, was a member of the

American patrician class. He graduated from Yale University and in 1889–1890 attended the French national forestry school at Nancy upon the urging of his father. Thus, he became the first American formally educated in the profession of forestry. Although Pinchot went on to enjoy an illustrious career as a politician—once even running for the U.S. Senate—it was his years as a forester and a pioneering leader of the conservation movement that he remembered most fondly. President Teddy Roosevelt named Pinchot as the first chief of the U.S. Forest Service and, under Pinchot's leadership, the country's first national forests were established. He believed that the sole purpose of natural resources was to serve the needs of humans and that humans had an obligation to conserve those natural resources for future generations. Pinchot was interested solely in maximizing the productivity of those resources in which humans had a direct interest. As a forester, he sought to produce an abundant and lasting supply of commercial timber with little regard for the larger ecological implications of that productive effort.[27] Pinchot echoed the utilitarian sentiments of English philosopher Jeremy Bentham when he said that forests should be managed "from the standpoint of the greatest good of the greatest number in the long run."[28]

During the first decade of the twentieth century, Muir and Pinchot became embroiled in a debate that would come to symbolize two major competing environmental worldviews: resource development versus preservation.[29] The specific cause of the debate was a proposal to build a dam and reservoir in the Hetch Hetchy Valley adjacent to California's Yosemite National Park. Pinchot favored the development of the reservoir for the provision of water to the people of San Francisco. Muir opposed the plan, believing that the Hetch Hetchy should be preserved in a natural state free from human development. In the end, Pinchot was victorious and the dam was constructed. Both men struggled mightily to assert their views in the debate. Perhaps because of this struggle, coupled with his crushing defeat, Muir soon retired from public life and died not long afterward.

Today, it is easy to cast Muir as a hero and Pinchot in the role of environmental villain. In their day, however, Muir was considered the supporter of a shortsighted, elitist preservationist philosophy and Pinchot, the progressive conservationist whose views were in step with the prevailing public sentiment that natural resources should be used to enrich the lives of all Americans, not just the wealthy. Today, a few scholars, such as Char Miller, even see Pinchot, through his work to preserve the nation's dwindling forest resources, as an early environmentalist.[30]

Albert Schweitzer

Albert Schweitzer (1875–1965), born in Kaysersberg, Alsace, France, was one of the most accomplished intellectuals of the twentieth century. He was educated as a philosopher, theologian, physician, classical musician, clergyman, missionary, and writer. During his life, he enjoyed success and acclaim in each of these endeavors. He is perhaps best remembered for his work in humanitarian causes. In 1913, he devoted his life to serving as a medical missionary in a hospital he helped establish in French Equatorial Africa (now Gabon).

Throughout his life, Schweitzer held a deep regard for nature, which was a powerful force in his life. Writing in 1944, he recalled,

> Even when I was a child I was like a person in an ecstasy in the presence of Nature, without anyone suspecting it. I considered Nature as the great consoler. In her I always found calm and serenity again when I was disturbed. . . . It is said that I am a man of action. But at bottom I am a dreamer, and it is in reveries, reviving the living contact with Nature, that I gather the powers that make me an active being.[31]

Schweitzer's interest in nature, coupled with his humanitarian concerns, led him in 1915 to enunciate his reverence for life philosophy, the central tenet of which is that it is good to promote and preserve life. To Schweitzer, life did not simply mean human life, but rather all life forms, both animal and vegetable. He is even said to have found it painful to kill bacilli for study under his laboratory microscope.[32] Reverence for life was an attitude of mind, not a set of rules that one should follow. It required the individual to make decisions about the worth of creatures and act accordingly. This philosophy offered Schweitzer both freedom and the burden of responsible choice. The freedom arose from following what he deemed to be a proper philosophy of life. The burden came from the constant guilt he felt as he made particular choices regarding the fate of creatures. Reverence for life permits no boredom, no superiority, no isolation, no detachment because everything is a subject of concern and nothing is beneath notice. Although reverence for life seemed irrelevant in Schweitzer's time, it was important to Rachel Carson; she dedicated *Silent Spring* to his memory.

Aldo Leopold

Aldo Leopold (1886–1948) was born in Burlington, Iowa. He graduated from the Yale School of Forestry in 1909 and spent most of the next nineteen years employed by the U.S. Forest Service. For fourteen of those years he worked in the U.S. Southwest, where he helped develop some of the first Forest Service game management and outdoor recreation programs. From 1924 until 1928, Leopold was assistant director of the Forest Service Forest Products Laboratory in Madison, Wisconsin. Tiring of his career as a federal bureaucrat, he eventually resigned from the agency and in 1933 joined the faculty of the University of Wisconsin as professor of game management, the first such position ever created in the United States. He remained in that job until his death.

During his life, Leopold wrote a number of eloquent essays that provided philosophical insights regarding ecology, conservation, and environmental management. One of his most famous essays, "Thinking Like a Mountain," relates the poignant story of Leopold's own conversion, as it were, from utilitarian forester to citizen of the environment. The essay told of a true episode from Leopold's early days in the Southwest when, as a part of game management activities, he was shooting wolves to prevent them from killing deer. Leopold came on a mortally wounded she-wolf just before she expired and saw the "fierce green fire" dying in her eyes. "I was young then" he wrote, "and full of trigger-itch; I thought that because fewer wolves meant more deer, that no wolves would mean hunters' paradise. But after seeing the green fire die, I sensed that neither the wolf nor the mountain agreed with such a view." Borrowing from Thoreau he continued, "in wildness is the salvation of the world. Perhaps this is the hidden meaning in the howl of the wolf, long known among mountains, but seldom perceived among men."[33]

Certainly the most influential of Aldo Leopold's essays was "The Land Ethic," which was published posthumously in a volume of essays titled *A Sand County Almanac and Sketches Here and There*. In oft-quoted lines, Leopold wrote, "Quit thinking about decent land-use as solely an economic problem. Examine each question in terms of what is ethically and esthetically right, as well as what is economically expedient. A thing is right when it tends to preserve the integrity, stability, and beauty of the biotic community. It is wrong when it tends otherwise."[34] The significance of Leopold's land ethic to modern environmentalism is its view that there is inherent worth in the integrity of natural ecosystems apart from any value they may possess for humans. This ecological perspective rejects the view of land as mere property. Leopold agreed with the notion that humans could use land to satisfy their needs. However, land was not an object to be used, and perhaps abused, in any way that humans may desire. Leopold's ideal was one of a harmonious relationship between humans and the land, in which the land was treated as a community deserving of moral standing.[35]

The preceding summary of the foundations of modern environmental thought began with the work of St. Francis of Assisi in the twelfth century and concluded just after World War II with the works of Aldo Leopold. This brings us to within a few decades of the publication of Rachel Carson's *Silent Spring*. The ideas of the early philosophers constitute a diverse range of opinions concerning the causes of and solutions to the world's environmental problems. Environmental scholars have often attempted to synthesize these disparate ideas into a simpler, more coherent whole. One prevailing view is that the various environmental philosophies can be separated into two broad philosophies known as ecocentrism and anthropocentrism.[36]

Ecocentrism emphasizes an ecological, Earth-centered worldview. Its roots are found in the romantic transcendentalists of the nineteenth century, and it draws particularly upon the thinking of Thoreau, Muir, and Leopold. Ecocentrism maintains that the world was originally in a natural state of equilibrium until humanity intruded. Since then, the intricate web of life has been broken through a succession of degenerative disruptions that will ultimately lead to the destruction of the world itself.

Ecocentrism preaches reverence and care for the Earth and the humility of humanity in the face of natural laws. It decries conspicuous consumption, bigness, and urbanization. It demands of its adherents a code of behavior based upon ecological principles. Originally a philosophical and moral crusade, in recent years ecocentrism has become a focal point of radical politics and activism. In theory, ecocentrism

- supports a code of moral behavior based upon the limits of nature and ecology rather than human need,
- favors restraints on the drive for economic progress,
- questions the relevance of the principles of democracy especially as they apply to minority groups who may hold unpopular views, and
- encourages anarchy to correct extreme environmental degradation.

Anthropocentrism, the opposing philosophy to ecocentrism, holds that any and all human actions are by definition anthropocentric (i.e., human-centered). Therefore, any attempt by humans even to conceive of a system of ecocentric rights is impossible because this can be done only in the context of human values. Anthropocentrism admires humanity, technology, cities, and the development of political and economic systems. The environment is regarded as a neutral entity without moral standing and is available for humans to use in order to attain their ends. The beginnings of anthropocentrism are traceable to a prehistoric separation of humans from nature, possibly coincident with the rise of agriculture following the end of the last ice age 12,000 years ago. Its philosophical roots are found in the biblical injunctions to be fruitful and multiply, subdue the Earth, and have dominion over life, and in the thinking of the various economists, especially the neoclassicists, as well as Pinchot. In theory, anthropocentrism

- supports the rational and objective rather than emotional appraisal of social goals,
- encourages managerial and economic efficiency that attempts to produce the most material output with the least effort,
- has faith and optimism in the ability of humans to understand and control natural processes, and
- does not hold a sense of wonder, reverence, or moral obligation toward nature.

The ecocentrism versus anthropocentrism classification provides a simple and convenient means for categorizing environmental thought. Indeed, for some scholars, the ecocentrism/anthropocentrism separation essentially defines the current struggle to improve environmental quality.[37] There is, however, a degree of artificiality in this rigid categorization. In life, the boundaries between environmental worldviews are much more blurred.[38] It is quite possible, for example, for an individual simultaneously to support some elements of anthropocentric thinking while supporting some ecocentric ideals. Indeed, even though George Perkins Marsh was in a strict sense anthropocentric, in *Man and Nature* he also demonstrated a concern for world ecology. Thus, we should avoid the temptation to rigidly divide the world into two groups, one bad and the other good. This only serves to mask the possible common ground between differing environmental opinions and minimize the chance for understanding and mutual accommodation.

The search for understanding and accommodation in environmental policies is, indeed, the theme of this book. This was what Rachel Carson advocated in *Silent Spring*. She never supported a total ban on all agricultural chemicals. Instead, she advocated "accommodation" between humans and nature,[39] an approach that requires understanding of opposing environmental worldviews. The challenge for humanity is to examine the array of possible environmental positions, avoid the radical and the reactionary, and choose a viable middle ground between extreme ecocentrism and extreme anthropocentrism that will accommodate both human need and respect for environmental integrity.

Chapter 2 establishes the socioeconomic setting in the United States just prior to and during the period 1962 to the mid-1970s. The United States during those years, just like Great Britain during the Industrial Revolution, was undergoing dramatic change. Appreciation of these changing socioeconomic conditions is important to a complete understanding of the development of modern environmentalism. Following the discussion of socioeconomic conditions are chapters on Rachel Carson's *Silent Spring* and on subsequent environmental authors. These authors are presented chronologically, allowing the reader to explore these works in the same order in which they originally appeared. The book concludes with a glimpse beyond the age of the environmental philosophers. By studying the principal works from the early years of modern environmentalism, readers concerned with the environment—policymakers, professors, students, and citizens—can better understand and appreciate environmental thought.

2
Post–World War II Socioeconomic Conditions

Silent Spring and the related literature that followed it helped instill in the public a lasting concern for the environment. The alarming messages about increasing world population, excessive consumption of natural resources, and pollution stood on their own merits. However, the changing socioeconomic conditions in post–World War II America certainly facilitated the public acceptance of that message.[1]

The era of 1960s and 1970s was truly one of the most socially tumultuous in U.S. history. It was a time of widespread disenchantment with traditional social values, questioning of authority, and rejection of a lifestyle based upon materialism and consumption. These attitudes were most evident among middle-class youth, as evidenced by the following words written in 1969 by Youth International Party (Yippie) leader and self-styled revolutionary Jerry Rubin:

> The Youth International revolution will begin with a mass breakdown of authority, mass rebellion, total anarchy in every institution of the Western world. Tribes of longhairs, blacks, armed women, workers, peasants and students will take over. . . . The White House will become one big commune with free food and housing, everything shared. . . . The Pentagon will be replaced by an LSD experimental farm. . . . People will farm in the morning, make music in the afternoon, and fuck wherever and whenever they want to. The United States will become a tiny Yippie island in a vast sea of Yippieland love. . . . Money is shit. Burning money, looting and shoplifting can get you high.[2]

The socioeconomic changes that occurred during this era were a crucial and inseparable part of the modern environmental movement. Environmental concerns were very often intertwined with other key issues of the 1960s and 1970s such that one served to reinforce the other. This chapter surveys those crucial social and economic changes in post–World War II America and explains their influence on the development of modern environmentalism.

Entering into the 1960s, the United States faced several prominent issues that would forever alter the national character: the Cold War, the civil rights movement, the Vietnam War, the growing affluence and consumer culture of the American people, the increased interest in outdoor recreation, and the increased influence of youth culture upon U.S. society.[3] Each of these factors contributed to the questioning of traditional values. From that questioning came the pressure for changes to what the public perceived as inequitable, unjust, and outmoded social policies. There was a growing distrust in all forms of national leadership—in politics, the military, and business—much of it stemming from the government's handling of Vietnam. The Cold War and the nuclear arms race engendered a sense that technology, while conveying great benefits, also carried huge costs. The U.S. civil rights movement provided a model for vehement protest against civil authority. The growing affluence of the American people afforded them the luxury of being able to protest. Americans' increased access to and interest in the outdoors heightened concerns about the environment. And the growing American youth culture provided a highly energetic force pressing for social change.

In order to examine the historical development of these issues, it is helpful to begin in 1932, just thirty years prior to the publication of *Silent Spring*. The U.S. population was then 124 million—less than one-half its present level—and the nation retained something of an agrarian character, with 20 percent of the labor force still living on farms. The United States was in the depths of the Great Depression, the most severe and prolonged economic downturn the nation had ever experienced. From the joyous prosperity of the 1920s, the economy had descended rapidly to near rock bottom. Gross national product (GNP) was declining at an average rate of 10 percent per year.[4] One of every four workers, both agricultural and otherwise, was unemployed. In the nation's factories, unemployment ran as high as 37 percent. Industrial manufacturing fell by 54 percent. Industrial stocks on Wall Street lost 80 percent of their pre-Depression value. The downturn affected everyone—millionaire, factory worker, and farmer alike—as the American promise of ever-increasing prosperity was seemingly shattered.

President Franklin Delano Roosevelt attempted to stimulate a recovery with his New Deal programs. Unfortunately, government programs were not enough to revive the moribund economy; it would take World War II to accomplish that.

By 1939, the war in Europe had begun to generate a mild economic recovery in the United States. The unemployment rate improved to 17 percent as factories scrambled to fill orders for war matériel destined for the United Kingdom. On December 8, 1941, the United States declared war on Japan following the bombing of Pearl Harbor. On December 11, Germany and Italy declared war on the United States, thereby prompting a full-scale war mobilization effort. Not only soldiers and their families, but the whole of American society became involved in the war effort, and industrial capacity soared to meet the challenge of the war years. The rapid metamorphosis of the United States from ailing patient to industrial juggernaut was astounding. In 1939, the United States had just 350,000 men and women in the armed services. By 1945 the total was 12.3 million, a thirty-five-fold increase. The United States began the war with a fleet of 2,500 airplanes and 760 ships. Just four years later, the nation's civilian workforce had constructed 300,000 airplanes, 124,000 ships, 100,000 tanks, 2.4 million trucks, 41 billion rounds of ammunition, and 434 million tons of steel.[5]

By the end of the war, the United States and the combined Allied forces had crushed Germany and Japan to a degree never witnessed in modern warfare. Commented Donald M. Nelson, chairman of the U.S. War Production Board, "the course of the war had been a scheduled, systematic, and inexorable obliteration of our enemies."[6] Clearly, the United States had triumphed. It had been a victory not just for the armed services, but for the civilian workforce as well. Indeed, victory would not have been possible without civilians' personal sacrifices and energetic, almost total participation. Images of patriotism, justice, efficiency, and strength were vivid in the American mind. The words of national leaders enforced this view. General Dwight D. Eisenhower said, "America's record in production, as well as on the battle line, is one that will fill our histories forever."[7] President Roosevelt called America "the arsenal of democracy."[8]

Following the war, during the period from 1945 to 1962, the United States experienced a period of sustained economic growth as GNP increased steadily at about 2.4 percent per year. Beyond the excellent economic growth rate was a fundamental change in U.S. patterns of spending and personal consumption. The percentage of family income spent on necessities such as food and clothing fell from 53 percent to 33 percent. In contrast, the portion of the typical family's income going to luxury items such as new automobiles more than doubled from about 6 percent to 13 percent. The acceptance of one new technology—television—was perhaps the prime example of Americans' new zeal for consumer goods. Only a few thousand televisions were in existence in 1946, the first year of commercial broadcasts. Just ten years later, in 1956, there were thirty-four million sets in American homes reaching one hundred million viewers. Veterans of the armed services improved their opportunities for affluence with the help of new federal educational and home-purchasing assistance programs. With the impetus of these programs, the number of college degrees per 1,000 adults jumped from about 50 to nearly 225. The number of new houses built annually more than quadrupled between 1945 and 1962, from 326,000 to 1,469,000 units. By 1962 the population had increased to 186 million, and just 7 percent of the workforce now resided on farms. Unemployment was modest, averaging only about 4 percent per year.

From the growing affluence of the American public came also an increased interest in outdoor recreation. With more leisure time and a new interstate highway system providing rapid access across the nation, Americans were able more than ever before to visit and explore U.S. national parks, national forests, and wilderness areas. Much of this new recreational activity was different from traditional outdoor activities such as hunting and fishing in the sense that people simply wanted to interact with nature rather than consume it. Large numbers of Americans now participated in hiking, backpacking, canoeing, rafting, camping, nature study, and photography.[9] This increased interest in the natural world brought about pressure for new federal legislation to ensure excellent outdoor recreation experiences for present as well as future generations. Examples of some resulting laws include the Wilderness Act of 1964, the National Trail Systems Act of 1968, and the Wild and Scenic Rivers Act of 1968.

Since the Depression, the United States had clearly become a more urbanized, better-educated, more affluent, and increasingly consumer-oriented society. Pent-up demand from the Depression era and World War II exploded as the United States began amply rewarding itself after more than fifteen years of abstinence. Mixed with the good life, however, were serious domestic and international tensions. Immediately following the war, the United States fell into conflict with the USSR over the latter's use of military force to install communist governments in the shattered countries of eastern Europe. Because this practice ran counter to U.S. interests and also to the principle of self-determination of governed peoples, the two nations entered into the Cold War, a period of continuing political struggle that would last until the collapse of the Soviet Union in 1989.

Nuclear weapons became a central focus of foreign policy for both nations during the Cold War. Rather than serving as offensive weapons, long-range ballistic missiles were manufactured and placed in strategic positions principally for the deterrence of military aggression. One country's nuclear warheads were matched by the other's, resulting in an ever-escalating arsenal. During the 1950s, the Cold War nuclear arms race created a national mood that bordered on the absurd. Some citizens began digging atomic bomb shelters in their backyards, federal agencies drew up plans for mass evacuations, air raid sirens were placed in towns to warn of impending doom, and special radio stations periodically broadcast civil defense test warnings. In public schools, children were put through drills instructing them what to do in the event of nuclear attack. All this activity had an air of black comedy as Americans tried to enjoy the newly found fruits of affluence while living with the threat of a nuclear holocaust.

Despite national paranoia regarding "the bomb," Americans continued to place much of their faith for the future in science and technology. After all, these factors had been largely responsible for victory during World War II. The major international science initiative of the 1950s was the International Geophysical Year (IGY). This eighteen-month period of intensive scientific study of the Earth began in 1957 and involved thousands of scientists from some sixty-seven nations who collaborated on various projects to explore the depths of the oceans and the heights of the atmosphere. One surprise event of the IGY, the launching of the space satellite Sputnik I, served not only to shock the American public but to heighten Cold War tensions as well.

On October 5, 1957, the Soviets put the twenty-three-inch diameter aluminum sphere into orbit. One month later they launched yet another satellite, this time containing a canine passenger named Laika, and the space race was fully underway. The people of the United States, still basking in the glory of their World War II successes, were stunned. It would take nearly a year and a half before the United States could put its own satellite into space, but by then national confidence in the United States' world leadership had been badly shaken.

Domestic tensions also mounted during the period from 1945 to 1962. While the majority of Americans were enjoying the benefits of a growing economy, a significant minority population was becoming increasingly restive because of their continued exclusion. Black Americans had been free and equal under the law since the adoption in 1870 of the Thirteenth Amendment to the Constitution, which prohibited slavery. In truth, they had never attained either social or economic equality despite their important contributions to the nation's culture and, ironically, their wartime efforts.

Since the 1940s, various organizations such as the National Association for the Advancement of Colored People, the National Urban League, and the Congress on Racial Equality had been using nonviolent action in an attempt to effect change, but with almost no major successes. In 1954, in *Brown v. the Board of Education of Topeka, Kansas,* the U.S. Supreme Court had ruled that segregated educational facilities were inherently unequal thus unconstitutional. However, changes in the social condition of blacks were not immediately forthcoming. This would be achieved only slowly, painfully, and with much litigation, persistence, and violence. In 1957 Reverend Martin Luther King Jr. organized the Southern Christian Leadership Conference in Atlanta, Georgia, bringing the civil rights movement to the region of the country traditionally deemed to be the least racially tolerant and catapulting him to the forefront of the movement as its unchallenged leader. Despite King's advocacy of nonviolent methods, the struggle for equality continued to create great divisions among the American public. Black Americans' demands for racial justice and equality would become increasingly strident and militant as 1962 approached.

In 1962, American involvement in Vietnam was relatively small in scale. Within just six years, however, the United States would have nearly 550,000 troops in Southeast Asia, and Vietnam would be un-questionably the most divisive issue facing Congress, the president, and the American people.

During World War II, Japan had occupied what was then known as French Indochina, which comprised the countries of Vietnam, Cambodia, and Laos. Following Japan's defeat in 1945, local Vietnamese forces declared the region an independent republic. The French contested this move and attempted to reclaim the region by force. The United States contributed substantial financial support to the French effort, but in 1954 the French were finally defeated and abandoned Indochina. Two Vietnamese republics were then established, one in the south and a communist government in the north. In 1956, motivated by the "domino theory" (that is, if one country falls to communism, its neighbors will soon fall too), the United States put 760 military advisors in South Vietnam. By 1962, the number of advisors had grown to 16,000. Most Americans were at first supportive of the attempt to stem communist expansion. Because of the policy position taken by the U.S. government, most citizens regarded the conflict as a just cause against a despotic, third-rate communist country. By 1973, however, public opinion regarding the war had changed dramatically. Totally frustrated by the inability to win a war that was costly in terms of both human lives and dollars, and plagued with questions about the morality of their cause, Americans would be as anxious to depart Vietnam as the French had been nearly twenty years before.

By the 1960s even consumerism, the ultimate symbol of the good life in post–World War II America, was coming under fire. The person most responsible for making consumer protection a major public issue was Harvard-educated lawyer Ralph Nader.[10] In 1965, Nader wrote a book, *Unsafe at Any Speed,* which stated that defective design was the primary cause of automobile accidents and injuries. The following year, Nader testified on automobile safety before the U.S. Congress. Through these and related efforts, he motivated a strong public interest in protecting American consumers. In addition, he occasionally used his position as national spokesman to chide the public for its insatiable appetite for consumer goods. Nader's activities spread to other areas of consumer interest, such as food and drug products, natural gas pipeline safety, radiation hazard controls, tax reform, health care, and insurance rates. In 1968, he mobilized a group of college students known as Nader's Raiders to assist in his investigations. Among their many consumer protection activities, Nader's Raiders kept a close eye on the relationship between government regulatory agencies and the corporations they were charged with overseeing. Nader's efforts led in 1972 to the creation of the Federal Consumer Product Safety Commission, which was charged with responsibility for reviewing public complaints regarding defective and dangerous products. His activities also led to the creation of many other private consumer organizations, which were eventually united under the Nader-headed Consumer Federation of America, a group of more than three hundred organizations that represent consumer interests to Congress.

Because of these volatile social issues, the years that followed the publication of Rachel Carson's *Silent Spring* were among the most turbulent the United States has ever experienced. It was a time when three prominent public figures—John Kennedy, Robert Kennedy, and Martin Luther King Jr.—were assassinated. Pressures from the Cold War and the nuclear arms race intensified with events such as the construction of the Berlin Wall and the Cuban Missile Crisis. The civil rights movement grew increasingly militant with the rise of such groups as the Black Panthers and the Black Muslims. The Vietnam War created deep rifts among various segments of society about the necessity and justification for American military involvement. And all of this social strife was occurring during a period of growing personal affluence. Between 1962 and 1970 GNP increased at an annual rate of 4.2 percent, the greatest rise since World War II. Unemployment fell to its lowest levels in the postwar period. Both personal consumption expenditures and new home construction continued mounting to record levels through the 1960s and into the 1970s.

The period from 1962 to the mid-1970s was also especially remembered as a time when college-aged young people began to protest as never before against the traditional goals and mores of American society. Environmentalism, along with the war in Vietnam, was a prime focus of the students' concern. Some scholars have suggested these protests were essentially a reaction against the values and philosophies of their parents.[11] These youth had little knowledge of the personal and social sacrifices their parents had made during the Great Depression and World War II. They were largely affluent urban dwellers who had never toiled on a farm. Yet, while young people were comforted on one hand by a general affluence, they faced on the other the threat of being drafted for military service in Vietnam, a war that society increasingly perceived as unjust. Experimental use of drugs such as marijuana and psychedelics such as LSD became widespread among children of the middle class. Three youthful music stars—Janis Joplin, Jimi Hendrix, and Jim Morrison—died of causes that were either known to be or suspected of being drug related. This was the time of Woodstock and the Age of Aquarius, "the pill" and demands for greater sexual freedom, hippies and "flower power." From Cornell to Berkeley, the nation witnessed violent college protests against the war, racial injustice, and nuclear arms. On May 4, 1970, national guardsmen killed four antiwar protesters and wounded nine others at Kent State University in Ohio. Ten days later, two more student protesters were killed at Jackson State University in Mississippi.

Amidst the great social unrest of the 1960s and 1970s, some people spoke of revolutionary change. To a few, this meant violent revolution as a means of correcting perceived social injustices. To others, the revolution was one of nonviolent change. In his 1970 book, *The Greening of America,* Charles Reich expressed the melodramatic revolutionary sentiment of the times:

> There is a revolution coming. It will not be like revolutions of the past. It will originate with the individual and with culture, and it will change the political structure as its final act. It will not require violence to succeed, and it cannot be successfully resisted by violence. It is now spreading with amazing rapidity, and already our laws, institutions and social structure are changing in consequence. It promises a higher reason, a more human community, and a new and liberated individual. Its ultimate creation will be a new and enduring wholeness and beauty—a renewed relationship of man to himself, to other men, to nature, and to the land.[12]

America's need for revolution, said Reich, was rooted in an array of social problems. These included

- lawlessness and corruption in all the major institutions of society,
- poverty amidst America's affluence,
- destruction of the environment,
- a sense of powerlessness on the part of citizens,
- the artificiality of American culture,
- an absence of community, and
- a loss of self.[13]

The revolutionaries' target, however, was never clearly identified. Most previous revolutions had been against a tyrannical monarch or an overbearing government. The revolt of the 1960s and 1970s was simply against "the system"; that is, contemporary American values and lifestyle. Writer Saul Alinsky expressed just this type of ill-focused yet intense revolutionary fervor in his 1971 book titled *Rules for Radicals:*

> Today's generation is desperately trying to make some sense out of their lives and out of the world. Most of them are products of the middle class. They have rejected their materialistic backgrounds, the goal of well-paid job, suburban home, automobile, country club membership, first class travel, status, security, and everything that meant success to their parents. . . . They have watched it lead their parents to tranquilizers, alcohol, . . . divorces, high blood pressure, ulcers, frustration, and the disillusionment of "the good life." They have seen the almost unbelievable idiocy of our leadership . . . today [our leaders] are all viewed with contempt. This negativism extends to all institutions, from the police and the courts to "the system" itself.[14]

The writings of Charles Reich and of Saul Alinsky capture the emotionalism, the tumult, and the desperate push for change in existing social institutions. It was indeed a time of great social upheaval, of undeniable change, of identifying social injustice. It was also a time when public attention began to focus, in part, on the environment. The time was ripe for the motivating words and thoughts of the environmental philosophers, and it all began with Rachel Carson's classic work *Silent Spring.*

3
Rachel Carson's *Silent Spring*

Following are excerpts from the first chapter of *Silent Spring*, titled "A Fable for Tomorrow":

> There once was a town in the heart of America where all life seemed in harmony with its surroundings. The town lay in the midst of a checkerboard of prosperous farms . . . where in autumn white clouds of bloom drifted above the green fields. . . . Then a strange blight crept over the area and everything began to change. . . . There was a strange stillness . . . a white granular powder . . . had fallen like snow upon the roofs and the lawns, the fields and streams. No witchcraft, no enemy action has silenced . . . this stricken world. The people had done it themselves. This town does not actually exist. . . . Yet every one of these disasters has actually happened somewhere.[1]

Few books published in this century could equal *Silent Spring* in its profound effect on public opinion. The product of nearly five years of intensive research by author-biologist Rachel Carson, its chapters first appeared in serialized form in the *New Yorker* magazine in June 1962. The book was released on September 17, and by November *Silent Spring* had risen to number one on the nonfiction best-seller lists. By January 1963, the book had become a runaway best seller with more than one-half million copies in print and soon was destined for publication in sixteen countries outside the United States.

The immense commercial success of the book was, of course, due to the startling and controversial message it contained: the natural environment was being poisoned by chemicals and "the people had done it themselves."[2] The issue was not entirely new; a few scattered scientists had earlier spoken of the threat posed by the careless use of agricultural chemicals. However, the world took serious notice only when, at last, the message was delivered by one who was both a competent researcher and a talented author. In *Silent Spring,* Rachel Carson put before the public the chilling possibilities of a neo-Malthusian catastrophe where humanity's demand for greater agricultural productivity would contribute to its own undoing.

As early as 1945, Rachel Carson had expressed concern over pesticide spraying and had even attempted unsuccessfully to interest *Reader's Digest* in an article on the subject. In 1958, after years devoted to other scientific endeavors, she received a letter from friend and fellow writer Olga Owens Huckins that finally convinced her a forceful public statement was urgently needed. The letter told of Mrs. Huckins' own observation of the horrible side effects that resulted when DDT was aerially sprayed to control mosquitoes in two Massachusetts counties. Grasshoppers, bees, and birds, with "bills gaping open and their splayed claws drawn to their breasts in agony," were killed by the sprays, which left the mosquitoes unaffected.[3] Carson's initial attempts to interest other scholars in writing a book on the dangers of indiscriminate chemical use did not bear fruit, so she alone undertook the challenging project.

Rachel Carson, in some respects, seemed a person perfectly qualified for taking on an issue so potentially explosive as chemical contamination of the environment. She had a graduate degree in the sciences, for many years had worked as a government biologist, and also had impressive literary credentials with three best-selling books to her credit. But in other ways she hardly seemed up to locking horns with strident commercial agricultural interests. Physically slight of build, Rachel Carson was a soft-spoken, retiring woman whose avocational interests included bird-watching, her pet cats, and a few friends. By her own admission, she never identified with other key social issues of the day, such as the feminist movement. With the exception of the preface to the 1961 edition of her book *The Sea around Us,* which briefly mentioned the hazards of nuclear waste disposal in the oceans, she had never taken a strong position on environmental matters. Although perhaps more a mild-mannered scholar than a crusader, she nevertheless tackled the task with determination.

From the outset, the problems involved in researching and writing a book about the environmental consequences of agricultural chemicals were considerable. Carson corresponded with countless experts to obtain research information not yet published. And even though mountains of published literature existed, much of it was difficult to obtain, and the coverage of human, animal, and plant effects was spotty. Besides the research difficulties, there were other significant and more personal problems. Soon after Carson commenced work, her mother died. This was a deep loss as the two lived together and shared a very close relationship. In addition, the death placed a greater burden on Rachel Carson in the rearing of her six-year-old great-nephew, Roger Christie. Although never married, Carson adopted young Roger in 1957 following the death of his mother, Marjorie, who was Rachel Carson's niece. In addition to these family matters, Rachel Carson herself had a seemingly unending string of illnesses during these years, including bouts with flu, difficulties with arthritis, an ulcer, and a staphylococcus infection. Finally, with a recurrence of breast cancer in 1960 she became aware that, at best, she had only a few more years to live. So she worked at a furious pace until the publication of *Silent Spring* in 1962. The resultant fusion of science and skilled writing proved, indeed, most potent.

Silent Spring focuses its ire primarily upon the widespread and indiscriminate use of agricultural insecticides and, to a lesser extent, on herbicides and fungicides. The book's essential argument is that, since these synthetic chemicals were first introduced during World War II, some five hundred related compounds had been developed to help humans gain control over the undesirable organisms in the natural environment. Their zeal to apply this new technology and their desire for profits had raced ahead of their ability to comprehend the full ecological effects of pesticide use. Chemicals were applied over forested, agricultural, and even urban areas with little research data on how long they might persist in the environment or how they might affect humans, nontargeted insects, and other animals.

Silent Spring further maintains that the general public had by and large been kept in the dark regarding the potential threat of pesticides. People had been lulled into a false sense of security by government agencies and some scientists who declared, virtually without evidence, that no threat existed. Even government-imposed tolerance levels for pesticide contamination of consumables such as fruits and vegetables were misleading because little was known of the human body's propensity for chemical accumulation.

Throughout, the book presents numerous research findings and eyewitness accounts to illustrate the dangers of careless chemical applications. One such story contained in the chapter titled "And No Bird Sings" warns of the insidious threat of pesticide accumulation that can occur through the food chain. In 1954, Professor George Wallace and his graduate student John Mehner began a research project to study robin populations around Michigan State University in the city of East Lansing. In the same year, DDT spraying programs were conducted around the campus to control elm bark beetles (carriers of the Dutch elm disease fungus) and mosquitoes. Almost immediately people noticed dead and dying robins, but in time the problem seemed to pass. By late 1957, however, Wallace and Mehner noticed that young robins were almost nonexistent whereas in earlier years there had been hundreds. Dr. Roy Barker of the Illinois Natural History Survey eventually solved the riddle of the robins' fate. Barker determined that DDT had accumulated on tree leaves, which subsequently fell to the ground and decayed into the soil. The contaminated leaf litter was ingested by earthworms, which were, in turn, eaten by the robins. The individual worms contained only minute amounts of DDT but as the birds consumed dozens each day, deadly levels of poison collected in their bodies.

In the chapter "Needless Havoc," Carson tells a story to suggest that the wholesale application of pesticides raises "not only scientific but moral" questions.[4] The incident involved a decision by the Illinois Agriculture Department to aerially spray dieldrin, a compound fifty times more lethal than DDT, in order to eradicate Japanese beetles. Between 1954 and 1961, 131,000 acres were sprayed around the town of Sheldon with some incredibly destructive side effects. The dieldrin virtually annihilated ground squirrels, fox squirrels, pheasants, robins, meadowlarks, and starlings; killed muskrats, rabbits, and cats; and sickened cattle. Many of the animals experienced particularly violent deaths; "the dead ground squirrels . . . exhibited a characteristic attitude in death . . . the head and neck were outstretched and the mouth often contained dirt suggesting the dying animal had been biting the ground."[5] The chapter closes with the bitter question, "By acquiescing in an act that can cause such suffering to a living creature, who among us is not diminished as a human being?"[6]

The arrogance and insensitivity of the government toward the rights of private citizens who oppose mass insecticide spraying is described in the chapter "Indiscriminately from the Skies." The U.S. Department of Agriculture, in an attempt to eradicate the gypsy moth, began spraying DDT on one million acres of forested and urban land in Pennsylvania, New Jersey, Michigan, and New York in 1956. Irate citizens sought to have the spraying stopped only to have government officials ignore their complaints. In 1957, the government expanded the program to three million acres that included densely populated portions of Long Island. A group of citizens sought a court injunction, which was denied, and they were again drenched with DDT. A lawsuit was eventually brought before the U.S. Supreme Court and, although the Court declined to hear the case, the event did bring national attention to the disregard for property rights of private citizens.

In the same chapter, Carson describes the Department of Agriculture's fire ant eradication program, one of the largest mass spraying projects ever undertaken. The fire ant, so-named for its stinging bite, was an imported pest that by the late 1950s inhabited most of the southern United States. Though a nuisance, the fire ant reputedly posed no serious threat to humans, livestock, wildlife, or plants. Nevertheless, the department, with the strong support of pesticide manufacturers who regarded the program as a sales bonanza, began spraying in 1958. The chemicals used were dieldrin and heptachlor, both many times more potent than DDT. Over the next several years, numerous reliable reports appeared of poisonings to wildlife, birds, and farm animals across the South. A Georgia veterinarian made perhaps the most startling discovery: calves were being sickened by heptachlor from their mothers' own milk. Ironically, the spraying was having very little effect on the fire ant population. Louisiana, for example, was reporting more acres infested than before the program began. Finally, in 1962 after twenty million acres had been treated in nine states, the fire ant eradication program was terminated as an expensive, damaging, and ineffective failure.

Silent Spring contains chapters and accounts regarding almost every aspect of human-caused chemical threats to the natural environment, including contamination of soils, surface water, groundwater, salt marshes, estuaries, and so forth. Perhaps the most provocative chapters, however, are those that deal with the human dimensions of the problem. With titles such as "Beyond the Dreams of the Borgias," "The Human Price," "Through a Narrow Window," and "One in Every Four," these chapters introduce the possibilities of immediate and long-term human health effects of chemical exposure. Dangers exist not only from the pesticides used in commercial agriculture ("Every meal we eat carries a load of chlorinated hydrocarbons"[7]), but also from those used directly in the home and in domestic gardening. The chapters present many frightening concepts that were at that time novel to the lay public, such as the tendency of toxins to accumulate in fatty body tissue, the carcinogenic nature of some chemicals, and the ability of some compounds to cause genetic mutation. Carson argued that "it is simply impossible to predict the effects of lifetime exposure to chemical and physical agents that are not a part of the biological experience of man."[8]

The final three chapters, titled "Nature Fights Back," "The Rumblings of an Avalanche," and "The Other Road," argue that indiscriminate pesticide use ruins nature's usually powerful ability to keep undesirable insects in check. Destructive insects develop resistance to insecticides through natural selection and, with predators diminished by the same poisons, their numbers increase more rapidly than ever. The only workable solution to the problem of pest control, maintains Carson, is "the other road"—the selective and prudent use of safer chemicals coupled with other, less threatening technologies such as biological control and insect sterilization.[9] Carson did not advocate a complete ban on chemical pesticides, but this point was largely lost on her critics. In conclusion, the book issues a stern warning that humans, in their arrogant attempts to control nature, had turned an arsenal of terrible weapons against the Earth and, in the process, were unraveling the very fabric of life.

Silent Spring challenged not only the irresponsible uses of chemicals, but the users as well. Carson explicitly criticized state and federal agricultural agencies, state agricultural universities, commercial food and agricultural interests, chemical manufacturers, and professional entomologists. The reaction to this challenge was swift and severe and, as one source so descriptively stated, "where the shot hit, the feathers fly."[10]

The uproar began, in fact, before the book was released. In response to the *New Yorker* articles, a tidal wave of mail fell upon Congress, the Agriculture and Interior departments, the Public Health Service, and the Food and Drug Administration. Velsicol Corporation, a major agricultural chemical producer, threatened to sue the publisher, Houghton Mifflin Company. Following the book's publication the pace of the onslaught quickened. Chemical and agricultural trade journals ran editorials and articles decrying *Silent Spring* as a return to the Dark Ages complete with pestilence and famine. Agricultural bulletins carried helpful hints on how to counter Carson when dealing with the public. Even the influential American Medical Association sent worried patients directly to the chemical trade associations as the best source of information on pesticide dangers.

Paul Brooks, Rachel Carson's editor and biographer, believes that the fury of the attacks on *Silent Spring* were motivated by what the chemical and agricultural interests perceived as a direct threat to their very existence. Said Brooks,

> Her opponents must have realized—as indeed was the case—that she was questioning not only the indiscriminate use of poisons but the basic irresponsibility of an industrialized, technological society toward the natural world. She refused to accept the premise that damage to nature was the inevitable cost of "progress." The facts she revealed were bad enough, but it was the point of view behind them that was really dangerous, and must be suppressed.[11]

Yet, while the criticism of *Silent Spring*'s message was loud and persistent, it came from a relatively small segment of society. The popular press and elected officials, in contrast to the chemical and agricultural interests, sensed that Rachel Carson had surfaced an issue of substance that at the very least merited serious and penetrating discussion. President John F. Kennedy, when questioned about the government's position on pesticide abuses, stated at a press conference on August 29, 1962, that "since Miss Carson's book" the Department of

Agriculture and the Public Health Service were taking a closer look at the matter.[12]

One notable exception to the favorable coverage in the popular press was *Time* magazine's article of September 18, 1962. In a scathing piece, *Time* accused Rachel Carson of "frightening and arousing her readers" and of using "emotion-fanning words." *Silent Spring,* they said, was "unfair, one-sided and hysterical." The article concluded, "her emotional and inaccurate outburst in *Silent Spring* may do more harm by alarming the non-technical public, while doing no good for the things she loves."[13]

Accusations of inaccuracy, such as those raised in the *Time* article, are the most injurious a researcher can receive. They suggest ineptitude, or worse, falsification, both of which are the equivalent of mortal sins in the scientific community. In addition to questioning her veracity, critics vilified Rachel Carson's personal character in other ways. She was called "a communist," "a priestess of nature," and "a devotee of a mystical cult," to name a few epithets.[14] To those who knew her, the claim that she was an unscientific, emotional polemicist was so far off the mark that it was hard to see how anyone could read the book and come to that conclusion. Indeed, this shadow cast on Rachel Carson's character seemed curiously at odds with her established reputation.

First as a child and later as a career woman, Rachel Louise Carson had approached life's tasks with dedication. She learned this serious view of work for the most part in her home. Born on May 27, 1907, she was reared with an older sister and brother on a farm just a few miles from Pittsburgh in the small town of Springdale, Pennsylvania. Her father, Robert, dabbled in the real estate business and was able to provide his family a comfortable but by no means affluent lifestyle. Any lack in material wealth, however, was certainly supplanted by a richly nurturing home life due largely to the efforts of Rachel's mother, Maria, who was herself an educated woman and a minister's daughter. A type of friendly formality existed among the Carson family members, whom a close childhood friend of Rachel's interestingly described as "intellectual" and "highly civilized people."[15] Mrs. Carson was exceptionally caring, if somewhat overprotective, and served as a powerful influence supporting Rachel's lifelong dual love for literature and nature.

As a public school student, Rachel Carson was a quiet but excellent student, bookish and precocious in her studies.[16] In her personal relationships she was regarded as something of a loner, private yet amiable. Without doubt, however, the most foretelling event of Carson's early life was the emergence of her considerable skill as a writer. Beginning at age ten, she published three essays for small payments in the then-famous children's magazine *St. Nicholas.* These pieces, though short in length, showed amazing clarity of expression and organization. Rachel's teachers also were impressed with her literary abilities and even more so with her maturity and deep insight.

Following high school graduation, Carson attended the Pennsylvania College for Women (later Chatham College) near Pittsburgh. The students at PCW were mostly from well-to-do families. In contrast, Rachel was forced to seek financial assistance every year that she attended college. As in public school, however, she was academically top-notch and ranked among the upper 10 percent of students. Besides her studies, Rachel was active with campus journalistic and literary organizations and published a number of prize-winning essays. Although not particularly athletic, she was an eager and enthusiastic goalie at field hockey. The student body of three hundred was perfectly suited not only for shy Rachel but also for Maria Carson, who managed to be with her daughter nearly every weekend.

Rachel originally majored in English when she enrolled at PCW, intending to make literature, her first love, her vocation. During her sophomore year, however, she took two semesters of required biology from thirty-four-year-old Mary Scott Skinker. Though initially cool to the subject, she quickly warmed to both the topic and the enlightening young teacher. In her junior year, despite the misgivings of college officials, Rachel changed her major to biology and launched herself headlong into organic chemistry, botany, field trips, and frog dissections. At the time she thought she was abandoning one career for another; writing and science seemed mutually exclusive. Only later in life would she realize that she had simply given herself something to write about. Though she had changed her major from literature to biology, Rachel's interest and skill as a writer remained strong during her time at PCW. In her junior year, while taking a composition class from Grace Croff, she produced some of her very best writing.[17]

Graduating magna cum laude from PCW with a bachelor of arts in biology in 1929, Rachel obtained a scholarship for graduate studies in zoology at Johns Hopkins University in Baltimore and also was selected for a program of summer study at Woods Hole Marine Biological Laboratory. The appointment at Woods Hole helped to fulfill Rachel's long-held dream to visit the sea. Since childhood, the ocean had occupied her thoughts and had even been the subject of some of her essays. Oddly, however, she had never seen it. The summer at Woods Hole changed all this by introducing her to the ocean, something she would come to know intimately during the next three decades.

Next year the Carson family, minus brother Robert, moved with Rachel to a new home in Baltimore. In 1932, she completed her master of arts in zoology and for the next three years worked as a teaching assistant at Johns Hopkins University and the University of Maryland. In 1935, with financial needs pressing, Rachel, in an important career move, obtained a temporary position preparing radio scripts about fisheries and marine life for the Bureau of Fisheries (later the U.S. Fish and Wildlife Service) in Washington, DC. Within a year the temporary appointment became permanent, and over the next sixteen years she advanced from assistant aquatic biologist to editor-in-chief of the agency.

During these years, it was primarily Rachel Carson's skill as a science writer that made her a valued government employee. Ironically, this very talent would eventually take her from the government. Working at home often into the early morning hours with only her cats as company, Rachel Carson began drafting pages of a manuscript about the sea. In 1941, she completed and published her book *Under the Sea-Wind.* Despite being beautifully written and critically acclaimed, the book initially sold poorly. Disappointed but undaunted, she soon began work on a second book, *The Sea around Us,* which was published in 1951. This time she had a smashing success. Eighty-six weeks on the best-seller lists and the subject of an Oscar-winning movie documentary, *The Sea around Us* made Rachel Carson both famous and financially independent. Soon *Under the Sea-Wind* was rereleased and it too became a success. In 1952, Rachel Carson departed government service for good to become a full-time writer. Three years later, in 1955, she published her third best-seller *The Edge of the Sea.*

All of Rachel Carson's first three books were exquisite literary gems. They dealt with complex scientific material, yet their clear, lyrical prose flowed gently from the page and captivated readers the world over. More than just enjoyable reading, however, Rachel Carson's work was also reliable science. She once estimated that during the three years required to write *The Sea around Us* she had studied more than one thousand scientific manuscripts and corresponded with innumerable experts in the field of oceanography. Rachel Carson's conscientious efforts garnered accolades and awards, including several honorary doctorates and the deepest respect of her professional colleagues.

Carson's research for *Silent Spring* was no less conscientious than that for her other books. For example, appended to the text of *Silent Spring* were more than fifty pages of citations listing the principal scientific sources she had used to build the case against pesticides and agricultural chemicals. However, the expenditure of physical and mental energy that had created this masterwork had also placed Carson under an enormous emotional strain. Heart-rending evidence of this stress is contained in a letter Carson wrote to her friend Dorothy Freeman shortly after the completion of *Silent Spring:*

> After Roger was asleep, I took Jeffie [her cat] into the study and played the Beethoven violin concerto—one of my favorites, you know. And suddenly the tension of four years was broken and I let the tears come. I think I let you see last summer what my deeper feelings are about this when I said I could never again listen happily to a thrush song if I had not done all I could. And last night the thoughts of all the birds and other creatures and all the loveliness that is in nature came to me with such a surge of deep happiness, that now I had done what I could—I had been able to complete it—now it had its own life.[18]

As the furor over *Silent Spring* grew, Rachel Carson's reaction was to distance herself as much as possible from the fray. Even if she had wanted to leap into the midst of the controversy, her health dictated against it. One exception to Rachel Carson's low public profile, however, was her appearance in April 1963 on the CBS report, "The Silent Spring of Rachel Carson." Her principal antagonist during the televised discussion was Dr. Robert White-Stevens of the American Cyanamid Company, a strong defender of pesticide use and equally strong critic of *Silent Spring*. Biographer Carol Gartner recalled Carson's demeanor that night:

> Carson's emphasis was on the lack of sufficient knowledge about the effects of pesticides . . . for coherent planning. Neither the pesticide industry nor the government could prove they really knew what they were doing. Carson's dispassionate factual statements . . . left viewers with a strong tilt toward [her] position, despite White-Stevens' intemperate attacks and continued misrepresentations.[19]

In May 1963, one month after the CBS special, the U.S. Office of Science and Technology released a report titled "Use of Pesticides." The study, prepared by a select panel of scientists, amounted to official scientific endorsement of *Silent Spring*. Industry and government agencies alike were roundly criticized for their lax handling and administration of pesticides. *Silent Spring* was, in turn, praised for having performed a valuable service by informing the public of the dangers of these toxic substances. Soon after the release of the government's report, the highly respected American Association for the Advancement of Science issued a statement saying "the pesticides report . . . adds up to a fairly thorough-going vindication of Rachel Carson's *Silent Spring* thesis."[20] As one official from the Department of the Interior said, "It became obvious that she was many, many times better informed than her critics . . . because she approached the problem from the viewpoint of basic science while [they] functioned at the technician level."[21]

The Office of Science and Technology report essentially hushed Rachel Carson's critics and cleared her name. In June, she appeared before committees of both the U.S. Senate and the House of Representatives to begin what she saw as the next critical step in the process *Silent Spring* had initiated: the push for legislation to regulate pesticide usage. The book's popularity continued to soar and by year's end it was on bookstore shelves in the United Kingdom, France, Germany, Italy, Denmark, Sweden, Norway, Finland, and The Netherlands. With the New Year came continued interest in *Silent Spring*'s message and more opportunities for Carson to travel and meet the public. But other aspects of her life were not going well. Weakened already by cancer and arthritis, she suffered a heart attack that left her all but an invalid. Though Rachel Carson attempted to write, read, and remain active, her life ebbed away during that spring. She died on April 14, 1964, at age fifty-six, in Silver Spring, Maryland. A traditional Episcopalian burial service read from the *Book of Common Prayer* was held for her in no less prestigious a venue than Washington National Cathedral.[22] Her body was cremated and a portion of her ashes buried next to her mother in a cemetery in Montgomery County, Maryland. The remainder were scattered near her summer home along the coast at Newagen, Maine. At the scattering, Rachel's dear friend Dorothy Freeman read a few lines from the T. S. Eliot poem "The Dry Salvages."[23]

Many events of the past quarter century stand as evidence of the truly enormous social impact of Rachel Carson's *Silent Spring*. Passage of the National Environmental Policy Act, creation of the Environmental Protection Agency (EPA), and the annual celebration of Earth Day are but a few examples. Rachel Carson's most important legacy, however, may be found not in the laws of Congress nor in the halls of Washington's bureaucracy, but in the minds of the people. She shocked us into awareness of the deadly threat posed to present and future generations when the air, water, and soil are used casually as repositories for toxic substances. In raising the alarm over human-caused pollution, Rachel Carson introduced the bellwether issue and most durable topic of the modern era of environmental concern.

In addition to its initiation of the modern age of environmentalism, *Silent Spring* helped to achieve Rachel Carson's immediate goal of increased study and control of pesticides. In 1970, the EPA was charged with the administration of the Federal Insecticide, Fungicide and Rodenticide Act of 1947 (FIFRA), which controls the manufacture and use of pesticides in the United States. The law was subsequently strengthened through amendments in 1972, 1975, 1978, and 1988. FIFRA requires the EPA to test the ingredients in commercial pesticides to determine whether they pose a danger in the form of cancer or other health risks. Once the EPA has demonstrated a health hazard from a particular pesticide, the pesticide is withdrawn from use and the burden is upon the pesticide manufacturer to demonstrate that the risk is minimal or that the benefits of continued use outweigh those risks.[24]

Under FIFRA, the EPA has banned some fifty pesticides that had previously been approved for use. Among the most notable of these pesticides are many classified as chlorinated hydrocarbons. This class includes DDT, dieldrin, and chlordane, some of the most effective yet most dangerous pesticides because of their persistence in the environment and the broad spectrum of organisms that they can kill. One of the great success stories resulting from the banning of DDT was the recovery of several endangered species of birds.[25] DDT had been developed in 1939 and used with great success for the management of insect pests that harmed crops and human health. However, biological scientists noted that during the 1950s and 1960s the populations of several species of fish-eating birds, such as the brown pelican, osprey, and our national symbol, the bald eagle, had declined precipitously in regions where DDT was used to spray crops. Research indicated that ingestion of the insecticide through consumption of contaminated prey impaired the birds' ability to place sufficient quantities of calcium in their eggshells. As a result, eggshells became excessively fragile and in many instances broke before the young hatched. Following the 1972 ban on DDT, most of the affected bird species have recovered and the bald eagle has been removed from the list of endangered species.

The control and use of pesticides continues to be a hotly debated issue. Proponents point out that these chemicals have conveyed huge, measurable benefits to society. These stem from the saving of human lives through elimination of insect pests that carry lethal diseases and also from the protection of crops. It would be impossible, they argue, to adequately feed and protect humanity without pesticide use. In contrast, opponents say that the threats to wildlife and to humans, especially individuals exposed to pesticides during manufacturing or use are simply too great.

One possible solution to the controversy is "the other road" suggested by Rachel Carson, which combines the use of pesticides with other methods to limit insect damage to agricultural crops. In fact, for the past two decades the U.S. Department of Agriculture and the land grant universities have sponsored research into an approach known as integrated pest management (IPM). IPM attempts to combine various tillage and farm management practices in order to minimize the need for pesticide use. IPM proponents claim it offers a viable alternative to heavy pesticide use. They say also that success and acceptance are limited mainly by the resources that the agricultural community is willing to devote toward their development.

Paul Brooks said that no better epitaph could be chosen for Rachel Carson than the final passage from her book *The Edge of the Sea:*

> Now I hear the sea sounds about me; the night high tide is rising, swirling with a confused rush of waters against the rocks below my study window. Fog has come into the bay from the open sea, and it lies over water and over the land's edge, seeping back into the spruces and stealing softly among the juniper and the bayberry. The restive waters, the cold wet breath of the fog, are of a world in which man is an uneasy trespasser; he punctuates the night with the complaining groan and grunt of a foghorn, sensing the power and the menace of the sea.
>
> Hearing the rising tide, I think how it is pressing also against the other shores I know—rising on a southern beach where there is no fog, but a moon edging all the waves with silver and touching the wet sands with a lambent sheen, and on a still more distant shore sending its streaming currents against the moonlit pinnacles and the dark caves of the coral rock. . . .
>
> Contemplating the teeming life of the shore, we have an uneasy sense of the communication of some universal truth that lies just beyond our grasp. What is the message signaled by the hordes of diatoms, flashing their microscopic lights in the night sea? What truth is expressed by the legions of barnacles, whitening the rocks with their habitations, each small creature within finding the necessities of its existence in the sweep of the surf? And what is the meaning of so tiny a being as the transparent wisp of protoplasm that is a sea lace, existing for some reason inscrutable to us—a reason that demands its presence by the trillion amid the rocks and weeds of the shore? The meaning haunts and ever eludes us, and in its very pursuit we approach the ultimate mystery of Life itself.[26]

4

Harold Barnett and Chandler Morse's
Scarcity and Growth

In 1963, just one year after the release of *Silent Spring*, two economists, Harold Barnett and Chandler Morse, released a book titled *Scarcity and Growth: The Economics of Natural Resource Availability*. Completed while the authors worked under the sponsorship of Resources for the Future, a highly respected Ford Foundation think tank located in Washington, DC, *Scarcity and Growth* was important to the modern environmental era because it provided an empirical test of natural resource scarcity, an issue that had concerned humans for a very long time.

In terms of commercial success, *Scarcity and Growth* was simply no match for the likes of *Silent Spring*. More a scholarly monograph than popular fare, it sold only about 25,000 copies over its life, and those mostly to libraries and academicians. Yet the findings and insights contained in *Scarcity and Growth* were a powerful influence on a generation of environmental economists who even today regularly cite the work. Despite its scholarly nature, however, Barnett and Morse's book contained clearly discernable ideas on what many regard to be the inevitable dilemma of resource shortages.

The study was born of a practical need stemming from World War II, when the United States had placed exceptionally heavy demands on its natural resources. Seven years after the war, in 1952, the President's Materials Policy Commission (also known as the Paley Commission for its chairman, the late William S. Paley, founder of CBS) was formed to investigate the prospects of resource shortages. The commission concluded that while most mineral, agricultural, and forestry supplies seemed to be presently available, the costs involved in obtaining these resources *might* escalate in the future. The implication was that U.S. industries could be caught in a squeeze due to increasing procurement costs and, if so, the standard of living of American citizens would suffer. In response to the Paley Commission's report, Resources for the

Future was formed as a nonprofit corporation for research and education in the development, conservation, and use of natural resources.[1] Economist Barnett was hired as principal investigator in 1955, and Cornell University professor Morse was hired part-time to begin work on this, the first major empirical investigation of resource scarcity.

Although events of World War II provided the impetus for *Scarcity and Growth*, the intellectual foundations were much older. One hundred sixty-five years prior to Barnett and Morse's work, two classical English economists, Thomas Robert Malthus and his friend and associate David Ricardo, began developing the theories the two modern economists would study. A third English economist, John Stuart Mill, also was an important influence on Barnett and Morse through his clarification of Malthus and Ricardo as well as his own original thinking on resource scarcities.

The theorem of Malthus, a plodding yet brilliant Anglican clergyman, was set forth in his monumental 1798 treatise titled *An Essay on the Principle of Population as It Affects the Future Improvement of Society*. The essential idea is well known and well understood even today. At least people *think* they understand Malthus. The generally accepted interpretation of Malthusian scarcity is more or less as follows: society has the ability to increase agricultural production only at an arithmetic rate while the number of mouths to be fed increases at a geometric rate. Hence at some point population will outstrip food supplies with calamitous results. This popularized version has often carried the connotation that the physical extinction of resources is what imposes limits on society. When they're gone, they're simply, well, gone. This simplified notion of resource extinction is a misinterpretation of Malthus that persists even today. What Harold Barnett and Chandler Morse saw in Malthus, however, was the much more sophisticated concept of *economic* scarcity of natural resources and its attendant effects on economic growth. Economic scarcity refers to the decreased availability of resources relative to the amount of effort required to obtain them.

To Malthus' way of thinking, land was one ingredient, like labor or tools, used in the process of growing crops. While Malthus argued that the quantity of arable land was fixed and someday might be completely occupied by farms, he also recognized that land could be improved and made more productive through intensive cultivation. With greater effort, farmers could gradually squeeze more produce from the same fixed amount of land but—and herein lies the rub—at decreasing rates. Thus each additional worker sent to the field produces incrementally fewer crops or, as later economists would say, diminishing marginal returns.

In addition to the musings of Malthus, Barnett and Morse also studied the theories of David Ricardo as expressed in his 1817 book *Principles of Political Economy and Taxation.* Ricardo was not only Malthus' contemporary, but his dear friend as well. Despite their close friendship of nearly fifteen years, however, the two men endlessly and sometimes heatedly debated questions of economic theory. Malthus was a priest hampered by a severe speech impediment and Ricardo a wealthy Jewish-born businessman who served in the House of Commons. An odd couple indeed, but the most notable pairing in the annuals of economic thought save, perhaps, Marx and Engels.

Ricardo agreed that diminishing marginal returns would characterize agriculture, but he disagreed with respect to the manner in which this process would occur. Ricardo, unlike Malthus, believed that agricultural land was not only limited in quantity, but also varied tremendously in quality. Because of differences in fertility or proximity to markets, there was, he observed, great variation in the usefulness of land for growing crops. Thus, as populations grew, farmers would use more intensive methods of cultivation while always relying upon land of lower and lower quality. Ricardo's scenario may have differed from Malthus' but the end result was the same—diminishing marginal returns.

So Malthus and Ricardo both predicted diminishing marginal returns as farmers sought ways to feed the ever-increasing masses. But how would this translate into economic scarcity, and how would economic scarcity, in turn, impinge upon economic growth? The economic scarcity would arise from the fact that society would have to sacrifice increasingly more to obtain less. Whether measured by the number of field hands and their hoes or by the money required to pay for that labor and equipment, the cost of extracting agricultural produce would increase. And as populations continued to grow and societies were harder pressed to feed them, there would come a time when these costs would dominate the entire economy. Per-capita economic growth would cease and then plummet as humans struggled just to scratch a living from the Earth. A gloomy paradigm indeed and the very one that later caused the Scottish essayist Thomas Carlyle to dub economics the "dismal science."[2]

Fifty years following Malthus' famous essay came *Principles of Political Economy* by John Stuart Mill. Mill was an extraordinarily gifted intellectual versed in languages, literature, and political economy, whose father, James, had been a friend of Ricardo's. Barnett and Morse examined the younger Mill's writings too in the context of *Scarcity and Growth* as a means of gaining greater insight into Malthus and Ricardo. According to Barnett and Morse, Mill was unable to deny absolutely the possibility of a Malthusian-Ricardian world of diminishing returns and resource scarcity, but he was equally unwilling to confirm its inevitability. Mill, so it seems, had some confidence that humans could voluntarily check population growth and, at the same time, better use resources so as to prevent catastrophic shortages. Said Barnett and Morse, Mill "saw many actual and potential ameliorations in the possibilities of technological and social progress."[3] It's not at all surprising that Mill anticipated this human resourcefulness and plasticity whereas Malthus and Ricardo did not. The latter two knew the industrial age only in its formative years. By contrast, the much younger Mill was afforded a longer look and no doubt was more able to fathom the potential for sweeping change.

Thus, to the authors of *Scarcity and Growth,* Mill's words raised doubts about the certainty of resource scarcity; there were at least theoretical possibilities that human cleverness could cope with the situation. In addition to his commentary on Malthus and Ricardo, Mill introduced a fresh concept which to Barnett and Morse seemed "strikingly relevant to the twentieth century."[4] This was the notion that personal solitude and natural beauty could be impaired through population growth and industry. Though humans might not experience shortages of conventional agricultural produce and minerals, they could, in the process of growing crops and mining, come to see a paucity of quality human habitat. As we shall see later, this idea would place an important caveat on the empirical results of Harold Barnett and Chandler Morse.

With Malthus, Ricardo, and Mill as a prologue, Barnett and Morse formulated and tested their hypotheses. The first was named the strong hypothesis because it was a faithful, thus strong, representation of the Malthusian and Ricardian theories. This hypothesis simply maintained that if natural resources were becoming scarce in the United States, then the cost of extracting those resources should be increasing with the passage of time. Barnett and Morse used *extraction cost* in a special sense. It referred to the amount of labor and investment capital needed to grow crops, mine minerals, or the like, and also the effort required to process and transport those raw materials to the consumer. To test the hypothesis, data were needed, and these were supplied by two other Resources for the Future researchers, Neal Potter and Francis T. Christy Jr. They collected data on the amount of labor and capital used for resource extraction in the period from the Civil War to 1957 for a great variety of natural resources, such as grains, sugar, cotton, vegetables, meat, milk, copper, lead, petroleum, coal, and lumber. From these data, Barnett and Morse calculated indices representing the unit extraction costs for the various resource commodities.

When Barnett and Morse plotted the cost trends for their great market basket of natural resource commodities, lo and behold, they found virtually all extraction costs trending not up as the resource scarcity theory had suggested, but down. Across the span of nearly one hundred years, agricultural costs had steadily declined and mineral costs had fallen precipitously. Only forest product costs had increased, but even then only during the early years from 1870 to 1919; since 1919, forestry extraction costs also had declined. Were Malthus and Ricardo wrong? Were resources becoming, in fact, not scarce but economically more plentiful? Apparently so, said Barnett and Morse. "On the whole, our strong hypothesis of natural resource scarcity fails; the evidence mainly shows increasing, not diminishing, returns."[5]

As further evidence, Barnett and Morse wanted to test a second, so-called weak hypothesis that was conceptually a bit more complicated than their first. The term *weak* derived from the fact that it adhered less rigorously to Malthus and Ricardo's bleak world of the strong hypothesis where rising absolute natural resource costs completely choked off economic progress. Under this less menacing hypothesis, economic activity might slow but would never stop, and the horrible societal decline envisioned by Malthus and Ricardo would certainly never occur.

The weak hypothesis examined as evidence both the ratio of extractive costs to nonextractive costs and the ratio of natural resource prices to other commodity prices. The use of relative extractive costs to test the weak scarcity hypothesis was motivated by the following logic: the historical data had indicated that extractive costs were declining, but then perhaps all production costs, extractive and nonextractive alike, had fallen due to technological improvement and general social progress; maybe natural resources were in fact becoming scarcer, hence more costly, but only relative to other goods. Besides relative costs, Barnett and Morse also examined as corroborating evidence the trends in the relative prices paid for extractive resources. "Price measure," they wrote, "is statistically independent of relative cost measurement, and thereby provides a check on its results."[6] Increasing costs, rising price ratios, or both would provide evidence of relative resource scarcity.

The result of the weak hypothesis test? It was very similar to that for the strong hypothesis. The relative costs and prices for agricultural and mineral products had declined or at least remained steady since the Civil War. Only forest products had exhibited weak economic scarcity through both rising relative costs and prices. However, because forestry accounted for only about 10 percent of all natural resource extractive costs, Barnett and Morse concluded that the United States had no reason for undue concern. Neither absolute nor relative economic scarcity seemed much of a problem or, as Harold Barnett remarked, "The evidence denies the doctrine."[7]

Thus, the widely accepted and long-held theory of natural resource scarcity was refuted by empirical evidence—at least for the United States. Of course, this was all very good news, but how could Malthus and Ricardo have missed the mark so badly? Why did the evidence deny the doctrine? Barnett and Morse explored these questions and found an explanation in human technological ingenuity. Americans, they averred, had simply proven adept at discovering and exploiting new resources. When raw materials became expensive, people imported, explored, and found substitutes, often of higher quality than the originals:

Recognition of the possibility of technological progress clearly cuts the ground from under the concept of Malthusian scarcity. Two decades ago Vermont granite was only building and tombstone material; now it is a potential fuel, each ton of which has . . . uranium equal to 150 tons of coal. The notion of an absolute limit to natural resource availability is untenable when the definition of resources changes drastically and unpredictably over time.[8]

Barnett and Morse saw this desire for progress and innovation as an integral part of the modern world motivated by the very threat of economic scarcity that was so feared:

> The scientific age differs . . . from the preceding mechanical age. Not only ingenuity but, increasingly, understanding; not luck but systematic investigation, are turning the tables on nature, making her subservient to man. And the signals that channel research effort, now in one direction, now in another—that determine innovational priorities—are usually the problems crying loudest to be solved. Sometimes the signals are political and social. More often, in a private enterprise society, they are market forces. Changes in relative costs, shifts in demand, the wish to develop broader markets—all aspects of growth—create problems which then generate solutions. Technological progress is no longer a mere by-product of man's efforts to win a decent living; it is an inseparable, organic part of that process.[9]

As for the welfare of future generations, Barnett and Morse argued that the solution was to educate humans, not to lock up resources. After all, hadn't technological progress provided a satisfying explanation of the past increases in the economic availability of natural resources? And none of this good fortune was by happenstance; it resulted, they said, from humans' investment in themselves. The two authors believed with apparent conviction that improvement of human capital, rather than legally mandated limitations on consumption, was our key to the future.

> Prescriptions for physical conservation of natural resources are not appropriate, however, for meeting the . . . obligation to the future. Resource reservation . . . will . . . have a perverse effect on future output and welfare. The reason, of course, is that the legacy of economically valuable assets which each generation passes on consists only in part of the natural environment. The

more important components of the inheritance are knowledge, technology, capital instruments, economic institutions. These, far more than natural resources, are the determinants of real income per capita.[10]

However, even Barnett and Morse had to admit that there were some instances when resource protection might be justified: "preservation of wild and scenic features of our natural environment for our own aesthetic benefit will presumably be appreciated by our successors."[11]

Besides providing strictly empirical results, *Scarcity and Growth* made other, although perhaps less obvious, contributions to our understanding of natural resources. One such contribution was the basic idea that resource scarcity was indeed an empirical issue incapable of being resolved by theoreticians alone. For more than 150 years, people had been willing to accept the untested reasoning of Malthus as proof positive that economic shortages and social collapse were inescapable. Barnett and Morse astutely noted, however, that "the occurrence . . . of natural resource scarcity . . . must be regarded as a hypothesis, not a self-evident fact."[12] And their analyses had ultimately rejected this hypothesis.

The work of Barnett and Morse also contributed to a general revitalization of academic interest in natural resource economics. Perhaps the best evidence of the influence of *Scarcity and Growth* was the publication in 1979 of *Scarcity and Growth Reconsidered,* and in 2005 of *Scarcity and Growth Revisited.*[13] The last volume featured the work of several preeminent resource economists who, decades after the original work, reprised and commented on some of Barnett and Morse's themes. But even considering new criticism and comments, there was little doubt that the original book had established the embarkation point for modern economic investigations of natural resource scarcity.

Even today, tests for resource scarcity, and thus tests of the Malthusian hypothesis, continue to be a part of modern economic inquiry. Such empirical tests, unfortunately, often yield complex and contradictory patterns of price and cost trends depending upon the resources examined, the time periods analyzed, and the influence of government policies.[14] Generally, such studies have shown that natural resource prices for petroleum, minerals, and forest products have tended to decline over the past century, thus signaling a reduction in economic scarcity.[15] Such examinations of the Malthusian hypothesis almost certainly will always be of interest to those concerned with natural resources and the environment, in part because of the controversial nature of the hypothesis. Ever since the time of Malthus, the hypothesis has stirred emotions because of what it implies about the inability of humanity to determine its own fate. Instead of freely making proper choices with respect to sexual reproduction and resource consumption, humanity is supposedly governed by its own ungovernable instincts, instincts that would lead to its eventual demise. In effect, Malthus seemed to say that humans were their own worst enemies. Even today, people embrace or deny this position with serious conviction.

The Malthusian theory will remain with us because, as Barnett and Morse noted, it is in fact not an eternal truth beyond challenge but a hypothesis subject to empirical testing. As such, researchers will always want to test it against each new data set on resource extraction costs and prices to determine if, at various times and places, natural resource scarcity is a problem.

Barnett and Morse ended their written work, as researchers often do, with some interpretation and reflections about its greater meaning for society. Much of that discussion centered upon the study's relevance to the world's developed and less developed nations. The findings of *Scarcity and Growth* suggested that the United States, and perhaps other industrialized nations as well, had little to fear in terms of resource availability. The two authors, however, saw primitive societies as being altogether different. Because of their simple technologies and limited capital, Malthusian-type scarcities in the Third World were not only possible but very probable. The authors also believed that poorer countries were more prone to runaway population growth, which you may recall, had been a linchpin in Malthus' theory. Despite perceptions that population growth was a problem limited to the Third World, the two men also recognized that all countries could benefit from the study of family planning.

From these conclusions it may seem that the United States and other western countries had escaped the natural resource dilemma unscathed, but such is not the case. Indeed, the ending to *Scarcity and Growth*, in an interesting twist, presents the industrialized world with a most remarkable warning: "The modern natural resource problem . . . it appears, is not diminishing returns, but . . . indirect effects of technological change and economic growth," including "pollution," "noxious gases," "lands denuded," and "radioactive fallout."[16] Thus, it is not the direct costs of natural resources that threaten the United States, but the indirect costs imposed by environmental degradation. Just as Rachel Carson had so eloquently argued, Barnett and Morse, in the closing pages of *Scarcity and Growth*, also acknowledge an insidious thread connecting social progress and environmental quality.

By the time *Scarcity and Growth* went to press, Chandler Morse had returned to Cornell University in Ithaca, New York, while Harold Barnett moved on first to Wayne State University in Detroit as professor of economics and then to Washington University in St. Louis as head of its Department of Economics. Each eventually retired from his respective institution with the status of professor emeritus. Harold J. Barnett died February 11, 1987; Chandler Morse passed away December 5, 1988.

5

Stewart L. Udall and *The Quiet Crisis*

The Quiet Crisis was published in 1963, the same year as Barnett and Morse's *Scarcity and Growth*. While it was certainly influenced by *Silent Spring*'s message of environmental concern,[1] its focus, like that of *Scarcity and Growth*, was more on the human use and consumption of natural resources than on environmental pollution. Stewart Udall approached this natural resource issue differently, however, than did Barnett and Morse. Whereas *Scarcity and Growth* dealt with the economic scarcity of extractive natural resources such as minerals and timber, Udall's book broadened the scope to include non-commodity natural resources. *The Quiet Crisis* was concerned with the disappearance of natural resources such as timber and grazing lands, but also with the loss of scenic beauty and the grandeur of public lands, particularly in the United States.

A concept Udall emphasized in *The Quiet Crisis* was the conservation of natural resources. *Conservation*, in Udall's usage, refers to the management for current and future generations of such natural resources as timber, fish, game, topsoil, grazing land, and minerals, as well as to the preservation of forests, wildlife, parkland, wilderness, and watershed areas for aesthetic enjoyment. Now a commonly used term, *conservation* traces its origins to American natural resource management of the late nineteenth century. Gifford Pinchot, the first chief of the U.S. Forest Service, and his forester Overton Price, seeking a single word to embody the concept of sustainable resource management, borrowed from the notion of east Indian forestry reserves, known as conservancies, to create the term *conservation*.[2]

The "quiet crisis" to which the book's title refers was the gradual loss of natural habitat, "a habitat that will, each day, renew the meaning of the human enterprise." Thus, according to Udall, Americans, in their pursuit since World War II of economic well-being and a more affluent lifestyle, had become engaged in a "lopsided performance" that undermined the alternative social goals of a healthy environment and the conservation of natural resources. The crisis was undoubtedly real because society was dependent upon the environment and natural resources for its continued existence. Yet the crisis was "quiet" because it had gone largely unnoticed by the public, who were deceptively "encouraged by a false sense of well-being."[3] Scientific and economic progress had lulled the public into a state of blissful contentment, causing them to ignore the perils of a steadily degrading natural environment.

Stewart Lee Udall was particularly well qualified to write about the U.S. environment and publicly owned natural resources.[4] At the time he wrote *The Quiet Crisis*, he was serving as Secretary of the Interior in John F. Kennedy's presidential administration. A prestigious political appointment such as this was a natural career step for Stewart Udall. He was born to a politically prominent family in St. Johns, Arizona, on January 31, 1920. He is the son of former Arizona Supreme Court Justice Levi S. Udall and Louise Lee Udall and his brother is the late U.S. Congressman Morris "Mo" K. Udall.

Udall's childhood and public school years were spent in St. Johns, a rural Mormon community founded by his grandfather. As a young man, he left St. Johns to attend the University of Arizona in Tucson. He interrupted his studies to spend two years as a Mormon missionary in New York and Pennsylvania, and to serve as a U.S. Air Force gunner in Europe during World War II. In 1946, Udall was a member of the first University of Arizona basketball team to play at the National Invitational Tournament at Madison Square Garden. Graduating from the university in 1948 with a law degree, Udall started his own practice, and a few years later, opened a law firm in Tucson with his brother, Morris.

In 1954, Stewart Udall was elected to the U.S. Congress from Arizona. He served on the U.S. House of Representatives Committee on Interior and Insular Affairs (1955–1960); the House Education and Labor Committee (1955–1956); the House Committee on Education and Labor (1957–1960), and a Joint Committee on Navajo-Hopi Indian Administration (1957–1958). Instrumental in persuading Arizona Democrats to support Senator John F. Kennedy during the 1960 Democratic Nomination Convention, Udall was appointed by President Kennedy as secretary of the interior, a position he held for nine years. His accomplishments as a cabinet member include passage of the Wilderness Bill and the Wild and Scenic Rivers Act; the expansion of the National Park System to include four new national parks, six new national monuments, eight seashores and lakeshores, nine recreation areas, twenty historic sites, and fifty-six wildlife refuges; and the creation of the Land and Water Conservation Fund (the principal fund for purchasing additional U.S. public lands). After leaving government service in 1969, he taught for a year at the Yale University School of Forestry as a visiting professor of environmental humanism.

Stewart Udall, in his foreword to *The Quiet Crisis,* mentions two events that inspired him to write the book. First, he had learned that famed poet T. S. Eliot had fallen gravely ill due to severe air pollution in London. Second, he had been informed that American poet Robert Frost's farm, which is mentioned in Frost's poem "West-running Brook," had been converted to an auto junk yard. Asked Stewart, "Is a society a success if it creates conditions that impair its finest minds and make wastelands of its finest landscapes? What does material abundance avail if we create an environment in which man's highest and most specifically human attributes cannot be fulfilled?"[5]

In his attempt to answer these questions, Udall pursued an investigative approach using historical inquiry:

> History tells us that earlier civilizations have declined because they did not learn to live in harmony with the land. . . . It is not too late to repair some of the mistakes of the past. . . . We can do it if we understand the history of our husbandry, and develop fresh insight concerning the men and forces that have shared our land attitudes and determine the pattern of land use in the United States. . . . [*The Quiet Crisis*] is dedicated to the proposition that men must grasp completely the relationship between human stewardship and fullness of the American earth.[6]

The fourteen chapters in *The Quiet Crisis* present a compelling history of American natural resource conservation. The first three chapters ("The Wisdom of the Indians," "The Birth of a Land Policy," and "The White Indians") trace this history from pre-Columbian times up to the settlement of the American West, paying homage to the Native Americans who first entered the North American continent some 10,000 years ago. As diverse as these native peoples were in language and customs, there was, nevertheless, one trait which was common to all in Udall's view: their reverence for the life-giving Earth.[7]

To the Native Americans, this homeland was the center of their universe. They held a deep affection for the Earth yet had no notion of private ownership. The idea that land could be bought, sold, and owned, said Stewart Udall, was an alien concept to them. Lands were almost always held in common; upon the death of an individual, the property used by that person would revert back to the community at large for redistribution.

Once the Europeans set foot on the continent, the drama between them and the Native Americans unfolded like a "Greek tragedy."[8] Initial friendship and cooperation were soon replaced with distrust and hostility. The invaders parceled out once-wild lands to private ownership and plundered the natural resources. The settlers' demand for land and resources proved insatiable; policy toward the Indians was governed solely by expediency. Forced removals, settlement on reservations, and genocide eventually sacrificed the Indians' way of life in order to "redeem" the continent from the wilderness.

As Udall noted, after long years, we now have an opportunity to measure the influence of the Indians and their culture on American life, and we find much to learn. Said Stewart Udall, "It is ironic that today the conservation movement finds itself turning back to ancient Indian land ideas, to the Indian understanding that we are not outside of nature, but of it . . . we have slowly come to some of the truths that the Indians knew . . . that unborn generations have a claim on the land equal to our own, that men need to learn from nature, to keep an ear to the earth, and to replenish their spirit through frequent contacts with animals and wild land."[9]

The Europeans brought to the New World a way of life that dramatically altered the use and stewardship of natural resources. The colonists immediately adopted a dualistic view of the land. On one hand, there was an abundance of resources unlike anything they had ever before seen. Yet, at the same time, they saw the land as wild, forbidding, and in need of taming. Witness this passage from the records of the Plymouth Bay Colony, in November 1620: "What could [the Pilgrims] see but a hideous and desolate wilderness, full of wilde beasts and wilde men . . . all things stand in appearance with a weatherbeaten face, and the whole country, full of woods and thickets, represented a wilde and savage hue."[10]

The Spanish, French, Dutch, and British each in their own way attempted to subdue the "wilde" land. Udall argued that once the Euro-Americans and their government gained the continent, two factors contributed more than any others to the shaping of future natural resource policy. First was the decision by the colonial governments following the Revolutionary War to place into the public domain all lands wrested from the British. Thus was created the origins of an enormous federal land base by which the government could, among other things, direct and influence the availability and consumption of natural resources. Second was the expansion of the public domain through the federal acquisition of land. The most important initial action in this regard was by Thomas Jefferson who arranged the Louisiana Purchase, which immediately doubled the size of the new country.

Explorations of the public domain by government-sponsored expeditions such that of Meriwether Lewis and William Clark and by independent mountain men such as Daniel Boone and Jed Smith evidenced what Udall refers to as "the circular process of history; the land determining the character of the men, who . . . were determining the future of the land." Furthermore said Udall, "The result of this interaction was the clearest possible example of the American ambivalence toward the land that continues to dominate our relationship to the continent and its resources. It is a combination of a love for the land and the practical urge to exploit it shortsightedly for profit."[11]

Chapter 5, "The Raid on Resources," reports on the culmination of this tendency by the citizens of the young nation to exploit the nation's natural resources for profit. The "raid" began with the mountain men and their beaver traps but would reach a series of high points in the last decades of the nineteenth century. Tree cutters were the advance men of agrarianism. Trees were an obstacle to settlement and woodsmen were, therefore, the pioneers of progress. Much of the initial wood harvest was simply wasted. But with the creation of lumber markets for housing and the construction of sawmills, lumbering soon became the United States' largest manufacturing industry.

Timber was not the only resource plundered. Soil that had been eons in the making was as thoroughly devastated as the forests. Mineral exploitation was, likewise, a source of land and resource destruction. California gold miners using canvas hoses and nozzles would wash away entire riverbanks in search of gold-bearing gravel. Oil and natural gas production was a strip-and-run business with enormous incidental waste.

The farmers' pursuit of a livelihood caused them to overgraze rangelands, plow the plains and former forest lands, and leave a path of destruction in their wake. Eventually, most of these farms failed because the farmers, in turn, failed to understand some basic facts about the land. Excessively farmed lands were depleted of nutrients and soil cleared of vegetation disappeared to water and wind.

The fickleness of fashion also contributed to the destruction of natural resources. Populations of fur-bearing animals such as sea otters, seals, and beavers were depleted to serve the coat and hat markets. Plume hunters, answering the demand of the millinery trade, destroyed entire rookeries of egrets and herons.

Perhaps the most inexcusable of these sad histories of resource depletion is that of the American bison. This magnificent emblem of the American frontier was nearly exterminated in an unprecedented campaign of animal butchery. The precise pre-Columbian bison population size is something of mystery, but informed guesses place their original numbers as ranging somewhere between an astounding 10 million and 100 million animals. Settlers wrote that continuous herds of the beasts would extend from six to ten miles in every direction.[12] Mass killings began following the Civil War motivated by several factors: to provide food for railroad workers, meat for city dwellers, or pure sport and, most tragically, from a desire to exterminate them as the primary food source of the Indians. The extent of this bison carnage exceeds comprehension. Of the millions of animals that had originally populated the nation, by the late 1880s, only a few hundred individual bison still lived . . . only a few hundred! Even President U. S. Grant, hero of the U.S. Civil War, when given the chance to sign a bison protection bill into law, vetoed it, thus casting his lot with the proponents of waste and butchery.

Udall felt that this era of exploitation was encouraged by belief in a myth: "It was the intoxicating profusion of the American continent which induced a state of mind that made waste and plunder inevitable. A temperate continent, rich in soils and minerals and forests and wildlife, enticed men to think in terms of infinity rather than facts, and produced an overriding fallacy that was nearly our undoing—the Myth of Superabundance. According to the myth, our resources were inexhaustible. It was an assumption that made wise management of the land and provident husbandry superfluous."[13]

The rapacious tendencies of these previous generations, fortunately, did not go unnoticed. Stewart Udall notes that, even prior to the mid-nineteenth century, people began to express concern regarding the destruction of nature. Individuals and groups would eventually use an array of approaches to resolve the problem of wanton destruction of natural resources. Some were philosophers, others relied upon science, yet others sought to influence government policy, while some argued for private individual action. The chapter titled "The Stir of Conscience" deals in part with the philosophical approach evident in the nature writings of Ralph Waldo Emerson and Henry David Thoreau.

Emerson (1803–1882), a native of Boston, Massachusetts, was an essayist and poet and a leader of the philosophical movement of transcendentalism (see chapter 1 for an explanation of transcendentalism). His principal essay, *Nature,* published in 1836, argued that humans should seek to develop a special relationship with the universe in order to regain a sense of "self," which he felt had been lost in the modern world. The best way for humans to develop this relationship, thought Emerson, was to become attuned to the sights and sounds of the natural world. Many of Emerson's essays were forest prose poems rooted in nature. Solitude, meditation, and communion with nature, to Emerson, were essential to developing a relationship with the universe.

Emerson's neighbor in Concord, Massachusetts, was Thoreau, who was Emerson's junior by fourteen years. Thoreau was a decidedly ungregarious fellow. Although a close friend of Emerson's, he eschewed most other personal relationships. He was said to have a "porcupine personality" and an eccentric manner of escaping the real world by wandering too much in the woods. Thoreau, however, would likely have debated what was meant by "the real world." He rejected the notion that life should be spent getting and spending, just as he looked askance at the engines and establishments of the Industrial Revolution. What would it profit, he asked himself, if people gained the whole continent but in the process lost contact with the wellspring of human renewal?[14]

In 1845, Thoreau began an experiment of sorts to test his theory of natural philosophy. He left civilization and repaired to a cabin on Walden Pond near Concord, where he spent twenty-six months living in a most frugal fashion. There, he minimized his ties with town life and maximized his contact with nature. Thoreau developed a relationship with the animals and the birds, watched the cycles of the seasons, and studied the ponds and rivers, trying to gain a deeper understanding of the natural world.

Thoreau's experience at Walden has no doubt been idealized in the modern mind. It did however serve a great social purpose by alerting a portion of the American public to the need to preserve nature as an essential component of human existence. As such, Thoreau became one of the first U.S. preservationists. He protested the destruction of landscapes and wildlife. He made a plea for national wildlife preserves. Indeed, men like Thoreau and Emerson were forerunners of the U.S. conservation movement. Even though their contributions were largely philosophical in nature, they succeeded in laying a foundation for the people of action who would follow.

Chapter 6 ("The Beginning of Wisdom") explains the key role that science played in setting the nation on a course toward natural resource conservation. One person profiled in this chapter was George Perkins Marsh (see chapter 1 for a biography). Marsh's natural curiosity led him to develop an interest in science related to ecology and the natural environment. In fact, he was one of the first to argue for establishment of the Smithsonian Institution as a government-sponsored research organization. In 1849, he was appointed as minister to Turkey and later, in 1861, as minister to Italy. These assignments gave Marsh an opportunity to expand his knowledge of the history of resource management and ecology to a world scale. While in Italy, George Perkins Marsh began to write *Man and Nature,* in part a lamentation over the past abuses of natural resources, but more important a treatise on world ecology underscoring the interconnectedness of the natural systems of the planet and calling on humans to seek a proper balance with nature.

Through *Man and Nature,* Marsh did more than any of his countrymen to disabuse the notion that the resources of the United States were self-renewing and inexhaustible. "It is certain," he wrote, "that a desolation, like that which has over-whelmed many once beautiful and fertile regions of Europe, awaits an important part of the territory of the United States . . . unless prompt measures are taken to check the action of destructive causes already in operation."[15]

With this book, George Perkins Marsh established both a scientific and moral foundation for a new approach to U.S. natural resource and land policy. Marsh's appeal for the scientific management of resources reached a small but very influential and politically connected group of people in the United States. In *The Quiet Crisis,* Udall devotes several key chapters to this fusion of science and politics which would play such an pivotal role in the American natural resource conservation movement. These chapters include "The Beginning of Action," "The Woodlands," and "Men Must Act" (chapters 7, 8, and 10, respectively).

Key among these individuals who melded science with politics was Carl Schurz. A German by birth, Schurz, in 1848, immigrated to the United States and, in 1877, was appointed secretary of the interior by President Rutherford B. Hayes. Schurz brought with him to the United States a knowledge of German practices of scientific forestry. Armed with this science plus his skills as an orator and journalist, he helped to persuade leaders of some groups, such as the American Forestry Association, that depredations of public forests needed to be halted. Schurz pointed out that, through their cut-and-run practices, American "timber barons," i.e., persons in the private economic sector who harvested public timber, were stealing not merely individual trees but entire forests.

Carl Schurz's observations on the rapidly declining state of America's public forests and the need for more stringent government control met with substantial opposition. Timber-state congressmen accused him of trying to promote "Prussian methods" in a democratic nation and of wanting to oppress honest entrepreneurs who were the backbone of the republic.[16] Schurz, as secretary of the interior, issued a science-based report on the condition of America's public forests that slammed the practices of the timber barons and argued for reform. Although substantive changes in public forest management were still a few decades away, Schurz's use of science and the political system was a milestone in U.S. conservation history.

While Schurz was secretary of the interior, another science-based report on natural resources came across his desk that would prove to be as important as his own on forestry: "A Report on the Lands of the Arid Region of the United States" by John Wesley Powell. Powell's report was essentially a land-use plan for the western United States. He pointed out that, with few exceptions, the land west of the Great Plains received little annual rainfall. The rainfall was so slight, in fact, that traditional agriculture could not be sustained and thus many of the homesteaders moving to that region were doomed to failure. He concluded that the farmers must be aided by river dam development and large reservoirs to provide irrigation water to their dry-land farms.

John Powell presents a tremendously compelling figure even today. After serving in the Union Army during the American Civil War, in which he lost an arm at the Battle of Shiloh, he subsequently spent ten years leading scientific expeditions in the Colorado Plateau region of the western United States. Excited by the land, he devoted one year to daredevil running of the Colorado River through the Grand Canyon to chart the then-unexplored region. It was a mission of science, and his observations were carried out in the face of physical hazards that terrified even the members of his expedition. But in the process of conquering the mighty Colorado River, Powell learned then what we now accept: that scientific management of natural resources, such as water, is the key to their conservation.

A pair of individuals who, likewise, combined science and politics in order to promote the conservation of natural resources was President Theodore Roosevelt and Gifford Pinchot. Indeed, this pair of names is today virtually synonymous with the conservation movement of the late nineteenth and early twentieth centuries. Whereas the timber barons had run roughshod over Carl Schurz, in Roosevelt and Pinchot, they found determined and formidable proponents of forest conservation who, in the end, would win the day.

Pinchot, a well-born, well-educated practitioner of scientific European forestry, was appointed as the Department of Agriculture's first chief forester in 1898. His charge, he was convinced, was to stop the destruction of America's forests and to inaugurate the practice of scientific forestry. Aided by an 1891 congressional act that established national forest reserves, Pinchot set about to develop forest management plans for these lands which would permit their use but with an eye to long-term, sustainable yield.

Pinchot's big break came when Teddy Roosevelt assumed the presidency in 1901. The two men, who were already well acquainted, joined forces to promote the idea that public forests could be used and sustained at the same time.[17] They scored a major victory in 1905 when Congress assigned the public forests to the U.S. Department of Agriculture, where they were designated as national forests.

Pinchot was a conservation fighter, argued Udall, who gave the resource raiders blow for blow. He had no use for abusers of the public domain. Grazers and loggers were assigned permits and assessed users' fees. Grass and trees, for the first time, were managed so that they could be replenished on a sustained-yield basis. Law and order came at last to the public lands and were enforced by Pinchot's forest rangers who served as agents for the current public as well as for future generations.

Gifford Pinchot, opined Stewart Udall, was one of the greatest conservation leaders in our history. He was the only federal bureau chief who was counselor to a president. Witness Teddy Roosevelt's words in his letter to Pinchot the day the president left the White House: "As long as I live, I shall feel for you a mixture of respect and admiration and affectionate regard. I am a better man for having known you. . . . I owe you a particular debt of obligation for a very large part of the achievement of this Administration."[18]

Yet for all the accolades that history can bestow upon a person with such vision, Pinchot was not without his weaknesses as a conservation leader. For example, he lacked sensitivity to wildlife and wilderness values. To him, untrammeled wilderness was a form of waste. The idea of national parks was likewise unacceptable to him. Thus, the stage was set for a head-on collision between the ideas of sustained resource use and their outright preservation.

Chapter 9 of *The Quiet Crisis*, titled "Wild and Park Lands," details the fight to reserve wild lands, located largely in the western United States, simply for protection of their aesthetic and scenic qualities. This philosophy of preservation stood in contrast to Pinchot's belief that forested and wild lands should be used for commodity production and not placed off-limits to lumbering, grazing, and other "productive" activities.

Although many personalities were involved in this struggle to preserve wild lands, none was more prominent nor more colorful than John Muir. In the spring of 1868, Muir arrived in California and first set his eyes on the summits of the Sierra Nevada. It was during an exploratory walk into this mountain wilderness that he first viewed the stupendous valley of the Yosemite. He was at the time thirty years of age; the Yosemite region would from that time forward become the focus of his efforts to preserve wilderness.

A portion of Yosemite Valley had, in fact, been set aside for protection by the state of California four years prior to Muir's arrival. However, lumbermen and cattlemen had continued to extract and use the resources of the land largely unhindered. Muir, desiring to permanently preserve Yosemite, within a few years would observe that a federal model for preservation was established when Yellowstone National Park, our first national park, was designated in 1872. Understanding the power of the press, Muir authored several articles on the Yosemite, thereby persuading the public and politicians that preservation of the unique area was warranted. Beginning in 1890, three unique areas in California—Yosemite, the Sequoia, and the General Grant forest reserves—were established as national parks.

Encouraged by his success, Muir established an organization of conservationists and mountaineers known as the Sierra Club, a group still active today in matters of natural resource protection. Muir, once a friend of Pinchot's, would eventually become involved in a bitter dispute with him over the protection of California's Hetch Hetchy Valley from damming to create a water reservoir (see chapter 1). Muir would eventually lose the fight to protect the Hetch Hetchy. Nevertheless, his push for preservation through the skillful use of lobbying and influencing public opinion would become a model for like-minded preservationists in the post–*Silent Spring* era.

Chapter 11, "Individual Action," and chapter 12, "Cities in Trouble," acknowledge the work of the private organizers and philanthropists who did yeoman's service for the conservation cause: George Bird Grinnell, William Dutcher, and T. Gilbert Pearson helped to form the National Audubon Society, which crusaded for key legislation to protect migratory birds. Grinnell, along with Teddy Roosevelt, helped to organize the Boone and Crockett Club, an elite group of hunters that established national standards for hunting, wildlife protection, and sportsmanship that endure to this day. John D. Rockefeller Jr., son of the Standard Oil Company magnate, channeled his considerable wealth and influence toward the acquisition of lands for the establishment of some of our most important national parks, such as Acadia, Great Smoky Mountains, and the Grand Tetons. Foresters Aldo Leopold and Robert Marshall, in 1934, helped to organize the Wilderness Society, a group that even today helps to promote the national interest in the preservation of wilderness areas. Frederick Law Olmsted, the renowned landscape architect who designed New York's Central Park, helped to promote an interest in improving the beauty and "livability" of our cities.

The Quiet Crisis was a significant environmental literary contribution during the post–*Silent Spring* era that helped to elevate public consciousness regarding the need to protect U.S. public lands for the enjoyment of present and future generations. Stewart Udall was unquestionably influenced by Rachel Carson and was, indeed, a great admirer of her contributions to environmentalism. An interesting historical note: Stewart L. Udall was an honorary pallbearer at Miss Carson's funeral held in Washington National Cathedral.[19] He continues to contribute to the nation's affairs as an author, historian, scholar, lecturer, environmental activist, lawyer, naturalist, and citizen of the outdoors. Today, he lives in Santa Fe, New Mexico.

6

Roderick Nash's
Wilderness and the American Mind

In 1964, the U.S. Congress passed and President Lyndon Johnson signed into law the Wilderness Act (16 U.S.C.A. 1131–1136). Adopted after nearly a decade of debate, during which time it was subjected to substantial opposition, the Wilderness Act at last created for the United States a national wilderness preservation system. At the time of its passage, this law represented one of the strongest commitments to environmental and natural resource preservation by any nation in the world.[1]

The Wilderness Act of 1964, while allowing the continuation of some existing uses and some limited resource development on designated wilderness areas, ensured the protection of wilderness on federal lands in its natural state for public benefit and enjoyment. The almost poetic language of the act spoke of wilderness as "an area where the earth and its community of life are untrammeled by man, where man himself is a visitor who does not remain . . . an area of undeveloped Federal land retaining its primal character and influence . . . which . . . has outstanding opportunities for solitude or a primitive and unconfined type of recreation."[2]

People have advanced many justifications for the preservation of land in a wild state.[3] Some argue that it provides a setting for religious experiences and serves as a refuge from modern civilization. Supporters regard it as an important part of American cultural heritage, as a commitment to ethical obligations to protect nature, and as a setting for a variety of recreational pursuits. For all these reasons, this establishment of "official" wilderness by the U.S. Congress was undeniably a pivotal point in the history of American environmentalism.

In 1964, Roderick Nash, then a doctoral student at the University of Wisconsin, completed his dissertation under the guidance of Professor Merle Curti. The subject of his dissertation, fortuitously, was American wilderness, more specifically, the concept of wilderness as a state of mind. The timing couldn't have been better, as Nash himself would later acknowledge. Said Nash, "I realize that I chose the topic [i.e., wilderness] to write about when it was becoming extremely important in American culture. I was lucky, I picked a subject that 50 years before might not have attracted much attention. . . . I just happened to be right there writing in the field at the beginning of environmental history . . . when wilderness was becoming highly important in American culture. . . . The Wilderness Act was passed the same year that I completed my dissertation."[4]

Fate may indeed have intervened in the completion date of Nash's dissertation. But the written work itself was pure inspiration and enduring scholarship. It was, as Nash would later say, "the big book."[5] It was so comprehensive in scope and so well researched that, when published by Yale University Press in 1967 under the title *Wilderness and the American Mind,* it would become the press's all-time biggest seller and a book rated number two in one survey of the greatest environmental books of all time (rated number one in that survey, incidentally, was *Walden* by Henry David Thoreau).[6]

Wilderness and the American Mind begins with a prologue, "The Condition of Wilderness," then contains twelve chapters and an epilogue. The prologue's principal function is to explore the varied definitions of *wilderness,* and it concludes that the term has "a deceptive concreteness." Wilderness has a subjectivity about it that makes a single definition elusive. As Nash said, "One man's wilderness may be another's roadside picnic ground. The Yukon trapper might consider a trip to northern Minnesota a return to civilization while for the vacationer from Chicago it is a wilderness adventure indeed." In general, however, Nash concluded that wilderness is land where the environment is predominantly nonhuman: "The presence of an occasional beer can, cabin or even road would not disqualify an area but only move it slightly toward the civilized pole."[7]

Chapter 1, "Old World Roots of Opinion," is concerned with historical European, and to a lesser extent Asian, concepts of wilderness.[8] From Old World writings, it is clear that European settlers in the New World were acquainted with the concept of wilderness even before they crossed the Atlantic. Their familiarity was due less to actual contact with wilderness than to their impression of wilderness as an abstract concept in Western thought, particularly in religious writings. Wilderness was a symbol that permeated the Judeo-Christian tradition. Both the Old and New Testaments were replete with references to wild, untamed lands.

The European settler understood wilderness as something alien to humans. It was an insecure and hostile environment against which humankind waged an unceasing struggle. As Nash wrote, "[Wilderness's] dark mysterious qualities made it a setting in which the pre-scientific imagination could place a swarm of demons and spirits. . . . This intellectual legacy of the Old World to the New not only helped determine initial responses but left a lasting imprint on American thought."[9]

Interestingly, many of the biblical references discussed by Nash describe the wilderness as a land reserved for sinners. When the Lord of the Old Testament wished to punish a sinful people, he often found the wilderness his most powerful weapon. The cities of Sodom and Gomorrah, for example, became parched wastes of salt pits and thorny brush to penalize their citizens for their sins. In general, Nash found that Western thought had generated a powerful bias against wilderness and that the New World offered abundant opportunities for the expression of this sentiment.[10]

Chapter 2 of *Wilderness and the American Mind,* titled "A Wilderness Condition," delves into the experiences of the first European settlers in the American wilderness. Nash captures this complex relationship rather succinctly in his description of William Bradford's impression when he first stepped off the *Mayflower.* Bradford called the new land a "hideous and desolate wilderness," thus initiating the settlers' tradition of repugnance for the wilderness.[11]

The first Europeans in America, according to Nash, held two mutually reinforcing views of the wilderness.[12] First, on a physical level, it constituted a threat to survival. Safety and comfort, even necessities like food and shelter, depended upon overcoming the wild environment. The dark forests hid savage creatures and wild beasts and even stranger creatures of the imagination. Second, the wilderness represented the dark and sinister symbol of a moral vacuum. Thus, to these early Europeans the New World represented a cursed and chaotic wasteland.

Settling the new land was akin to a morality play where pilgrims made their claim to the land in the name of nation, race, and God. Civilizing was a process of bringing moral light to darkness, ordering chaos, and changing evil to good.

The early pioneers, opined Nash, simply lived too close to the wilderness to appreciate it. As the French political writer and statesman Alexis de Tocqueville noted following his 1831 visit to the United States: living too close to the wilds had produced a bias against them.[13] With the rare exception of the frontiersman who would forsake safety, comfort, and even culture to live in the savage land, the new Americans were prejudiced against the wilderness. It would be their children and grandchildren, far removed from the wilderness condition, who would appreciate its aesthetic values.

Not long after the initial settlement of wild America, wilderness would take on a decidedly more appealing public image. Nash recounts this process of image transformation in chapter 3, "The Romantic Wilderness." The roots of change were found in Romanticism, a literary movement found in virtually every country of Europe, the United States, and Latin America; lasting from about 1750 to about 1870, it was characterized by reliance on the imagination and an idealization of nature.[14]

With Romanticism wilderness would lose much of its repulsiveness. The same qualities—solitude, mystery, and chaos—that to previous generations had made wildness an object of scorn were now coveted as traits of beauty and strength. They had the power to inspire and motivate humans and to serve as an elixir for the soul.

The advent of Romanticism, said Nash, was motivated by breakthroughs in European science, specifically in the areas of astronomy and physics.[15] As scientists revealed a universe that was complex yet harmonious, they strengthened the belief that creation had a divine source and order. This led to a striking change in the concept of nature. It was now seen as fruitful, comfortable, and well ordered. Primitivism, as an extension of the Romantic ideal of nature, argued that humans' happiness and well-being decreased in direct proportion to their degree of civilization. A literary example of Primitivism is found in Daniel Defoe's *Robinson Crusoe*. While Defoe left no doubt that wilderness had its disadvantages, Crusoe's life on the deserted island nevertheless contained an element of charm that implied shortcomings of modern civilization.

Thus with Romanticism, the public's opinion of nature began to change, even if only gradually. The appreciation of nature, importantly, began in the cities. Said Nash, "The literary gentleman wielding a pen, not the pioneer with an axe, made the first gestures of resistance against the strong currents of antipathy. . . . To be sure, indifference and hostility toward wilderness remained generally dominant. . . . Yet by the mid-eighteenth century a few Americans had vigorously stated the case for [wilderness] appreciation."[16]

Chapters 4 through 7 are titled, respectively, "The American Wilderness," "Henry David Thoreau: Philosopher," "Preserve the Wilderness," and "Wilderness Preserved." They recount the impact of changing public opinion regarding wilderness which, in turn, led to the first statutory preservation of natural areas by the U.S. Congress. Important elements in altering public opinion toward wilderness, as Nash notes, were the fine arts and literature and a new sense of nationalism in the American public.

The wilderness of the United States was much grander than anything Europeans had ever experienced. Immediately following independence, the new American citizens began to investigate the nature of their new country. They found its wildness unmatched by anything in their previous cultural experiences, which evoked a sense of national pride regarding natural lands that even supplanted the emotions raised by the Romanticists. Then as now, the media brought these images of wildness to the citizens. And in those times "the media" meant the fine arts and literature.

Accomplished painters such as Thomas Cole of the Hudson River School, Frederic E. Church who portrayed on canvas the beauty of Maine's Mt. Katahdin, Albert Bierstadt who painted the grandeur of the Rocky Mountains, John James Audubon who created *Birds of America,* and Thomas Moran whose huge canvas of the Grand Canyon still hangs in the Senate lobby graphically conveyed the splendor of the American wilderness to politicians and the public. Even today, these powerful, magnificent paintings can evoke strong, sympathetic feelings in the viewer. During the nineteenth century, they had an equally dramatic impact on elected officials who were in a position to protect America's natural wonders.

Like the fine arts, literature also played a key role in influencing public opinion about wilderness during the nineteenth century. Henry David Thoreau's *Walden,* James Fenimore Cooper's colorful stories of frontiersman Natty Bumppo, Francis Parkman's recounting of his western frontier adventures in *Oregon Trail,* and William Cullen Bryant's poems, such as "Thanatopsis," helped to engender in the public a concern for the preservation of disappearing wild America.

The combined forces of literature and art had an impact on the preservation of natural areas. The establishment of Yellowstone National Park on March 1, 1872, was the first official act of wilderness preservation, not only in the United States but in the world. On that date, President U. S. Grant signed an act designating two million acres of northwestern Wyoming as "a public park or pleasuring ground for the benefit and enjoyment of the people. . . . [The secretary of the interior] shall provide for the preservation . . . of all timber, mineral deposits, natural curiosities, or wonders within said park . . . in their natural condition."[17] Nash argues, however, that Yellowstone was not set aside specifically for wilderness preservation. Wilderness was merely a by-product of concern over the protection of geysers, hot springs, and waterfalls from commercial exploitation. Only later would people realize that the establishment of Yellowstone had also preserved wilderness. Thirteen years after Yellowstone was established, the state of New York created a 715,000-acre forest preserve in the Adirondacks to be "kept forever as wild forest lands."[18]

The preservation of Yellowstone and the Adirondack Forest Preserve in the late nineteenth century, while an important beginning for wilderness preservation, occurred almost by accident.[19] What was needed to sustain the momentum of those early successes, said Nash, was a national movement and, of course, leaders to initiate that movement. One such leader was John Muir, whose contributions to the wilderness preservation movement Nash chronicles in chapter 8, "John Muir: Publicizer." Muir not only publicized the movement through his articles in national magazines such as *Atlantic Monthly,* he also helped to define more clearly the differences between wilderness preservation and the practice of forest management, which was also emerging as a national issue during the late nineteenth century.

The goal of forest management was to use forest resources for commodity production but without harming the long-term productive capacity of the land. Wilderness preservation, in contrast, eschewed the harvesting of natural resources for any purpose and aimed at keeping the forest wholly subject to natural processes. Initially, Muir supported forest management, apparently seeing no incompatibility between forestry and wilderness preservation. Muir's early views on the subject led him to establish collegial relationships with both Gifford Pinchot and Teddy Roosevelt (see chapters 1 and 5 in this book), both proponents of commercial forestry. As the months passed, however, the political positions of the parties became delineated and Muir broke with both Pinchot and Roosevelt.

Nash describes the final meeting between Muir and Pinchot, which occurred in the summer of 1897 in a Seattle hotel. The issue at hand was that of sheep grazing on public forest lands. Muir profoundly opposed the "hoofed locust," as he called sheep, as intolerable on forest preserves. In contrast, Pinchot had just released a statement to a Seattle newspaper in support of the grazing of sheep on forest lands. In the hotel lobby, Muir approached Pinchot and asked him if he had been correctly quoted by the newspaper to which Pinchot answered in the affirmative. Muir shot back, "Then . . . I don't want anything more to do with you . . . you yourself [had previously] stated that the sheep do a great deal of harm."[20] Muir's outspokenness and disarming frankness, said Nash, was directed not only at the likes of Gifford Pinchot, but at the president as well. Aware of Roosevelt's love for hunting, Muir once chided the president, "When are you going to get beyond the boyishness of killing things . . . are you not getting far enough along to leave that off?"[21] These personal encounters symbolized the conflict over values that later characterized the differences between the commercial forestry and wilderness factions.

By the close of the nineteenth century, at least a portion of the American public had developed such a fascination with the wildness of nature that Nash termed this national emotion "The Wilderness Cult" (which is the title of his chapter 9). The cult had three principal facets according to Nash.[22] First was the belief that many of the desirable national traits of the American people—such as independence, innovativeness, and self-reliance—were derived from association with the wilderness during the United States' frontier past. Second, the wilderness was seen as a source of virility, toughness, and savagery, qualities that defined fitness in Darwinian terms. And third, a number of Americans saw the wilderness as a place invested with aesthetic and ethical values which, in turn, afforded a setting for contemplation and worship.

One person who made significant intellectual contributions to advance the wilderness cult was Frederick Jackson Turner (1861–1932). Turner was an American historian born in Portage, Wisconsin, and educated at the University of Wisconsin and Johns Hopkins University. He taught at the University of Wisconsin from 1885 to 1910 and at Harvard University from 1910 to 1924.[23] Turner, through his books and articles, argued that the frontier had made Americans not only different from Europeans but better. Indeed, he stated that the forest wilderness was responsible for forging a particularly strong and desirable form of democracy. Turner argued that living in the wilderness, in the most primitive conditions, had fostered individualism, independence, and confidence that encouraged self-government.[24] Thus, Turner linked in the minds of his fellow citizens the wild nature of their native land with the most sacred American virtues. Turner also noted that the end of the nineteenth century marked the first decade that the country was without a frontier. Turner's tone in his writings, said Nash, "suggested a pessimism and contributed to a general sense of nostalgic regret over the disappearance of wilderness conditions,"[25] thus encouraging Americans to preserve the wilderness qualities that remained.

The greatest showdown during the early twentieth century over the preservation of wilderness was undoubtedly California's Hetch Hetchy dam incident (the subject of Nash's chapter 10; see also chapters 1 and 5 in this book). The city of San Francisco was pushing to dam the Tuolumne River, which flows through Hetch Hetchy Valley, in order to supply its water needs. The damming would, of course, obliterate the valley, which was akin to neighboring Yosemite Valley in its grandeur. The damming did take place, but only after a bitter public battle which featured, among others, Pinchot, Roosevelt, and the developers opposing Muir, the preservationist. To be fair, however, Nash reports that Roosevelt was hardly strident in favoring the dam. Indeed, he seemed to have had quite mixed emotions favoring both preservation and development, but ultimately he supported the latter.[26]

The Hetch Hetchy dam project was finally approved by President Woodrow Wilson on December 10, 1913. In signing the act, he declared that "the bill was opposed by so many public-spirited men . . . that I have naturally sought to scrutinize it very closely. I take the liberty of thinking that their fears and objections were not well-founded."[27]

The key change stemming from the Hetch Hetchy incident, argued Nash, was that even though the damming did proceed, the American public was becoming increasingly concerned about destroying nature. Said Nash, "Muir [and others] were able to create a protest [about the proposed dam] because the American people were ready to be aroused. Appreciation of wild country and the desire for its preservation had spread in the closing decades of the nineteenth century from a small number of literati to a sizeable segment of the population." Furthermore, stated Nash, "very few favored the dam because they opposed the wilderness. Even the partisans of San Francisco phrased the issue as not between a good [i.e., civilization] and an evil [i.e., wilderness] but between two goods. . . . For three centuries they had chosen civilization without hesitation. By 1913 they were no longer so sure."[28]

As the citizens of the United States moved into the twentieth century, the interest in preservation of wilderness was indeed growing. The wilderness movement, or "cult" as Nash called it, had produced leaders and made a few key accomplishments. However, what was needed in order to produce substantive future results was an ethic—a philosophy as it were—to guide the movement. The person who would provide this philosophy, according to Nash, was Aldo Leopold (chapter 11, "Aldo Leopold: Prophet").

Graduating in 1908 as a forester from Yale University, Leopold worked for a time as a wildlife manager with the U.S. Forest Service in New Mexico and Arizona when they were still U.S. territories. During his formative years with the Forest Service, Leopold developed what would become a lifelong passion regarding the establishment of wilderness areas. Because of his interest and persistence, agency officials allowed Leopold to develop guidelines for the preservation of areas for wilderness recreation which, in turn, led to the establishment of the first official wilderness area, the Gila located in New Mexico. Leopold also inspired the development, in 1929, of a Forest Service policy for preservation of other wilderness areas in the national forest system.[29]

Perhaps even greater than these accomplishments, however, was Leopold's development over a period of years of a guiding philosophy regarding land ethics. Through journal articles and books such as *Sand County Almanac* Leopold, said Nash, argued that modern humankind needed a fundamental "change in attitude toward the natural world." Humans, said Leopold, needed "to see the land as a whole . . . to think of it in terms of community rather than group welfare, and in terms of the long as well as the short view."[30] Aldo Leopold therefore argued for the development by humans of a "land ethic" that "enlarges the boundaries of the community to include soils, waters, plants, and animals, or collectively the land." According to Leopold, the adoption of this land ethic "changes the role of *Homo sapiens* from conqueror of the land-community to plain member and citizen of it."[31]

Leopold's "land ethic" and his concern for the protection of wilderness even today inspire wilderness advocates. Said Nash, "So persuasively and eloquently did Leopold press these points that they quickly became gospel among preservationists and were woven into the fabric of the justification of the continued existence of wilderness."[32]

Robert Marshall was another twentieth-century personality important to the wilderness movement whose contributions Nash discusses in chapter 12, "Decisions for Permanence." Marshall, the son of a wealthy New York City attorney, early in life developed a strong interest in the outdoor life. As early as his junior year in high school, Marshall declared, "I love the woods and solitude. . . . I should hate to spend the greater part of my lifetime in a stuffy office or crowded city."[33]

While Marshall may not rank among the most original students of the meaning of wilderness, few have exceeded his zeal and effectiveness in crusading for preservation. His great strength was in translating ideas into action. Among his many notable contributions to the wilderness movement was founding and financing from his own personal funds The Wilderness Society, a Washington, DC–based environmental organization that even today is responsible for protection of forest and wilderness areas in the United States. Tragically, Marshall died of heart failure in 1939 at the relatively young age of thirty-eight years. In his will, he left a bequest of $400,000 to The Wilderness Society,[34] the equivalent of almost $5 million in 2003 dollars. In his epilogue to *Wilderness and the American Mind*, Rod Nash briefly discussed the National Wilderness Preservation System established by the Wilderness Act of 1964. Nash's brief mention of the system and the act is understandable in that they were created in the same year that his book was published. As already noted, the Wilderness Act of 1964 represents the strongest commitment by any nation to the preservation of wilderness. The act defines wilderness as an area of the Earth that is essentially untrammeled by humans, where the primary effects are of nature and the human imprint is unnoticeable; where there are opportunities for solitude, with designated areas being at least five thousand acres in size; and which may contain features other than wilderness which are of scientific, ecological, or historic interest.

The 1964 act designated nine million acres of "instant" wilderness and set in motion programs to study other areas for inclusion in a National Wilderness Preservation System.[35] An official act of Congress is required for the designation of any new wilderness area. Each new area is governed by the original Wilderness Act and by the specific statute that designated it as wilderness. The National Wilderness Preservation System includes land located across many federal agency landholdings: the National Park System, the National Wildlife Refuge System, the National Forest System, and the Bureau of Land Management. The managing agencies are required to preserve the wild character of the land, although some existing activities may continue (e.g., grazing, mining). New structures, roads, and motorized vehicles are forbidden except where used for rescue or emergency purposes. Mineral leasing is banned and timber harvesting is generally not allowed except for the control of fire, disease, or insects that may endanger adjacent ownerships.

Many have acclaimed the importance and contribution of Rod Nash's *Wilderness and the American Mind*. The *Los Angeles Times* hailed it as one of the "one hundred most influential books published in the United States in the last quarter century." *Outside Magazine* called it "one of the books that changed the world." Furthermore, it has been called "a book of genesis of modern environmentalism."[36]

A descendant of the Canadian river explorer Simon Roderick Fraser, Roderick Nash earned a Ph.D. in history from the University of Wisconsin–Madison. He subsequently enjoyed a thirty-year career as a professor of history and environmental studies at Dartmouth College and the University of California at Santa Barbara. At the latter institution, he offered the nation's first courses in environmental history. His efforts to organize an environmental studies major led to one of the first interdisciplinary programs in the United States, a program he also chaired. Nash has written several other noteworthy books, including *The Rights of Nature: A History of Environmental Ethics* (1989), which has been translated into six languages. One of the first commercial river guides in the American West, Nash drew on his experience navigating legendary whitewater rivers to write *The Big Drops: Ten Legendary Rapids of the American West* (1989). Nash retired from the University of California at Santa Barbara in 1994 to focus on whitewater boating, powder skiing, and ocean cruising. His work as an advocate for environmental responsibility and wilderness preservation continues.

7

A. C. Pigou, Ronald Coase, and the
Development of Environmental Economics

In response primarily to *Silent Spring*'s message of environmental concern, the academic community soon began generating literature on the subject. Political scientists, biologists, sociologists, everyone so it seems, got into the act. By the mid-1960s, academic economists had even created the field of study called environmental economics. This intriguing new direction was a search for an improved economic theory as to why humans abused the land, water, and air.

Yet to say that environmental economics was a new field of study in the mid-1960s is in fact a half-truth. The origins of environmental economics had emerged several decades earlier in Victorian England. At that time, the classical economic theories of Adam Smith, Thomas Malthus, and David Ricardo were undergoing intense scrutiny by economists. The unofficial leader of this emerging neoclassical school of thought was the great Cambridge University economist Alfred Marshall. Among the concerns of Marshall and his followers was to identify an economic measure of societal well-being. The term they used to describe this branch of neoclassicism was *welfare economics,* a phrase that did not have the present-day connotation of government help to the indigent. Welfare economics focused on the measurement of human satisfaction resulting from the production and consumption of goods and services.

Using the same analytical methods then in vogue for solving engineering problems, Marshall and his contemporaries constructed mathematical abstractions of the economic world to aid them in their studies. By creating new devices such as market supply and demand curves and by using marginal solutions derived from differential calculus, the neoclassicists were able provide a deeper, more orderly understanding of economics. Generally, they also held a more optimistic view of the distant future than their predecessors had. Whereas Malthus and Ricardo had expressed doubts about the availability of resources, and hence the ultimate viability of civilization, this new breed of economists saw humankind as capable of coping with the problems of a risky world. The basis of their faith was, as also expressed by Harold Barnett and Chandler Morse, that humankind could use the constant flow of information coming from a well-functioning marketplace to make long-term adjustments and improvements. Consumers could change their consumption patterns in response to changing market prices. Likewise, producers could adapt to market signals by altering production inputs and outputs and, importantly, through the adoption of new cost-saving production technologies. Thus, the marketplace itself was seen as a sort of economic gyroscope always correcting and compensating as society hurtled into the future.

From the neoclassical studies of economic welfare eventually emerged a two-part, market-based measure of social well-being. The first part, producer's surplus, is in essence a measure of profits, that is, the difference between the price received for an item in the market and the cost of producing it. Thus, producer's surplus is said to be the best measure of the well-being of the business sector. The second measure, consumer's surplus, is conceptually a bit more complicated. It is the difference between the value of the satisfaction a consumer receives from the consumption of a good and the price that must be paid for it. For example, if the consumer pays $1.00 for an item and receives $1.50 worth of enjoyment from it, the resulting consumer's surplus is 50¢.

Producer's and consumer's surpluses provided a place for economists to begin analyzing societal welfare, but the conceptual framework was incomplete. Still lacking was some means of accounting for market-external occurrences, such as pollution, which also affected human welfare. The missing piece was supplied by a student of Marshall's named A. C. Pigou in his book titled *The Economics of Welfare*. Pigou's text, first published in 1920, was a rich and comprehensive work consisting of nearly one thousand pages of turgid—and trying—post-Edwardian-era prose. He agreed with his fellow neoclassicists that the principal measure of economic welfare was the money value of human satisfaction derived from the production and consumption of goods and services:

Economic welfare [is] broadly taken to consist in that group of satisfactions and dissatisfactions which can be brought into relation with a money measure.... For the most general purposes of economic analysis, therefore, not much harm is likely to be done by the current practice of regarding money demand price indifferently as the measure of ... satisfaction.[1]

If Pigou had stopped there, history might have forgotten him, but fortunately he probed deeper. There existed, he said, "a number of violent paradoxes" to this definition of economic welfare. Among these paradoxes he listed "the frequent desolation of beautiful scenery through the hunt for coal or gold, the desecration widely wrought by uncontrolled smoke from factories and by the injury done to natural beauty by public advertisements."[2] A. C. Pigou thus recognized that there were certain activities occurring off the balance sheet of monetary trade which affected human welfare as much as the value of the goods and services people produced and consumed. And, in order to get a true measure of society's economic welfare, these hidden activities had to be taken into account.

Pigou also realized that these amendments to welfare could cut both ways, yielding both beneficial and detrimental effects. These effects he called "uncompensated services and disservices," and he described how they arose:

Here the essence of the matter is that one person A, in the course of rendering some service, for which payment is made, to a second person B, incidentally also renders services or disservices to other persons C, D and E, of such a sort that technical considerations prevent payment from being extracted from the benefited parties or compensation being enforced on behalf of the injured parties.[3]

Thus, person A is the producer while person B is the consumer. Other persons C, D, and E are third parties external to the market transaction who receive the uncompensated services or disservices. He provided examples of an uncompensated service (i.e., beneficial side effect) and disservice: "It is true in like manner of land devoted to afforestation, since the beneficial effect on climate extends beyond the borders of the estates owned by the persons responsible for the forest" and "smoke from factory chimneys . . . in large towns inflicts a heavy uncharged loss on the community, in injury to buildings and vegetables, expenses for washing clothes and cleaning rooms, expenses for the provisions of extra artificial light and in many other ways."[4]

Pigou referred to the directly measurable value of output as trade net product. When his uncompensated services and disservices were added to or deducted from the trade net product, he called the result social net product. Social net product was then Pigou's true economic measure of human welfare because it accounted for not only the monetary value of goods and services, but the indirect environmental impacts as well.

The Cambridge professor also recognized that equating trade with social net products through adjustment for uncompensated effects was a condition necessary for maximizing social welfare. And since the normally functioning market was incapable of accomplishing this, argued Pigou, it was the responsibility of governments to correct any inequity between trade and social costs through the imposition of "bounties and taxes."[5] To exercise this responsibility would bring about an overall improvement in human welfare through the restoration of a well-functioning market. Thus, governments would tax polluters in order to force them to adjust production and thus eliminate disservices while paying subsidies (bounties) to encourage the production of desirable services, such as natural aesthetics, for which no cash market existed. With these theories Pigou laid the foundation for the modern economic study of the environmental crisis.

With respect to his personal history, Arthur Cecil Pigou was born of French Huguenot parents in 1877 on the Isle of Wight just off the southern coast of England. In 1897, he went to Cambridge to study history and economics under Alfred Marshall. With Marshall's retirement in 1908, the thirty-year-old Pigou was named to succeed his former teacher as professor in the Chair of Political Economy at Cambridge. In 1914 Pigou was called into the armed forces to serve in World War I but refused as a conscientious objector. Instead he served in a ambulance unit run by the Society of Friends. His war experiences apparently had a deep emotional effect on Pigou and, as a result, he began a slow social withdrawal which progressed until, by life's end, he was a recluse. Curious evidence of this reclusiveness is the fact that, as a professor, he dictated through a half-opened door to a secretary seated in the next room. The manuscripts were then typed and returned to him the following day through campus mail.[6]

Through the years, Pigou's ideas were passed from professor to student, collecting a few additions along the way. New names were applied to Pigou's uncompensated services and disservices. They were called, respectively, external economies and diseconomies, and collectively were referred to simply as economic externalities. The process by which externalities were reduced through taxes and subsidies was called internalizing. Also, imaginative analytical techniques were developed for assessing damages to those aesthetic and psychological values that are not normally traded in markets.

By the 1950s, economists came to recognize the very important fact that most externalities existed due to the problem of open-access property. Thus, air and water pollution were not necessarily a matter of persons with evil intentions maliciously inflicting harm on others. Air and water were receptacles for pollution simply because, as open-access property, they were freely accessible. In effect, they constituted a free garbage dump—free at least to the polluter. The concept of open-access property was perhaps what Pigou had in mind when he said "technical considerations prevent payment from being extracted" for pollution damage.[7] But where Pigou had come close, later economists such as Scott Gordon, a Canadian, hit the target dead center.[8] The nut of the problem was unassigned property rights. People polluted because it was to their economic advantage and because there were no means of preventing them from doing so. Economists coined the term *market failure* to describe the process by which open-access property prevented a natural market price from being set for pollution deposition.

By the close of the 1950s, the theories of Pigou stood as unchallenged economic dogma. Government was seen as the party responsible for correcting economic externalities due to open-access property–induced market failure. However, in 1960, a British economist named Ronald H. Coase, then a professor at the University of Virginia, published a seminal paper titled "The Problem of Social Cost" which offered an alternative to Pigou's solution of government involvement. The fundamental difference in Coase's theory was his unique visualization of the problem. In his search for a remedy to pollution and the open-access property problem, Coase was not concerned with justice in the conventional sense; that is, in the sense that someone must be punished for polluting. Instead, his desire was to seek a state of economic fairness where all parties could benefit. His goal was to make all participants as economically well off as possible without worsening the condition of any of them. This economic state is referred to by economists as potential Pareto optimality after the Italian economist Vilfredo Pareto, who originated this definition of economic fairness.

Coase offered as his solution the idea of a negotiated settlement between parties. This, he said, was superior to one enforced through taxation as Pigou had suggested. To begin with, he saw enormous problems in simply determining the proper amount of the tax. The tax, said Pigou, should be equal to the economic damage, but the value of the damage, thought Coase, was virtually impossible to measure. And even if government officials could accurately determine the size of the tax, there were still problems in achieving a Pareto optimal state. The polluting firm, when facing the tax, would reduce its industrial production. While this would help achieve an optimal reduction in pollution damage to third parties, a problem would arise because the firm would lose profits and consumers would forego the benefit of consuming some of the firm's output. The net result: one winner and two losers. The most efficient solution, argued Coase, was a negotiated settlement sans government involvement, provided that the cost of negotiation was not too great. Those suffering pollution damage would receive compensation for their losses, while producers could continue previous output levels and consumers likewise could maintain their satisfaction from product consumption. The implication stemming from Coase's work, in the legacy of neoclassical optimism, was that humans could live with some environmental degradation if they were willing to rely on a free-market approach—negotiated damage compensation—to correct a malfunctioning market system.

Coase also addressed the issue of which party, prior to negotiation, should initially possess the rights to the common property. Should it be the sufferer or the polluter? After all, said Coase, didn't the producer have as much right to produce as the sufferer did not to be polluted? Good common sense would suggest to most people that the sufferer should own those rights. And the sufferer, accordingly, should tell the polluter to stop using the common property for pollution disposal and to pay for the damages caused thereby. Coase's remarkable conclusion, however, was that it did not matter which party was initially assigned the rights to the common property. If the two parties were compelled to negotiate a solution then, in theory, the same amount of pollution reduction would occur regardless of to whom the property rights had been originally assigned. It mattered not whether the pollution sufferer was assigned the property rights and the company had to compensate the sufferer for pollution damages or, alternatively, the company was assigned the rights and the sufferer had to bribe it in order to stop the polluting. The resulting reduction in pollution would be identical in both cases. Thus, the question of who should own the common property was irrelevant to an economically efficient decision. With regard to income distribution, however, the assignment of property rights could have an enormous impact.

In formulating his celebrated theorem, one that would eventually garner for him the 1991 Nobel Prize in Economics, Coase had used Pigou's thoughts as an intellectual springboard. It was Pigou's notion of uncompensated services and disservices and his remedy of government intervention through taxation that had motivated Ronald Coase. In the closing pages of his text, however, Coase expressed less than laudatory opinions of his fellow countryman's work:

> Indeed, Pigou's treatment of the problems considered in this article is extremely elusive and . . . his views [raise] almost insuperable difficulties in interpretation . . . it is difficult to resist the conclusion, extraordinary though this may be in an economist of Pigou's stature, that the main source of this obscurity is that Pigou had not thought his position through. It is strange that a doctrine so faulty as that developed by Pigou should have been so influential, although part of its success has probably been due to the lack of clarity in exposition. Not being clear, it was never clearly wrong.[9]

This criticism notwithstanding, the work of Pigou coupled with that of Coase put mainstream economists on an inside track when *Silent Spring* launched the modern environmental era. Indeed, with the environmental movement, their economic theories had at last found an application. By the mid-1960s, interest in the study of environmental economics was increasing in universities, government agencies, and private organizations such as Resources for the Future. Renowned natural resource economists such as John V. Krutilla and Allen V. Kneese began to build award-winning careers in the field. Several textbooks on environmental economics would eventually appear, and some two dozen scholarly journals each year would carry hundreds of articles on the subject. Issues dealt with in that growing body of literature include environmental pollution, global warming, outdoor recreation, fisheries, common-access property, and a host of theoretical topics.

The importance of Pigou's and Coase's contributions becomes clearer with the realization that economics, as much as any field of learning, is defined by its theory. This has always been the tradition in economics where empirical studies were largely a late-developing, post–World War II phenomenon. For most of the Western world's first two centuries of formal economic thought, data and high-speed computers were lacking and therefore theoretical analysis was the only study method available. Even today, prestigious academic stature in the field is determined mostly by how well one understands and utilizes that theory. Economists have used the elegant contributions of Coase and Pigou to conduct perhaps the most systematic examinations of any group of environmental scholars. Their discoveries and jargon have spread to other academic disciplines; it is not at all uncommon to hear non-economists speak, for instance, of "internalizing externalities."

Yet despite their achievements, environmental economists have typically played a subordinate role in influencing public environmental policy. Neither taxes nor market-like negotiations have found much real-world acceptance. Instead, direct regulation of polluters, an approach disdained by most economists, has been by far the most widely used method of pollution control. Certainly, some people may point to examples of economic-based mechanisms to remedy pollution—such as the carbon emissions trading markets as a solution to global climate change and the so-called transferable discharge permits which appeared in the U.S. Clean Air Act of 1990—as evidence of acceptance of the theories. With transferable discharge permits, an acceptable total level of pollution is designated for a large geographic area and each polluting firm in the area is then given permits to emit a prescribed portion of the total allowable pollution.[10] Individual firms may subsequently transfer (i.e., buy or sell) these permits in order to allow them to pollute more or less, but the total amount of pollution emitted by all firms is held constant. Discharge permits remain, however, an unproven approach to pollution control. In fact, environmental groups have even threatened legal challenges against the Clean Air Act if the use of pollution permits persists. Another instance of the lack of acceptance of economic theory in resolving environmental problems is found in large federal research programs. Even in billion-dollar federal environmental programs such as the National Acid Precipitation Assessment Program and the U.S. Global Change Program economists were invited to play only minor roles.

There are at least two explanations for the less than profound impact of neoclassical economics on environmental policy. First is the perception that environmental economics is a purely theoretical and perhaps even incomprehensible body of knowledge. Practitioners frequently invoke conditions that are impossible to duplicate in the real world. For example, the idea of getting parties together to negotiate pollution settlements seems far-fetched to many. Such a process, if not entirely impossible to conduct, would be very costly, thus violating one of the assumptions Coase had stipulated must be true. The theory itself, even for academicians, can be intellectually inaccessible. The writings of Coase, for instance, though devoid of higher mathematics, had to go through several interpretations by other economists before they were generally intelligible. And, as we recall, even Coase said he had difficulty understanding Pigou. Too, the compulsion of economists to present their ideas in the form of complex mathematics has not helped their cause. For all but a few, the formulations are arid and obscure.

Perhaps the greater obstacle to acceptance of the pollution remedies raised by Pigou and Coase, however, is their political unpalatability. The notion that taxes or market mechanisms should be used to achieve an "optimal level" of pollution is difficult for many public officials to accept. Indeed, even to suggest that there exists an optimal level of pollution could be construed as blasphemy. An optimal level of pollution would mean that society will always condone some environmental damage because total elimination is not cost-beneficial. Optimizing behavior is unquestionably an accurate description of public choice with respect to many phenomena. Society does not, for example, attempt to eliminate all crime or place traffic signals at every intersection. Instead, an optimal level of citizen protection is selected based upon perceived benefits, costs, and associated risks. But pollution is a different matter. Environmentalists certainly object to the notion that it is permissible to pollute. Even the typical citizen would likely find this idea repugnant. Thus, for a good portion of society the only acceptable political goal, unrealistic though it may be, is the virtual elimination of pollution.

Environmental economists today represent the most influential group within the general field of economics working on issues related to environmental quality. The neoclassical school of economics along with the theories of Pigou and Coase still constitute the principal theoretical underpinnings for those involved in mainstream environmental economics. As for the two early contributors, Arthur Cecil Pigou passed away in 1959, while Ronald Coase is now professor emeritus retired from the University of Chicago.

8

Kenneth Boulding and Spaceship Earth

In 1966 University of Colorado professor Kenneth Boulding published "The Economics of the Coming Spaceship Earth." The principal subject of this brief yet complex essay was the decreasing availability of the world's natural resources, especially energy resources, and the economic implications of these changes. His analysis was novel in that it used concepts from physics to examine the Earth's energy, matter, and information systems. This introduction of the laws of physics into environmental thought would prove to be a lasting contribution.

The theories that Boulding favored were not neoclassical as might be expected from a practicing professor of economics. He was, in fact, surprisingly critical of some standard mainstream economic concepts and analytical practices. Instead, as he discussed the transition from the frontier to the coming spaceman economy, Boulding expressed neo-Malthusian concerns regarding the planet's dwindling energy supplies. "Spaceship Earth" also called on society to voluntarily reduce resource consumption, the same recommendation John Stuart Mill had first stated formally in his writings.

Boulding believed that humans were progressing from a world of seemingly limitless open systems of energy and natural resources to a world with bounded, closed systems. The consequence of the closed system, feared the professor, was that the Earth's civilization would ultimately be doomed due to energy shortages dictated by the laws of physics. Through his writing he provided environmentalism with a clever metaphor—the spaceship—to describe the finite character of our planet. Too, his title captured the urgent and anxious mood of a global population racing headlong toward an uncertain but potentially disastrous future. Within a just few years, "Spaceship Earth" was a frequently cited essay destined to become a classic in the environmental literature.

Kenneth E. Boulding was born in 1910 in Liverpool, England, the son of a gas fitter and a housewife.[1] In his youth, he developed a deep interest in pacifism and, consequently, became a Quaker. Throughout his life he remained a dedicated, active Christian who drew great consolation and insight from his faith. Boulding excelled as a student, attending first Liverpool Collegiate then Oxford University, where he took up the study of economics. In 1932, he won a scholarship to continue his economics training at the University of Chicago and later attended Harvard. He returned to Great Britain for a brief time to teach at the University of Edinburgh, but finally returned permanently to North America, where he achieved professional prominence at a succession of U.S. and Canadian universities: Colgate, Fisk, Iowa State College, McGill, Michigan, Stanford and, finally, Colorado.

As a professor of economics, Boulding was regarded as a creative but unorthodox personality. Many of his views and ideas were never fully accepted by his professional colleagues. In truth, his professional interests and abilities ranged far beyond the narrow, rational world of supply and demand curves, and this set him apart from his peers. Nominated at different times for Nobel Prizes in both peace and economics, Kenneth Boulding was known best for his prolific publishing and his perceptive moral insights that challenged his fellow social scientists. His spiritual and philosophical concerns eventually led him far beyond the confines of conventional economics. During his career, he wrote three dozen books, eight hundred articles, and, interestingly, three volumes of poetry. Boulding's long white mane, stammering speech, and pointed wit made him a popular and entertaining lecturer. A colleague once remarked, "Imagine someone who was half Milton Friedman and half Mahatma Gandhi. His talks, his writing were so full of brilliant asides that no summary does them justice."[2]

In the pages of "Spaceship Earth," Boulding referred to the passing era of limitless resources as the "cowboy economy." This phrase captured, he thought, the reckless image often associated with the exploitive behavior characteristic of mature societies. To be sure, humans had known for centuries that they inhabited a spherical, closed Earth. But with respect to land and natural resources at least, the Earth had appeared boundless. This vision of the Earth as an endless, exploitable frontier was one of the oldest images held by humankind. Thus, said Boulding, it was a difficult concept to erase. But the times were bringing change. The global community was in transition, moving quickly from frontier conditions toward the realization of the closed and resource-limited spaceman economy.

The principal difference between the old and the new economies, said Boulding, was in their attitudes toward the consumption of energy and other natural resources. In the cowboy economy, consumption and production were regarded as laudable. In fact, the success of society was commonly measured in its amount of throughput, that is, in the amount of resources consumed as factors of production. GNP, the most widely used measure of economic activity during Boulding's day, was nothing more than a measure of the money value of total material throughput. The goal, then, of the cowboy economy was to maximize GNP and, thus, maximize natural resource consumption.

In contrast to the cowboy economy, the coming spaceman economy would try to minimize material throughput. Greater emphasis would be placed upon the preservation of stocks of natural resources; that is, the untapped reserve of resources as differentiated from throughput. Throughput represents the flow of resources to the consumer. The cowboy economy, for example, places value upon oil or timber extraction and their movement through the marketing channels to the final consumer. It makes no attempt to include in national income accounts the value of the stocks of resources that remain in place. In contrast, the spaceman economy is less concerned with increasing the rate of flows than with maintaining resource stocks in reserve.

Boulding thought that this emphasis on resource stocks could be incorporated into national measures of economic performance such as GNP. In the spaceman economy, Boulding suggested that society would want to distinguish between that portion of GNP which is derived from exhaustible as opposed to renewable resources. The portion of GNP that depletes exhaustible resources would constitute a deduction from the value of national wealth because it consumed resources that could not be replaced. That part of consumption and production activities which generated pollution would also be deducted from GNP. Such compensation for resource depletion and pollution in the calculation of GNP, Boulding believed, would provide a more meaningful measure of social well-being.

Boulding put some of the responsibility for a smooth transition to the spaceman economy on his fellow economists. The transition would require from them a change in philosophy regarding traditional economic practices. In particular he focused on the economist's practice of time-discounting future events. Economists have traditionally discounted (i.e., reduced) the value of future events relative to those that occur nearer in time. Indeed, the value of an event, such as a cash payment, that occurs fifty to one hundred years hence is reduced practically to nil by the mathematics of discounting. To illustrate, a loss of natural resources valued at $1 million that occurs one hundred years in the future would equal only about $7,600 when discounted to the present time by just 5 percent per year. Time-discounting therefore implies that the welfare of future generations is less important than that of present generations because it diminishes the future impact of today's environmental damage and excessive resource consumption. This callous disregard for intergenerational environmental impacts could lead to the dissolution of society. Said Boulding, "A society which loses its identity with posterity and which loses its positive image of the future loses also its capacity to deal with present problems and soon falls apart."[3]

The focal point of Boulding's essay was an exploration of a phenomenon known as entropy with respect to three types of closed Earth systems: energy, matter, and information. In a general sense, entropy refers to disorder or randomness within a system. More specific to Boulding's interest was the concept of entropy as used in thermodynamics, the branch of physics dealing with heat as a form of energy. The second law of thermodynamics states that heat energy will always flow from a hot body to a colder body and never in reverse. The second law says, further, that mechanical energy can be converted into heat, but that heat can never be completely turned back into mechanical energy. Within a closed thermodynamic system, entropy—that is, unavailable energy—will always increase and never decrease.

According to the second law of thermodynamics, without the introduction of new energy sources to our planet, the existing supply of energy, because of entropy, will dissipate and thus eventually become unavailable for use. In theory, then, entropy places an absolute limit on the viability of civilization. The second law dictates that we will eventually run out of useful energy. And with no energy there can be no civilization.

Boulding also explored the question of entropy with respect to matter and information: Would matter and information also, because of entropy, eventually become unavailable for human use? Because of another principle of physics, the law of conservation of matter, Boulding saw no limit placed on human existence due to the dissipation of material resources. This law states that matter can neither be created nor destroyed. Later, however, Paul Ehrlich would see the conservation of matter as posing a certain environmental dilemma for society (see chapter 10).

Neither did Boulding foresee a problem with information entropy. Instead he saw human knowledge as not only the most resilient system of all, but the most important as well: "We can see this preeminence of knowledge very clearly in the experiences of countries where material capital has been destroyed by war, as in Japan and Germany. The knowledge of people was not destroyed, and it did not take long . . . for most of the material capital to be reestablished again."[4]

Among his contemporaries, Kenneth Boulding had earned a reputation as an imaginative, productive iconoclast. In this respect, "Spaceship Earth" mirrored the mind of its creator. Rather than being a well-polished, linearly organized treatise, it was more a smorgasbord of thoughts relevant to the environment and future civilization. Despite its organizational jumble, however, it gained lasting currency in academic circles, but more so among ecologists and biologists than mainstream economists.

The notion of entropy did not, of course, originate with Boulding. It had been part of the science of physics since its introduction in 1824 by French engineer Sadi Carnot, who had been studying the thermal properties of engines. However, Boulding does seem to be one of the first writers to apply the idea to the environment. Over the years, entropy would continue to be a perplexing topic revisited time and again by various authors in the environmental literature. In current environmental studies textbooks, for example, the laws of thermodynamics and of conservation of matter are routinely discussed with regard to their environmental implications.

In a sense, entropy as an environmental issue is a new version of the older Malthusian theme of resource consumption and economic scarcity. With entropy, the problem results from the scarcity of energy due to its physical properties. To many environmentalists, the second law of thermodynamics is undeniable scientific proof that humanity's time on Earth is fixed. Strict constraints on energy consumption are the only hope for at least extending the existence of civilization.

In 1971, just five years after "Spaceship Earth" appeared, Professor Nicholas Georgescu-Roegen published "The Entropy Law and the Economic Process," which delved even further into the issue first raised by Boulding. Georgescu-Roegen, like Boulding, was an unorthodox economist. "Unorthodox," in fact, was precisely the term he used to describe himself.[5] Georgescu-Roegen began his essay with a commentary on the changing relationship between humans and their environment. Since the beginning of the Industrial Revolution, he said, humans in general had become so awed by technology that they had largely forgotten about the natural environment. They apparently believed that any problem related to natural resources could be overcome by technological advances. Likewise, economists beginning with the neoclassicists had ceased to consider the natural environment and were instead intrigued with the possibilities of technology. He argued, however, that there was a linkage between nature and the human economy and, furthermore, that it was essential for the good of civilization that the world understand this linkage.

The principal linkage between the economy and the material environment to Georgescu-Roegen was, of course, energy entropy. The goal of the economic system was to provide for human need and enjoyment. In this process, humans converted energy resources to mechanical energy, which has a higher state of entropy, leading to a permanent loss of heat energy within the closed thermodynamic system. The constant push for economic development dictated increasing amounts of energy and thus an escalating loss of energy to entropy. This constant race toward greater economic development demonstrated for Georgescu-Roegen the lack of human foresight: the higher the degree of development, the shorter was the life span of civilization. Instead of squandering energy and effort on luxuries, humanity would be much better served by producing only those goods and services essential for human existence. "The upshot is clear," he said, "every time we produce a Cadillac, we irrevocably destroy an amount of low entropy that could otherwise be used for producing a plow or a spade."[6]

Energy entropy became a permanent topic in the environmental literature through the work of first Boulding and later Georgescu-Roegen. It seemed to be the one inescapable Malthusian stumbling block placed before human civilization. Humans could work their way out of any environmental pickle in which they might find themselves except this sticky problem of energy entropy. When all energy had become bound up due to entropy, civilization would inevitably decline.

But what about time and the entropy problem? How long would it take this process to play itself out? Would it take ten years or ten billion? Peter Auer, in a response to Georgescu-Roegen, reflected on this important issue of time, arguing that human existence would not be limited in any practical sense by energy entropy.[7] The abundance of the sun's energy, the availability of radioactive materials for nuclear fission, and the possibilities of nuclear fusion would support current levels of human activity for longer than the anticipated life of the Earth itself. Even if the Earth's human population were to increase tenfold, Auer said, and its appetite for energy to increase by a similar amount, solar energy, fission energy, or fusion energy each represented virtually inexhaustible supplies. Thus, in Auer's opinion, the Malthusian fears of Boulding and Georgescu-Roegen were unfounded.

Boulding had raised a complex issue in suggesting that GNP was an inappropriate measure of social well-being. To begin with, few economists who understand the true definition of GNP would ever suggest that it was intended to be a measure of social well-being. Since its adoption in 1946 as a part of U.S. national income accounting, GNP was simply intended to measure the annual money value of the final goods and services produced by a country, not to constitute a complete quality-of-life metric. It is a measurement of society's production and consumption of market goods and services—nothing more or less. To suggest that GNP was a faulty attempt to measure social welfare was, therefore, misleading.

If GNP is mistakenly regarded as a true measure of well-being, however, and its maximization becomes a principal social goal, then this, too, is equally misleading. Clearly, GNP is a measure only of business activity and not of overall social happiness. Indeed, it is easy to illustrate that GNP by itself is a perverse measure of well-being. Take pollution as an example. When a company installs equipment to reduce the smoke generated from its factories or when the government spends billions to clean up a marine oil spill, then GNP will increase because the monetary flow of goods and services has increased. Thus, in order to increase GNP, we need merely to increase pollution and pollution cleanup. But surely no reasonable person would argue that pollution enhances social well-being. The problem is that GNP is an excellent measure of business activity but an inadequate measure of social well-being, health, and happiness, especially with regard to the environment. For this reason, Boulding suggested, a more appropriate measure is needed.

Since 1991, GNP has largely been replaced by gross domestic product (GDP) as the official measure of U.S. economic productivity. The difference between GNP and GDP is related to the ownership of production facilities. Under GNP, only output from production facilities owned by the country's citizens is counted. In contrast, GDP counts all output from domestic-based firms, regardless of the nationality of ownership. This change may seem innocuous, but it does have implications for environmental accounting.[8] It has been argued, for example, that U.S. companies that are located in less developed countries appear under GDP to be enhancing the economic output of those countries. However, the natural resources and profits flow to the United States, after being recorded as a gain in GDP for the less developed nations, thus overstating the true economic gain to the latter.

Boulding's suggestion that GNP be reformulated to approximate a quality-of-life measure foreshadowed an effort by researchers nearly a quarter of a century later to do just that. In 1989, Robert Repetto and his colleagues associated with the World Resources Institute in Washington, DC, developed a more robust measure of social well-being called net domestic product (NDP).[9] This measure is calculated by deducting from the GDP an allowance for the depletion of in situ stocks of natural resources such as petroleum, forests, and soils. NDP is regarded by some as an important experimental step in overcoming what they see as the biased way governments presently think about the value of their natural resources.

Another organization called Redefining Progress has also proposed an alternative to GDP. This index, called the genuine progress indicator (GPI), includes some twenty indicators of economic, environmental, and social quality of life currently ignored by GDP. Among these twenty items is an allowance for reductions in economic well-being due to resource depletion and degradation of the environment. But not everyone favors such an index. A West Virginia congressman said if the GPI includes depletion of coal reserves and the effects on air pollution, "somebody is going to say . . . that the coal industry isn't contributing anything to the country."[10]

NDP and GPI may provide improved quality-of-life measures, but they also present some messy measurement problems compared to GDP. Determination of GDP for a country is, at least conceptually, a straightforward process. The government need only measure the annual physical flow of final products and services through the national economy and multiply the components by each of their respective current market prices. NDP, on the other hand, raises some real problems in calculation because the government must now measure and value *stocks* of environmental and natural resources rather than simply the flow of products.

The measurement of physical stocks is a significant problem. Determining the total amount of oil, forests, or some other resource within a nation has always presented a challenge requiring the combined efforts of government and the private sector. Yet as difficult as physical measurement may be, there is an even more troublesome problem in determining the value of such resources. What value should society place on the environmental services natural resources provide? What value should we place on the oxygen-producing and carbon-storing capabilities of our forests? Furthermore, how do we express the value of "resources" when their social use might radically change in the future?

The problem of defining the future use and value of a natural resource is not trivial. To illustrate, recall the quotation in chapter 4 from Barnett and Morse concerning Vermont granite: "Two decades ago it was only building and tombstone material; now it is a potential fuel." So should we value the stock of Vermont granite as tombstone material or as potential fuel? The difficulty of valuing environmental and natural resource stocks is more than theoretical; it represents a significant barrier to the meaningful realization of Kenneth Boulding's dream of a better measure of social well-being.

Yet, even if governments were able to solve these nettlesome problems and produce an improved index of social well-being, the question remains, would the index be accepted by the public? Indeed, how would American families react to government numbers that purport to measure their collective happiness? One can imagine that an attempt to provide such indices would be greeted with some cynicism. A complaint against traditional GNP and GDP measures has been that they are not value neutral. In other words, they are more than just numbers indicating economic performance. They are also an expression of the values of the government and citizens. Likewise, one must wonder, are much more complex indices such as NDP and GPI any less value laden?

Time-discounting was another issue raised by Boulding that has caused some rethinking even on the part of environmental economists. The practice of discounting future events, both natural resource–related and otherwise, has long been a standard practice in economics. Its justification is based upon what economists call time-preference; events occurring nearer in time are preferred to those that occur in the distant future. A commonly used example is that of a cash loan: would you give someone a dollar today and expect only a dollar in return a year hence? The standard response is no. The borrower should pay interest on the debt because the lender's use of the money has been deferred. Some academics, like Boulding, have challenged the application of this notion to environmental and natural resource issues, however. In the case of global climate warming, for example, Ralph D'Arge and his associates have maintained that discounting is inappropriate because it devalues the welfare and rights of future generations.[11] Thus, if present generations consume fossil fuels and thereby contribute to the greenhouse effect through carbon dioxide emissions, then they should take into full account (i.e., without discounting) the impact of their actions on those innocents yet to inhabit this planet.

Kenneth Boulding's "Spaceship Earth" has been an important contribution to environmental thought because of the provocative ideas it introduced, especially with regard to the issue of entropy. It also presented significant challenges to the community of mainstream economists regarding environmental matters. Kenneth Boulding completed his career as an economist at the University of Colorado. He died of cancer on March 19, 1993, following a lengthy illness. He was survived at the time of his death by his wife, Dr. Elise M. Boulding, five children, and sixteen grandchildren.

Georgescu-Roegen examined the entropy issue relative to the environment in perhaps even greater depth than did Boulding. Sadly, during his life Georgescu-Roegen was never able to attract attention to his scholarly accomplishments or the subject of entropy to the degree he thought was deserved. An obituary essay written by Herman Daly soon after Georgescu-Roegen's death October 30, 1994, noted that "his latter years were marked by bitterness and withdrawal, brought on in part by the failure of the profession to give his work the recognition that it truly merited. . . . So great was his bitterness that he even cut relations with those who most valued his contribution. . . . But," continued Daly, "none of that diminishes the great importance of his lifework. . . . He demanded a lot, but he gave more."[12]

9

Lynn White and "The Historical Roots of Our Ecologic Crisis"

The American Association for the Advancement of Science (AAAS) is one of the world's great scholarly societies. Its principal publication is *Science,* a prestigious journal whose pages are typically filled with articles bearing complex, lengthy titles about molecular biology, organic chemistry, DNA structure, and other arcane science topics. For most researchers, publishing a manuscript in *Science* is a much sought-after and often elusive career goal.

In 1967, the pages of *Science* carried an article that was not cast in the usual mold. This work, titled "The Historical Roots of Our Ecologic Crisis," by Lynn White jr. (the lower-case letter *j* was his preference), was not about traditional science. It was more about sociology and history with a focus on the human motivations that led to degradation of the environment. Specifically, it dealt with the influence of organized religion and technology—or at least White's view of that influence—on the Western world's "unnatural treatment of nature."[1] White's objective in writing this article was to explore the root causes of humans' abuse of the environment and, thus, perhaps provide some clues as to the solution.

White's environmental philosophy, as expressed in his literary works, was decidedly neo-Malthusian. He believed that our "man-centered view of the nature of things and of the things of nature" was leading to our doom. And the end, he suggested, was not too distant: "We are in worse danger than we seem." White wrote of humans' ability to alter the future course of history by changing our philosophy toward the Earth. But White's hopes for such a philosophical about-face were not high: "We may be on the verge of a change of value structures that will make possible measures to cope with the growing ecologic crisis. . . . But the auguries are not encouraging."[2]

White's thesis that technology and religion were the causes of environmental degradation had gained some notoriety even prior to its publication in *Science*. He had presented a talk on the subject to the annual meeting of the American Academy of Arts and Sciences in Washington, DC, on the day after Christmas in 1966. Fifteen months later, in March 1967, the article was published and a much larger portion of the academic community was able to read White's provocative ideas concerning the relationship among religion, technology, and environmental degradation.

Lynn Townsend White jr. was born in San Francisco in 1907. In 1928 he graduated from Stanford University then earned a master's degree from Union Theological Seminary in New York. He later obtained a master's degree from Harvard, and in 1934 received his Ph.D. from the same university. After completing graduate school, he went on to establish himself as a distinguished academician, associating at times with such learned luminaries as Aldous Huxley. He served for fifteen years as president of Mills College, a small Oakland, California, institution for women. White's principal career accomplishment, however, was as a scholar of medieval history and technological innovation. On these topics he published numerous papers in both technical and popular journals, as well as several award-winning books. At the time he contributed his article to *Science*, the rotund, silver-haired professor was employed by the Department of History at the University of California at Los Angeles (UCLA).

The article began with White's discussion of some major ecologic disturbances that humans had wrought over the centuries: overgrazing, the excessive cutting of forests, the elimination of wetlands in the Netherlands, and the construction of the Aswan Dam in Egypt. The full scope of changes—their timing, location, and effects—were not well understood, said White, but "as we enter the last third of the twentieth century . . . concern for the problem of ecologic backlash is mounting feverishly."[3]

White's search for the causes of and solutions to environmental problems began with a discussion of the relationship between science and technology. He argued that natural science and technology had coexisted for centuries with no apparent ill effects. However, about four generations ago (i.e., presumably in the late nineteenth century), the balance began to shift when scientists in western Europe and North

America managed a marriage of the two. Humans' newfound ability to gain rapid, widespread control over the natural world led to a situation where "the impact of our race upon the environment has so increased in force that it [i.e., the environment] has changed in essence." "Surely," he said, "no creature other than man has ever managed to foul its nest in such short order."[4]

White identified many past attempts to reduce or eliminate environmental degradation but claimed none had been effective because the approaches were traditionally piecemeal. Instead, they offered partial solutions to a problem so immense that a comprehensive answer was needed. To find that comprehensive solution, said White, we should try to clarify our thinking by looking, in a historical context, at the presumptions that underlie modern technology and science.

Among his peers, Lynn White was a respected scholar of the history of science and technology, and his writing gives evidence of his facility with the subject. He enumerated some important facts that characterize modern science. First, modern science, in the strictest sense, is a product of Western civilization. Europe and North America, according to White, can claim credit for virtually every substantive achievement in science and technology. Second, he contended that the origins of modern science predate the Industrial Revolution by several centuries. White set these beginnings during the eleventh century, a time when the earlier scientific writings of the Greeks and Arabs were first translated into Latin. Latin texts stimulated the Western mind and by the thirteenth century, Europe had come to dominate scientific discovery and innovation. Later accomplishments by the likes of Copernicus, Galileo, and Newton firmly underscored Western preeminence in technical matters. Nothing of this sort, said White, was to be found in the East.

Having asserted that modern science was a phenomenon rooted in medieval Western civilization, White introduced the second principal element, Christianity, which began to grow and flourish at the same time and, in White's view, became intertwined with the development of modern science and technology. "The victory of Christianity over paganism," said White, "was the greatest psychic revolution in the history of our culture." Christianity emerged as the dominant Western religion and, according to White, shaped our collective thinking and behavior toward the natural world. "Modern Western science," he said, "was cast in a matrix of Christian theology."[5]

Christianity, according to Lynn White, establishes for Christians, and thus Western civilization, their relationship with the natural environment:

> Christianity inherited from Judaism not only a concept of time as nonrepetitive and linear but also a striking story of creation. By gradual stages a loving and all-powerful God had created light and darkness, the heavenly bodies, the earth and all its plants, animals, birds, and fishes. Finally God had created Adam and, as an after thought, Eve to keep man from being lonely. Man named all the animals, thus establishing his dominance over them. God planned all of this explicitly for man's benefit and rule: no item in the physical creation had any purpose other than to serve man's purpose. And although man's body is made of clay, he is not simply part of nature: he is made in God's image.[6]

Thus, argued White, Christianity brought about a separation between humans and nature. The Christian faith insisted that it was God's will for man to exploit nature to his own ends. This, claimed Lynn White jr. was the root cause of our present ecological crisis. Christianity quite simply had given Western civilization a mandate to exploit the Earth and the natural environment. With this mandate came the inevitable abuses that were now so troubling.

The acquisition of additional scientific and technological knowledge, he opined, would not get us out of the present ecologic crisis. And this came from one who was considered a world expert on technological innovation. "We shall continue to have a worsening ecologic crisis," he wrote, "until we reject the Christian axiom that nature has no reason for existence save to serve man."[7]

White's blaming of traditional Christianity may have been startling, yet it was also very much in step with the iconoclasm of the late 1960s. During this time, many Americans, and especially academicians, were beginning to challenge the contemporary relevance of social institutions. Universities, the military, political leadership, traditional value systems—everything and everyone—was subjected to critical examination. It is important to realize when reading the words of Lynn White jr. that his writings did not surface in a social or intellectual vacuum. Rejection of traditional institutions was very much in vogue, and at times there almost seemed to be competition to identify the next target for criticism.

With regard to a solution, White suggested that Christians look again toward religion: "Since the roots of our trouble are so largely religious, the remedy must also be essentially religious." As a model for reform, he said to follow the example and teachings of St. Francis of Assisi whose view of nature was reputedly quite different from that of the typical Christian. St. Francis envisioned that humans and nature were linked by means of a "pan-psychism of all things animate and inanimate, designed for the glorification of their transcendent Creator. Furthermore, said White, "Saint Francis . . . tried to substitute the idea of the equality of all creatures, including man, for the idea of man's limitless rule of creation. He failed. Both our present science and our present technology are so tinctured with orthodox Christian arrogance toward nature that no solution for our ecologic crisis can be expected from them alone."[8]

Upon its publication, "The Historical Roots of Our Ecologic Crisis" engendered both enthusiasm and rage.[9] The enthusiasm came mostly from scholars and theologians, while the rage came largely from practicing Christians and their clergy. White had expected that his thesis would be unacceptable to many Christians, but he underestimated the depth of their indignation. One of his former graduate students, Bert S. Hall, noted that a tide of protest from angry churchmen flowed across White's desk like a stream.[10] One critic went so far as to call him "a junior Anti-Christ probably in the Kremlin's pay."[11] The public outcry caused Professor White to jest, "I should have blamed the scientists."[12] His fellow Christians (for Lynn White identified himself as a religious Christian) clearly did not want themselves nor their religion blamed for environmental exploitation.

The academic community was generally less hostile to White. In fact, many theologians agreed with his central notion that religious attitudes affect human behavior toward the environment. Despite their general agreement with White they did challenge some specific aspects of his study. In particular, White was criticized for not considering factors other than religion that influence human behavior toward the environment. Environmental scholars also recognized that non-Christian cultures had certainly caused their share of ecological damage, a fact White did not explicitly acknowledge. In general, academicians found that Lynn White's conclusions were value laden and lacking in objectivity.[13] As a result, his assertion that Christianity alone had caused our ecologic crisis lacked credibility.

White's writing also contained ambiguities. For example, it was difficult to determine if he placed the ultimate blame for environmental degradation on the faith or the faithful. Did he think that there was something inherently wrong with Christianity, or just with the way people had practiced it? A clue to this ambiguity was his comment that Western society should "find a new religion or rethink the old one."[14]

One subtle yet critical inconsistency within Professor White's article was his reference to the Aswan Dam as a prime example of environmental degradation due to technology. Later in the paper, he said that Christianity was the root cause of all environmental problems. Yet the Aswan Dam was financed by an atheistic government, the former Soviet Union, and constructed in Egypt, a Muslim nation. With this one ill-considered example the professor had unwittingly rejected his own hypothesis.

Because of the controversy and scholarly problems in the article, Lynn White jr. had to rethink his position on religion and the environment. The result of this reconsideration was presented in his 1973 essay "Continuing the Conversation." The theme of this essay suggests an attempt to gracefully salvage a piece of scholarship that had missed its mark. However, it was to White's credit that he revisited the topic. In his words, "it is better for a historian to be wrong than timid."[15]

In "Continuing the Conversation," White still maintained that the United States was facing a serious ecological crisis. "I have not discovered anyone who publicly advocates pollution," he said, "Everybody says that he is against it. Yet the crisis deepens because all specific measures to remedy it are . . . undercut." And he still implicated technology in the crisis: "Today's ecologic situation is the by-product of a forward surging technology that first emerged in the Middle Ages."[16]

White, however, was forced to abandon his original thesis that Christianity had been the sole cause of technological progress and, hence, our ecological crisis. His new position was that Christianity had not caused but instead only facilitated the advancement of technology: "Christianity obviously is not the necessary base for a dynamic technology. . . . Christianity . . . provided a set of presuppositions remarkably favorable to technological thrust."[17]

No longer able to defend his original thesis, White turned the debate away from Christianity. He now maintained that, if not Christianity specifically, then religion in general had been the most important factor influencing human interactions with the environment:

> We shall not cope with our ecologic crisis until scores of millions of us learn to understand more clearly what our values are, and determine to change our priorities so that we . . . are able to cope effectively with all aspects of pollution. This means far more than simply rethinking and revising our economic political systems. . . . Every culture . . . is shaped primarily by its religion.[18]

White's new position seemed to suggest that his original thesis had been only partially incorrect. That is, his general suspicion that religion was somehow involved in environmental degradation was essentially correct and only the earlier narrow focus on Christianity had been wrong.

Under close scrutiny, however, White's new thesis also seemed to have problems. The difficulty was in his definition of religion. His definition was as sweeping as the conclusions he had drawn in "Roots of Our Ecologic Crisis." He went far beyond the traditional notion of religion as the philosophy concerning the relationship between humanity and its creator to encompass the entire spectrum of human values. Thus, all social values fell under the rubric of religion. An example of White's liberal redefinition was his implication that Marxism was an expression of religion: "The history of Marxism demonstrates that . . . religious values are fundamental in the dynamics of cultural and social changes."[19] To say that Marxist philosophy is a religion ignores its traditional political and economic foundations, however. With religion so broadly defined as to include all human values, it was virtually impossible for White not to accept his thesis that religion was the principal factor causing environmental decay. As in his first article, White's argument seemed flawed.

More than a quarter century after "Roots of Our Ecologic Crisis," historian Elspeth Whitney examined the impact of Lynn White jr. on environmental thought. Her judgment was that White's influence on environmental philosophy had been huge, despite the recognized weaknesses in his theses. He is largely given credit for the "greening" of theology; that is, the introduction of theology into the environmental debate. His influence has helped shape ecotheology, a modern movement involving theologians and the laity that attempts to bring religion into the resolution of environmental issues. Most theologians and other religious people who have tried to make sense of humans' relationship to the environment generally agree with White that care of the environment is at its core a moral and religious issue. Bringing this connection between religion and the environment to public attention was White's principal contribution to environmental thought.

While theologians may agree that the condition of the environment is basically a moral and religious issue, they have not however always agreed with White's view that religious doctrine has given humanity a mandate for environmental exploitation. Indeed, the current view of many theologians is that God, in giving humanity dominion over the Earth, assigned a role of stewardship rather than exploitation. Thus, with the privilege of dominion came the responsibility of caring for the Earth. Some now interpret acts of violence against nature as being as sinful as acts of violence against humans.

Today, there is still interest in the relationship between religion and the environment. Admittedly, however, the direct impact of religion on environmental policy may not have been particularly significant. Perhaps the most convincing evidence of this chasm between interest and action was found in the series of Global Forums of Spiritual and Parliamentary Leaders, which have been convened several times at international venues between the years 1988 and 2004. An impressive number of the world's great political and religious leaders have attended past meetings: Mother Teresa, the Archbishop of Canterbury, the Dalai Lama, European prime ministers, U.S. senators and representatives, and more. The July 14, 2004, meeting in Barcelona, Spain, focused on many global issues, one of which was the protection of water resources for both human consumption and aesthetic purposes.

In the United States, the mainstream Christian denominations continue to show an interest in environmental matters, an interest that is often linked to other important social issues of the day such as economic justice and feminism. Church-affiliated groups with names such as the National Religious Partnership for the Environment and the National Ministries Office of Environmental Justice hold conferences and promote activities which explore the relationship between economic enterprise and environmental quality. Another group is the North American Coalition on Religion and Ecology, a nonprofit educational organization located in Washington, DC. On the world level, the International Consortium on Religion and Ecology is a network of organizations working on the ethical dimensions of global environmental issues.

Even though many Christians may welcome the fusion of religion and the environment, some do not. One such dissenter is Paulist Father Robert A. Sirico, former president of the Acton Institute for the Study of Religion and Liberty in Grand Rapids, Michigan. Father Sirico has been critical of what he calls the "distinctly religious tone" of some aspects of environmentalism. He believes that many people now regard environmentalism as a sort of religion in itself in which followers have tried to superimpose an exalted view of nature on the traditional teachings of the church. This, said Father Sirico, undermines the basic purpose of religion, which is to avoid personal sin and to attain salvation. Playing perhaps unwittingly to Lynn White's original hypothesis, Sirico said, "It is not a part of the Jewish and Christian understanding of faith that nature in itself has an independent and metaphysical right to be untouched, preserved and adored." But he added, "The capacity of the land to continue to produce should not be permanently injured . . . but the well-informed conscience knows the difference."[20]

Father Sirico also condemned as a pagan religion the rising popularity of Gaia (pronounced "GUY-uh"), the belief that the Earth is a living being. Gaia comes from the Greek and means "mother earth." The notion of Gaia was first set forth in 1972 by atmospheric scientist James Lovelock from the University of Reading in England.[21] In developing the Gaia hypothesis, Lovelock claimed that the Earth *acted as if* it were alive because of its self-regulation of the atmosphere and climate. The Earth's climate has adapted to accommodate life, and this accommodation has followed a track too narrow and purposeful to be coincidental, he said. Also, argued Lovelock, the Earth's present atmosphere had departed so far from any abiological chemical makeup that it must have consciously conspired to support life. Lastly, he said that if life were to disappear from the Earth, the Earth would voluntarily change its atmosphere to that of a lifeless planet. Lovelock concluded that Earth was like a very large living creature—Gaia—who has planned the air, the oceans, and the surface to suit herself. Lovelock's implication was that Gaia would take care of herself despite human abuse. Whereas Lovelock only suggested that the Earth behaved as if it were alive, many present-day adherents of the Gaian philosophy as well as New Agers regard the Earth as possessing actual intelligence.[22]

In 1988, the American Geophysical Union held a conference of well-known scientists to consider the merits of the Gaia hypothesis. Those in attendance ranged from skeptics to true believers, and together they examined the evidence for and the utility of the hypothesis. James Kirchner saw Gaia as a nest of hypotheses ranging from the self-evident to the highly speculative. At the self-evident end, the concept simply repeated some well-known linkages between biogeochemical and biological processes. The speculative end—that is, that biological processes regulate the physical environment—Kirchner asserted could neither be tested nor proven. Nevertheless, the Gaia metaphor has become popular as a means for uniting the common destinies of people, organisms, and inorganic substances.[23]

There is no doubt that Lynn White's articles have had a profound impact on environmental thought. Said Elspeth Whitney,

> Almost immediately after its publication . . . "Roots" became a standard feature of anthologies and textbooks for use in college courses in environmental studies, the history of technology, and science, society, and technology. Reprints of the article have also appeared in numerous publications directed toward the general public ranging from *The Boy Scout Handbook* and *The Sierra Club Bulletin* to *The Whole Earth Catalogue* and *The Environ-*

mental Handbook and from the hippie newsletter, *The Oracle,* to the far more staid *Horizon Magazine.* In 1970 both *Time Magazine* and *The New York Times* featured reprisals of White's essay. The great historian Arnold Toynbee paid White the ultimate compliment by appropriating his argument twice without acknowledgement. Overall, the thesis in "Roots" has been repeated, reprised, and criticized in over two hundred books and articles by historians, environmentalists, and philosophers of technology between 1967 and the present. . . . [It has] been described as a part of environmental "folklore."[24]

Even though many people have studied White and agreed with his belief that sustaining society and the global environment is essentially an issue of moral and religious philosophy, few hold much hope that morality will prevail. Echoing neo-Malthusian fears, these people believe that political and economic interests will prevail in the immediate present at both the international and local levels.[25]

The issue raised by Lynn White jr. about the importance of the relationship between religion and the environment continues to have modern social relevancy. After the publication of "The Historical Roots of Our Ecologic Crisis," Lynn White jr. continued his productive academic career for seven more years on the faculty at UCLA. In 1974 he retired with the status of professor emeritus. Professor White passed away of heart failure on March 30, 1987, just one month short of his eightieth birthday.

10

Paul Ehrlich and *The Population Bomb*

The opening lines of Dr. Paul Ehrlich's 1968 book *The Population Bomb* conveyed an explicit and, regrettably, all too accurate picture of miserably overcrowded life in the Third World:

> I have understood the population explosion intellectually for a long time. I came to understand it emotionally one stinking hot night in Delhi a couple of years ago. My wife and daughter and I were returning to our hotel in an ancient taxi. . . . The streets seemed alive with people. People eating, people washing, people sleeping. People visiting, arguing, screaming. People thrusting their hands through the taxi window, begging. People defecating and urinating. People clinging to buses. People herding animals. People, people, people, people.[1]

Distressing though it was, the author's passionate message about the problem of world population found an attentive audience in the American public. By 1970, *The Population Bomb* had become a block-busting best seller with nearly one million copies in print. Fame followed fortune as Ehrlich became world population expert nonpareil, enjoying primetime celebrity status. Ehrlich appeared on Johnny Carson's *Tonight Show*, his personal appearances were booked a year in advance, he logged eighty thousand miles of air travel annually, and he received two dozen speaking requests each day--this was just about as close to stardom as an academician could get.

During the time he wrote *The Population Bomb*, Paul Ralph Ehrlich was professor of entomology and director of graduate studies in the Department of Biological Sciences at Stanford University. His professional life had been spent studying and teaching about insects. Entomology, he claimed, was his first love. A native of Philadelphia born May 29, 1932, he had written two previous books, *How to Know the Butterflies* (1960) and *Process of Evolution* (1963), and authored seventy other scientific publications—a number that would increase more than sevenfold over the next four decades. Six feet two inches tall, lank and lean, with a professorial slouch, Ehrlich was a man of enormous energy who routinely worked blistering sixteen-hour days. And, although he claimed not to be a crusader by temperament, he enthusiastically accepted what some called his new "messianic role" as spokesman against population growth.[2]

Ehrlich seemed to have written *The Population Bomb* with lay readers in mind. After all, it was their souls he wished to bestir concerning the horrors of global overpopulation. Composed in just three weeks, the popularized text was relatively brief, slightly more than two hundred pages in paperback, and contained only modest amounts of the usual supporting information such as footnotes and bibliographic citations. As a scholarly document, *The Population Bomb* does not impress as does, say, *Silent Spring* or *Scarcity and Growth*. But then, it probably wasn't intended to. Ehrlich's target was more the heart than the head.

Following a foreword by the Sierra Club's David Brower, a sponsor of the publication, came chapter 1, titled simply "The Problem." The message here was purely apocalyptic: There were too many people on the Earth and, because of a decrease in the "doubling time" of population growth, the situation was worsening every day.[3] This was especially true for what Ehrlich termed the "undeveloped" nations. He reckoned that within the next nine years (by 1977) the world would see acute food shortages where one in every seven persons would die from nutrition-related causes. And the dreadful effects of overpopulation would not be limited to starvation. The environment would deteriorate too, as humankind used more fertilizers and pesticides, cleared forests, increased the siltation of streams, encountered the greenhouse effect, and engaged in nuclear warfare.

In the second chapter, "The Ends of the Road," Ehrlich underscored the book's desperate tone by presenting several of his own rather fantastic scenarios of future world conditions:

- Struggles over wheat supplies lead the United States to make tactical nuclear strikes against China.
- The president's environmental advisers recommend sterilization of all persons with IQs less than 90.

- After a thermonuclear war in 1979, two-thirds of the Earth is uninhabitable and only cockroaches survive.
- Under Ehrlich's most optimistic scenario, one-half billion of the planet's population starves.

After presenting these nightmarish views, Ehrlich defied his readers to envision a more optimistic future.

The third chapter, "What Is Being Done," spoke of society's failures at population control, which according to Paul Ehrlich, were many. "People in positions of power," he said, "have either ignored the problem or have recommended solutions that are inadequate in scope or proven failures." A key target for criticism was the Roman Catholic Church for its support of the so-called rhythm method of contraception, a technique Ehrlich referred to as "Vatican roulette." Traditional family planning was also condemned as an abysmal failure. By contrast, he viewed fetal abortion as a "highly effective weapon in the armory of population control."[4] In this chapter, Ehrlich also discussed the possibilities for increasing food production to feed the masses. He saw very little promise in trying to cultivate marginally fertile lands or in turning to less conventional forms of agriculture such as sea farming. However, he did express some optimism over the prospects of improved varieties of agricultural crops, especially grains. The chapter concluded with some warnings about environmental degradation, and several pages were devoted to criticism of the U.S. Department of Agriculture's fire ant eradication efforts. (Recall that Rachel Carson in *Silent Spring* had at length discussed the damages caused by this federal pest control program.)

The book's fourth chapter, "What Needs to Be Done?" got down to the difficult business of finding solutions to overpopulation, a task the author said was "complex beyond belief."[5] Yet if the solutions were difficult, the place to start implementing them was, by comparison, easy to pinpoint—the United States. Ehrlich argued that because of its preeminent status in the global community, as well as its gluttony at the natural resources trough, the United States needed to assume the lead role in population control. He considered sterilants in the water and economic incentives designed to encourage fewer offspring. He also called for federal laws guaranteeing the right of every woman to an abortion and sex education in the schools that would emphasize "sex as . . . mankind's major and most enduring recreation, as the fountainhead of his humor."[6]

In this chapter Ehrlich also recommended the establishment of a powerful federal agency, the Department of Population and Environment, to be the "policeman" of his new movement to make the world more livable.[7] The Catholic Church hierarchy was taken to task yet again—this time for seven full pages—for their conservative views on abortion. He harshly condemned the motivations of the free enterprise system and, indeed, attempted to link environmental problems to that economic system. Christianity was impeached as a force that made us dominate and exploit nature; "the roots of our trouble," said Ehrlich, "are so largely religious."[8] He also urged the United States to demand that undeveloped countries implement population control programs as a condition of receiving food aid and, in those nations, said sterilization should be implemented by coercion if necessary.

The penultimate chapter, "What Can You Do?" was a call to action urging the public to carry forth the fight to control population growth. People were provided guides for mass mailings to elected officials and also given sample conversations with clever rebuttals for use on population bomb agnostics. "Above all," exhorted Ehrlich, "raise a stink." To that end he recommended to parents, "Give your kid an IUD to take to 'show and tell.'"[9]

The book's brief final chapter was titled "What If I'm Wrong?" Ehrlich thought that the chances of his errancy regarding the threats from population growth were incalculably small: "Naturally, I find this highly unlikely; otherwise I would not have written this book." He added, however, "If I am wrong, people will be better fed, better housed, and happier, thanks to our efforts."[10]

The initial public reaction to *The Population Bomb* was divided between those who welcomed the message and those who opposed it. But the criticism of those who did oppose Ehrlich's views was scalding. *San Francisco Chronicle* columnist Charles McCabe said Paul Ehrlich was "worse than Hitler."[11] Militant black leaders regarded his birth control schemes as nothing more than a program of genocide aimed at racial minorities. Religious Catholics were incensed by his condemnation of their faith and its ordained leaders.

These vituperative outpourings were certainly understandable; *The Population Bomb* had savaged some of the most cherished values of Western culture. Ehrlich was not asking the public merely for a little fine tuning to resolve the problems of population growth and environmental degradation. Instead, he was calling for a major societal restructuring. He was prepared to pitch out not only the baby with the bathwater, but the tub as well.

Most of the criticism aimed at *The Population Bomb* stemmed from the book's position on social issues. However, in places its scholarship could also have been questioned. Indeed, many of the book's major ideas seemed hastily conceived and, in places, a bit naive. For instance, Ehrlich defined the "optimum population size" as the "one permitting any individual to be as crowded or alone as he or she wished."[12] This is simply another way of saying that people should be provided all the space they want. All well and fine, but how is such a societal goal implemented? To whom do people complain when they are too crowded, and how do officials rectify the situation? And the concept provides precious little guidance in solving the global population problem.

Neither was *The Population Bomb* a strong contributor toward the development of new theories concerning population growth. In fact, many of the book's key concepts were hauntingly reminiscent of the Malthusian doctrine. For example, the book claimed that population "doubling time," that is, the amount of time required for the Earth's population to double, had continually shortened, thus leading to exponential population growth.[13] Thomas Malthus used the identical concept and terminology in 1798 in his famous *Essay on the Principle of Population.* Curiously though, in what appears to be a glaring omission, *The Population Bomb* never refers to Malthus.

Moreover, the text was frequently rambling, diffuse, and repetitive, perhaps an inevitable consequence of its having been written in just three weeks. For whatever reason, topics surfaced then submerged only to resurface time and again. Ehrlich's continual lambasting of the Roman Catholic Church was an example of this repetition. In addition, on various occasions the author appeared to contradict himself. Throughout the book Ehrlich attempted to name "the root cause of our problem," but the root cause seemed to vary—first population then religion, too many automobiles, the year-round sexuality of the human female, the evolution of the family, and so on.

Criticism notwithstanding, *The Population Bomb* garnered a large following. The academic community in particular seemed pulled to Ehrlich's message. A group of university colleagues, in response to McCabe's likening of Ehrlich to Hitler, drafted a letter voicing their support for the Stanford professor. His peers also voted to grant Ehrlich some of the most prestigious awards the scientific community can bestow on one of its own. Ehrlich was named a member of the National Academy of Sciences, a fellow of the American Academy of Arts and Sciences, and president of the American Institute of Biological Sciences, and he was elected to the boards of directors of a dozen or more environmental and public interest organizations. *The Population Bomb* was also embraced by college students, many of whom were among the first to join the Ehrlich-inspired organization Zero Population Growth.

The Population Bomb was only a beginning for Ehrlich. Aware of the book's deficiencies as an academic work, he sought the much-needed improvements. With the help of his wife and coauthor Anne Howland Ehrlich, a biological illustrator and Stanford University research assistant—ensconced at a desk just outside her husband's office —Ehrlich set out to produce "a thinking man's *Population Bomb*."[14] The resultant second-generation work was *Population, Resources, Environment: Issues in Human Ecology*, a textbook published in 1970. The newer text used *The Population Bomb* as a rough blueprint, but it was greatly expanded and much more thoroughly documented.

The first half of *Population, Resources, Environment* contained enlightening discussions on population, science, technology, and ecology. One such discussion dealt with the law of conservation of matter and the second law of thermodynamics, an interesting bit of physics which to many environmentalists serves as conclusive proof that industrial development and economic growth place absolute limits on civilization. (Recall that Kenneth Boulding in "The Economics of the Coming Spaceship Earth" had already raised these issues relative to physics and the environment.) The law of conservation of matter states that matter can neither be created nor destroyed. The second law of thermodynamics says the fraction of total energy available for use is constantly being diminished within a closed system. Conservation of matter thus implies that pollution placed in the environment will have a tendency to persist, while the second law of thermodynamics argues that there is some ultimate limit on the amount of energy available for work. Thus, the two laws together suggest that human generation of pollutants and rapid consumption of energy resources carry inescapable negative environmental consequences governed not by human laws but by the laws of physics.

About midway through the book, the Ehrlichs wrote, "It may be in vain that so many look to science and technology to solve our present day ecological crisis."[15] With this pronouncement, their emphasis shifted from science and technology toward social institutions as the key remedy for population growth and environmental ills. Ehrlich's earlier statements in *The Population Bomb* concerning social issues had been bold enough to ruffle feathers, and this book was no less restrained, saying for example that "laws could be written that would make bearing a third child illegal and that would require an abortion to terminate all such pregnancies. Failure to obtain the abortion could be made a felony."[16] The Ehrlichs also called for an upper age limit of sixty-five on elected officials: "the actual work of running the country in our complex world is simply too great a strain for older men."[17] Western culture and Christianity once again took a fierce pounding. Yet despite its irreverent tone—or perhaps because of it—*Population, Resources, Environment* was heartily endorsed by such famous personalities as former Secretary of the Interior Stewart Udall and two-time Nobel laureate Linus Pauling.

As an academic document, *Population, Resources, Environment* was a significant improvement over *The Population Bomb.* The metamorphosis was not yet complete, however; there was one more step to go. In 1977, Paul and Anne Ehrlich, joined by coauthor John P. Holdren, professor of energy and resources at the University of California at Berkeley, published their final entry in this literary trilogy. This latest work, titled *Ecoscience: Population, Resources, Environment,* was written primarily as a textbook.

Ecoscience's basic organization did not differ markedly from that of the previous book. Its beginning chapters dealt with matters of population, science, and technology, while the concluding sections discussed social issues and policy solutions. But despite the structural similarities, *Ecoscience* had a breadth of coverage unseen in its predecessor. In more than one thousand pages of fine print and copious literature citations, the book treated a remarkable array of topics such as demographic history, Malthusian rates of population increase (at last we see mention of the Reverend Malthus), land-use patterns, energy technologies, material scarcities, and disruptions of ecological systems. A small army of graduate students must have toiled like ants on this magnum opus.

Yet, even with the extended discussion of technical issues, *Ecoscience* held tenaciously to the view that population growth and environmental degradation could be halted only through a change in social institutions: "It is clear . . . no combination of policies and technologies can significantly ameliorate the predicament unless they overcome the non-technological roots of the problem."[18] Yet in this final volume the authors' tone softened to a degree and the corrective social measures proposed seemed less draconian. Gone was much of the shrill, caustic social commentary. Missing were Ehrlich's recommendations that third pregnancies be treated as felonies and terminated with mandatory abortions. The elderly were now regarded with dignity: "the problem with old people is . . . that they have been neglected. If . . . encouraged . . . older people would be able to continue making valuable contributions to society well into their advanced years." This was a far cry from Ehrlich's earlier calls for forced retirement of aging members of Congress. And the selective condemnation of Western culture seemed also to abate: "'Be fruitful and multiply, God will provide,' this view is common to both Western and Eastern religions."[19]

Ecoscience concluded with a brief final discussion of "cornucopians versus neo-Malthusians,"[20] as the authors termed what they identified as the two major schools of thought regarding environmental matters. The cornucopians were characterized as technological optimists—individuals who expect that humankind can and will make the necessary technological advances to ensure future supplies of energy and natural resources with minimal damage to the environment. Neo-Malthusians were those with less faith in technology as the salvation of the human race. The authors placed themselves squarely in the neo-Malthusian camp. Yet, in their final summation, they stated that problems of population and the environment could be resolved only through the concerted effort of both groups: "the real question, for those concerned about realistic solutions, is whether scholars and decision makers of all varieties can devise ways to bring human behavior into harmony with physical reality in time."[21]

Despite the academic shortcomings of *The Population Bomb*, it did bring public attention to the problem of world population as perhaps no other publication since Malthus' treatise of 1798. Certainly today, human population trends continue to be a major concern for most of the world's governments. This concern was evidenced by the 1994 United Nations International Conference on Population and Development held in Cairo, Egypt, which attracted some 20,000 representatives from 180 UN member nations and various nongovernmental organizations (NGOs), consisting largely of women's rights organizations. The ten-day conference resulted in a sixteen-chapter program that outlined a comprehensive strategy for stabilizing world population growth (visit the Cairo Conference website at http://www.iisd.ca/cairo .html). The most contentious issue dealt with in the program was abortion. Islamic, Catholic, and feminist groups lobbied aggressively on the issue, and there was a great deal of speculation as to which side would triumph. In the final document, the program's position was that the need for abortion must be avoided, and that abortion should in no case be used as a method of family planning.

The present-day angst regarding world population, as in Malthus' time, stems from its rapid rate of growth and the possible impact this will have upon natural resources and the environment. In 1798, when Malthus wrote his famous essay, the world population was an estimated 900 million people. The current world population is approximately 6.4 billion, an astounding sevenfold increase in just two hundred years. The recent high annual growth rate of world population was just over 2 percent, occurring in the early 1970s; as of 2004 the annual growth rate had declined to 1.21 percent. Although the situation has thus improved somewhat, projections suggest that the world's population will still be more than nine billion people by 2050 (data and projections available on the UN Department of Social and Economic Affairs, Population Division at http:/esa.un.org.unpp).

The pressures of population growth are most critical in the less developed regions of the Earth, such as Africa, Latin America, and Asia, where 82.3 percent of the world's current population lives. Africa has an annual population growth rate of 2.18 percent, Latin America 1.42 percent, and Asia 1.21 percent, all of which are at or above the current world average of 1.21 percent. Such high growth rates could have severe effects within just a few years. For example Africa, with its 2.18 percent annual rate would double its population in about forty years. In contrast, the annual population growth rates for the United States and Europe are 0.97 percent and 0.00 percent, respectively.[22]

U.S. population growth, at 0.97 percent per year, is low by world standards but is the highest among the industrialized nations.[23] At this rate, the United States would double its current 298 million inhabitants by the year 2080. In recent years, the U.S. population has shifted from the northeast and north to the south and the west and especially to coastal areas along the Pacific, Gulf of Mexico, and eastern Florida. This population shift has had particularly negative impacts on the wetlands of those regions due to increases in chemical pollutants, sewage, and urban runoff.

India and China are two developing nations with notable population problems. Together, India with 1.1 billion inhabitants and China with 1.3 billion account for about 37 percent of the world's total population. Both countries have recognized the negative impacts of large populations and have implemented national programs that attempt to reduce annual growth rates. China's efforts, however, have been more successful than those of India. India's annual growth rate, at 1.5 percent, is well above the world average, while China has managed to reduce her growth rate to about 0.65 percent. The apparent key to China's success rests on the fact that its strong population control programs are targeted directly at prospective parents.[24] Chinese couples are encouraged to postpone marriage. Married couples have ready access to abortion, sterilization, and contraceptives. Couples who have no more than one child are rewarded with a variety of financial incentives while those having more than one child lose these benefits. In contrast, Indian programs although in place for more than thirty years, have met with little success because of bureaucratic inefficiency and a lack of administrative and financial support. In addition, successful though it may be, China's one-child population policy is controversial. The strong social preference for male children has allegedly led to the deaths of millions of female fetuses and infants. Also, there is rumored to be a thriving foreign trade in the sale of unwanted female babies.

Some of the more frequently suggested means of reducing population growth rates within developing nations are economic development, family planning, economic rewards, and changes in women's roles.[25] The use of economic development as a method for slowing population growth stems from the theory of national economic development and demographic transition, namely, that a society's transition from a preindustrial to industrial state results in decreasing rates of birth.

Family planning has been recognized since the 1940s and 1950s as an effective means of reducing population growth, especially in developing nations. Since that time various national and international groups such as the UN Fund for Population Activities, the World Bank, and the U.S. Agency for International Development have promoted family planning. Their efforts have been helpful not only in reducing rates of population growth, but also in contributing to the general health and well-being of native populations.

Some experts have argued that while economic development and family planning have been successful, even stronger methods are sometimes needed to reduce more quickly the birth rates in developing nations. Thus, economic rewards and penalties are suggested as means of modifying human reproductive behavior. The case of China has already been discussed in this regard. The most successful programs tend to encourage rather than force couples to have fewer children and do not seriously violate existing cultural norms regarding birth and reproduction.

The final method of population control that has received a great deal of attention recently has been the changing of women's roles. In some societies, women are afforded few legal rights yet are required to perform a large share of manual labor, handle childbearing and child-rearing responsibilities, and in return often receive little formal education. Through education, it is hoped that women in such circumstances will become aware of opportunities for their lives other than bearing children and will have the skills to accept employment outside the home. Thus, education for women, especially in developing nations, offers possibilities for reducing population growth rates and indeed may be the most promising means of attaining this goal.

Paul Ehrlich's pessimism regarding the state of the environment and the future prospects for human population has had its detractors. But none was more outspoken than Julian Simon, a professor of economics at the University of Maryland. Indeed, for more than twenty years the acrimony and debate between the "doomster" and the "boomster" concerning the future of the world was one of modern environmentalism's most interesting sideshows. In opposition to Ehrlich's glum projections, Simon argued that humanity has never had life so good. Simon insisted that resource shortages posed no real problems, threats of environmental pollution had been vastly overblown, death rates were plummeting, and increasing human population, far from being a threat, provided the engine to drive progress.[26] So deep ran the philosophical differences and personal animosity between the two that they publicly mocked each other for their opposing views. The two men in the 1980s even made a wager about the future prices of certain mineral resources a decade hence. Simon said they would be cheaper, while Ehrlich insisted they would become scarcer and hence more expensive. In 1990, Simon was declared the winner of the bet and Ehrlich had to pay him $576.07.[27]

Paul Ehrlich's *The Population Bomb* was an important contribution to the environmental literature because it stimulated people to think seriously about problems of world population. Ehrlich remains active as a researcher and advocate of population control and environmental quality. He has authored or coauthored more than five hundred publications related to his interests. Since 1977, he has been Bing Professor of Population Studies at Stanford University. Julian Simon passed away on February 8, 1998.

11

Garrett Hardin and
"The Tragedy of the Commons"

On December 13, 1968, one year and nine months after the appearance of Lynn White jr.'s provocative article on religion and ecology, the journal *Science* featured yet another article that was destined to have a truly major impact on contemporary environmental thought. This work, titled "The Tragedy of the Commons," was authored by Garrett Hardin, then a professor of biology at the University of California at Santa Barbara. Hardin's treatise concerned the search for a solution to the problem of global overpopulation. Human population was, of course, a recurring theme in the environmental literature. Hardin's views on the subject were then novel, at least to a large portion of the scientific community.

At the time Garrett Hardin wrote "The Tragedy of the Commons," he was in his early fifties. He had been born in Dallas, Texas, in 1915 but as a child had frequently crisscrossed the Midwest as his father pursued a career as a clerk with the Illinois Central Railroad. At the age of four, Hardin was stricken with polio, which left him with a shortened right leg and forced him to wear leg braces throughout his life. His ability as an actor, along with some talent as a violinist, made him for a time consider the theater as a possible career. However, he eventually settled upon a life in higher education, first obtaining a degree in zoology from the University of Chicago and then, in 1941, a Ph.D. in biology from Stanford University.

After graduation from Stanford, Hardin spent five years as a researcher investigating the production of food from algae. Sensing his own lack of motivation and perhaps skill as a bench scientist, Hardin eventually moved from the laboratory into the classroom, where over the years he won acclaim as a teacher and author of college biology textbooks.

Beginning in the late 1960s Hardin's professional life underwent another change as he was drawn toward the concerns of the environmental movement. During the ensuing years, he published several articles in academic journals dealing with the ethical and moral dimensions of environmentalism and, in particular, human population growth. In contrast to an apparently unassuming physical appearance, which caused a journalist to liken Hardin to "a tourist from Kalamazoo," his writings served up some startling notions that left more than a few of his readers reeling. He was an outspoken advocate of legalized abortion who defended the practice as simply analogous to "smashing acorns."[1] Masses of poor people living in hopelessly squalid conditions, he thought, constituted an impossible impediment to a freer, more democratic lifestyle.

Perhaps the most candid expression of his ethical views on overpopulation appeared in the journal *Bioscience* in a 1974 article titled "Living on a Lifeboat." In this piece the author likened the world situation to one where well-fed people from wealthy countries drifted about in a lifeboat, while in the surrounding ocean swam those from poor and destitute countries, continually begging for entrance. Hardin said that if the wealthy nations continued to let the swimmers aboard—that is, in an allegorical sense to provide food and aid—then eventually everyone, rich and poor alike, would go under. The only solution, in Hardin's mind, was for those in the lifeboat to row away, leaving the unfortunate to perish. If his remedy seemed unfair, Hardin reminded the reader that survival in nature was not governed by social justice. The moral of the story was that continued aid to poor nations would simply exacerbate their population problems and ultimately destroy the helping nations as well.

Hardin's philosophy about human population alienated social critics of both the political left and the right as well as some scholars among his peers. Not surprisingly, Hardin's ideas led one editorialist for the *Saturday Review* to call him an "infection in the moral consciousness."[2] Others labeled him an insensitive elitist. However, although they might disagree with his ideas, members of the academic community regarded him as a bright and erudite mind and a gifted writer.

Garrett Hardin's most important article in terms of its intellectual contribution to the environmental movement was "The Tragedy of the Commons." The article contained a number of themes that were economic in nature, although Hardin himself was a biologist. His philosophy was in part neo-Malthusian, in that he envisioned calamitous results from population growth and the overuse of natural resources. However, he also explored the ideas of the neoclassicists, including issues such as resource valuation, decision criteria, taxes, subsidies, and the establishment of property rights. Ironically, while he spent a good many words impeaching mainstream economic thinking in "The Tragedy of the Commons," Hardin rarely referenced the economics literature.

Hardin opened his article by stating that modern technology had at times created social problems for which no apparent technical solution existed. By "no technical solution," Hardin meant that neither science nor technology could provide a remedy and that, instead, a change in human values and morality was needed.[3] He hypothesized that human overpopulation was such problem.

Before exploring his hypothesis, Hardin offered some views on the futility of human population growth in our finite world. His discussion focused on a social goal that he attributed to the English philosopher Jeremy Bentham (1748–1832) of achieving "the greatest good for the greatest number." Hardin criticized Bentham's goal on two counts. First, it was mathematically impossible simultaneously to maximize any two interdependent variables, such as human population and human satisfaction. Second, any attempt to maximize population would doom humankind to a kind of bland existence with, said Hardin, "no gourmet meals, no vacations, no sports, no music, no literature, no art."[4]

The optimum population, then, would have to be something less than the maximum, but how, asked the professor, could society determine what the optimum population was? It was a matter of tastes and preferences because, after all, different people preferred different things. Some wanted wilderness, others wanted factories, and since these goods were incommensurable (i.e., non-comparable) how was society ever to determine the appropriate mix? The answer, said Garrett Hardin, would lie in the development of (1) a criterion for judgment, and (2) a system for weighting different social needs and desires. Until these two issues were resolved, said Hardin, there would be no solution to the problem of optimal global population. The development of the judgment criterion and the weighting system was perhaps possible, but would happen only in the distant future.

Professor Hardin then took a literary swipe at yet another economist—this time at no less than the father of capitalism, Adam Smith. Hardin stated that optimum population growth would never be realized unless and until "we explicitly exorcize the spirit of Adam Smith."[5] The "spirit" Hardin referred to was Smith's "invisible-hand" hypothesis, set forth in his monumental work of 1776—indeed the cornerstone of capitalism—*An Inquiry into the Nature and Causes of the Wealth of Nations.* It suggested that the public welfare was best served by individuals making free economic decisions within a system of laissez-faire governance, as if led by an invisible hand. This notion of freedom of choice, especially with respect to population control, opined Hardin, was quite likely incompatible with the public interest, and thus required reexamination.

The perfect rebuttal to Adam Smith's invisible hand, said Hardin, was found in work of an obscure amateur mathematician named William Forster Lloyd (1794–1852). Hardin called Lloyd's idea "the tragedy of the commons" and explained it like this:

> Picture a pasture open to all. It is expected that each herdsman will try to keep as many cattle as possible on this commons. . . . What is the utility of adding one more animal . . . ? Since the herdsman receives all the proceeds from the sale of the additional animal, the positive utility [to the herdsman] is nearly +1. . . . Since, however, the effects of overgrazing are shared by all the herdsmen, the negative utility of any particular decision-making herdsman is only a fraction of -1. Adding together the partial utilities, the rational herdsman concludes that the only sensible course for him to pursue is to add another animal to the herd. And another; and another. . . . Therein is the tragedy. Each man is locked into a system that causes him to increase his herd without limit—in a world that is limited. . . . Freedom in a commons brings ruin to all.[6]

Hardin cited several examples of the problem of the commons: cattlemen leasing federal lands for livestock grazing in the western United States and in the process creating soil erosion and degrading the vegetation; the fishing of the seas by maritime nations until the stocks of fishes are exhausted; the opening of U.S. national parks to everyone without limit until the sought-after condition of solitude is gradually lost.

The problems of air and water pollution were also a type of tragedy of the commons said Hardin, but were the reverse of the aforementioned grazing issue. Instead of taking something out of the commons, polluters are putting things in—sewage, chemicals, radioactive wastes, noxious fumes, and even unpleasant advertisements. As with the grazing situation, rational humans discover that the social cost of placing these wastes in the environment is far less to them than the cost of waste purification and so, like grazing, pollution continues.

Hardin explicitly identified four areas in which he contends society must "abandon the commons." First, we must abandon the commons in food gathering. Farmland and pastures must be enclosed, as must hunting and fishing areas. This problem, says Hardin, exists more in developing than in developed nations. Second, the commons must be abandoned as a place for disposal of waste and pollution from automobiles, factories, insecticide sprayers, fertilizing operations, and atomic energy installations. Third, we must avoid the use of the commons as a means for pleasure. As examples of pleasure, Hardin listed publicly played shopping music (such as Muzak, no doubt), the noise from supersonic transports, and radio and television advertising. The fourth and final area was the abandonment of the commons in breeding. By this Hardin meant that society must relinquish the right to procreate at will. "The only way," he said, "we can preserve and nurture other more precious freedoms is by relinquishing the freedom to breed."[7] Sadly, however, he never provided a list of those "other more precious freedoms" for which people are asked to sacrifice the freedom of individual choice.

To Hardin, abandoning the commons involved two actions on the part of society. First, it required the assignment of property rights to all appropriate resources. Said the professor, "the tragedy of the commons . . . is averted by private property, or something formally like it."[8] Thus, he was interested in some legal means of excluding people and animals from gaining access to property and thereby limiting environmental damage and misuse of property. By property, he meant not only forests, farms, and pastures, but the water and air as well.

The second required action was what he termed "mutual coercion, mutually agreed upon by the majority of the people affected."[9] Thus, by means of majority rule, the governed would elect to limit—through the imposition of taxes, penalties, or some other sort of coercive device—their own freedom to breed or to pollute. This mutual coercion, thought Hardin, was essential for the protection of certain resources that could not be protected by fences or other physical barriers.

In devising the specific legal instruments for control of human actions, Hardin advised that society must be innovative and creative and depart from old notions of justice. "The laws of our society follow the pattern of ancient ethics," said Hardin, "and therefore are poorly suited to governing a complex, crowded, changeable world." And neither should the morality of social actions inhibit their implementation: "the morality of an act is a function of the state of the system at the time it is performed."[10] In simpler terms, what was forbidden one hundred years ago might be perfectly acceptable today because, according to Garrett Hardin, morality should be regarded as relative to contemporary events.

Hardin said that, as an alternative to coercion, we might at first be tempted to use an appeal to conscience as a means of limiting population growth and environmental damage. However, this effort was doomed to failure for at least two reasons. First, those who responded to such an appeal would, within a few generations, be out-bred by those who did not, and thus we would be right back where we started. Also, any attempt to induce pangs of conscience—to send people on a guilt trip, so to speak—would accomplish little more than making society's excess breeders "psychologically pathogenic."[11] Thus, unlike John Stuart Mill, Hardin had no faith in humans' ability to prevent environmental destruction through an appeal to conscience.

In the end, said Dr. Hardin, we must soon take action or face the tragedy. To take no action was to take some action, which is what we have done for thousands of years. An alternative to the commons need not be perfectly just to be preferable. Indeed, "injustice," said the professor, "is preferable to total ruin." Above all, we must "admit that our legal system of private property . . . is unjust—but we put up with it because we are not convinced . . . that anyone has invented a better system."[12]

The issue that Garrett Hardin had raised, the common property nature of natural resources, is a key concept in environmental thought. Indeed, it could be argued that common property is the greatest obstacle faced by society in the maintenance of natural resource stocks and environmental quality. As Hardin noted, the problem affects society in two ways. First, it contributes to overharvesting or overutilization of resources. When numerous users have unlimited access to a finite resource, they have little incentive to refrain from overuse. Because the individual users have no means of preventing access by others, they are unable to reap the rewards of any conservation efforts they may make.[13] This is the situation often seen in fisheries and on forest and grazing lands, where resource exploitation tends to be the rule. Second, common property contributes to pollution problems. As we have seen, the common property nature of water and air invites people to use them as waste receptacles free of charge. In both instances, the negative impact on the individual exploiter or polluter is less than the impact on society at large.

"The Tragedy of the Commons" quickly gained notoriety among the academic community. The consensus among academicians was that Hardin had raised an important environmental issue. The article generated discussion and stimulated inquiry into the common property issue. Despite the general appeal of Hardin's contribution there were detractors. One such negative response appeared in the same technical journal, *Science*, two years following Hardin's article. In the rebuttal, Beryl Crowe criticized Hardin's work on two points. First, he said that the idea was not original, and second he disagreed with Hardin's solutions to the problem of the commons.

With regard to the lack of originality, Crowe said that Hardin's "'rediscovery' of the tragedy was in part wasted effort, for the knowledge of the tragedy is so common in the social sciences that it has generated some fairly sophisticated mathematical models."[14] Without doubt, the common property problem had been previously recognized as a key environmental issue. Hardin himself had even credited the idea to William Lloyd, an obscure nineteenth-century mathematician. Key ideas in "The Tragedy of the Commons" were also strikingly similar to ones in a more contemporary paper by economist Scott Gordon titled "Economics and the Conservation Question," published in 1958. Gordon had researched the problem of common property for some years, looking mainly at ocean fisheries. He, too, had said that common property would lead to overexploitation of natural resources. Gordon sought remedies to the problem, advocating correction of "institutional defects" through the establishment of property rights as preferable to government intervention, presumably with quota systems. In his article, he also mentioned Jeremy Bentham's principle of utility (which Gordon credited both to Bentham and to American forester Gifford Pinchot who had used a similar phrase 125 years after Bentham had originated it).[15] Gordon, like Hardin, discussed the futility of trying to maximize "the greatest good for the greatest number" simultaneously.

Besides stating that Hardin's contribution was not original, Crowe also found fault with three key assumptions in the article: (1) that a criterion of judgment and a common value system must be developed in order to facilitate decisions regarding resource allocation; (2) that "mutual coercion mutually agreed upon" would prevent people from exploiting the commons; and (3) that a government-administered system could effectively protect the commons from overuse.[16] Crowe said that a criterion of judgment was impossible because the modern United States had become too socially fragmented and pluralistic. No longer was the country the great "melting pot" with a unified view of the world. There was no longer a shared value system that allowed all people to agree upon a single criterion of judgment. With regard to mutual coercion, Crowe said history had demonstrated that people would not be easily forced to do that which they did not voluntarily choose. Opposition to the war in Vietnam and the nascent civil rights movement had proven that people could not be coerced. Finally, Crowe felt that government regulatory agencies, while giving assurances that they would protect the commons, in fact, tended to cater to special interests rather than serve the public good. Therefore, Crowe thought that federal agencies were probably incapable of preventing ruin to the commons.

Beryl Crowe thought that Hardin's solutions to the common property problem were inadequate. He agreed, however, that the world situation with respect to exploitation of the commons was hopeless, saying "we stand 'on the eve of destruction.'" Yet, despite the "nearly remorseless working of things" he felt that science could to some extent alleviate the problem by monitoring the condition of resources and by developing new resource-extending technologies.[17] On this point, Beryl Crowe and Garrett Hardin were hopelessly at odds. Crowe looked toward technology as a partial solution to the tragedy of the commons, whereas Hardin's initial point in his essay had been that the commons presented a problem for which no technical solution existed.

There have been efforts, as Garrett Hardin suggested, to develop criteria of judgment and weighting schemes to assist in resource allocation problems. One example is the practice of cost-benefit analysis. This type of economic analysis searches for the so-called optimal level of project investment, which maximizes the difference between the benefits derived from a project and the cost of obtaining those benefits.

To conduct a cost-benefit analysis requires several steps. First is to measure the various costs associated with the project, say for example, a project to control air pollution. Pollution control costs are determined by a challenging yet relatively straightforward process of adding up the costs of the pollution prevention equipment to be placed in factories and motor vehicles. In addition to knowing the costs for all the possible mechanisms of control, the economist must also determine the effectiveness of each option in reducing emissions and hence environmental damage. It is often quite difficult to derive this information. Typically, more money spent on the control effort will result in lower amounts of pollution damage although, in typical economic fashion, the marginal damage reduction from cleaner air will decrease with each additional dollar spent.

After pollution control costs are determined, the benefits of pollution control must be estimated. In practice, the estimation of benefits tends to be a much more difficult task than the measurement of costs. Usually this phase of the analysis is hypothetical in that the damage estimates are based upon projections of damages that have not actually occurred. Benefits are calculated by subtracting the value of environmental damage that would occur with no pollution control from the value of damage which would occur at each of the various optional levels of control. Benefits are therefore the value of the environmental damages *avoided* at each level of pollution control.

If benefits, or for that matter control costs, occur as a stream of cash flows over the life of the project, the analyst will typically discount these values to the first year of the project. At least, this has been the standard practice. As we have seen, in the analysis of environmental damages some economists have questioned the practice of discounting because it implies that the welfare of future generations is less important than that of the present. The economic objective of cost-benefit analysis is to find the level of pollution control that yields the maximum difference between benefits (i.e., damages avoided) and pollution control costs. This is also said to be the most economically efficient level of control, meaning simply that the expenditure for control generates the largest level of benefits.

The spectrum of damages accounted for in the calculation of benefits can in theory be broad. It can include, for example, deterioration of human health, losses in agriculture and forestry, reduction of water quality in lakes and rivers, and damage to buildings and other human-made objects. The traditional practice, however, was to include only "tangible" benefits in the accounting framework—that is, to include only those things which have market prices, such as losses of marketable timber or agricultural crops, or damage to buildings and other human-made structures. Intangibles, those things not traded in cash markets, are usually listed for decision makers but not included in the quantitative analysis.

The problem of valuing benefits is analogous to Garrett Hardin's concern about the need for a system of weights to permit a fair comparison of the many choices society is presented regarding environmental resources. The development of a weighting, or valuation, system has had a long history in the economic literature. The problem has two parts: first, to determine what medium shall be used to express value, and second, to determine what the values themselves will be. Debates about valuation often confuse these two issues.

With regard to the medium, the tendency has been to use money to express social value.[18] Recall that A. C. Pigou had said that money price was a good place to begin valuation. Money has been chosen because it is the most generally accepted medium of exchange. Indeed, this has been the principal function of money over recorded history, to provide a universal medium of exchange so that all values can be readily compared. Not surprisingly, some people disagree with its use for valuation of the environment on ethical grounds:

The idea of putting money value on damage done to the environment strikes many as illicit, even immoral. The justification for monetary valuation lies in the way in which money is used as a measuring rod to indicate gains or losses in utility or welfare. It must not be confused with more popular concepts about . . . money . . . as the pursuit of Mammon. Some attempts have been made to find other units—notably energy units—but . . . money units remain the best indicator [of preferences] we have.[19]

The most challenging issue, however, is not what medium constitutes the weights (whether it be money or even units of energy) but rather how the weights—that is, the relative values—are determined. Economists have traditionally tried to let markets determine values. Yet analysts have, of course, long recognized that market prices do not exist for many of the things society values. And, even if prices do exist, they may not reflect the true social value of resources. Markets with externalities are one instance in which prices fail to reflect true social value. In those cases, some price adjustment based on the magnitude of the externality would then provide a more accurate estimate of the true social value of the resource.

In some instances, the market cannot establish values because no market exists for the good or service in question. There are many examples of socially desirable goods and services that are not traded in formal markets. Clean air, a scenic view, or a bird in flight cannot be readily valued because no cash market exists for those items. Other values are even more elusive. Examples are the value that people place upon simply knowing that wilderness exists, the value that someone may place on a particular natural resource for its use by future generations, or even the value of human pain and suffering. Society has been increasingly insistent that these intangibles be explicitly accounted for in cost-benefit analysis. It is not difficult to see that valuation in the absence of markets presents a formidable challenge.

In instances where markets do not exist, and therefore values cannot be observed, analysts have resorted to alternative methods for estimating social values.[20] One such technique is the Hedonic price approach. This method assumes that the value of an environmental resource is determined by the various attributes of that resource. The analyst uses statistical models to partition the contribution of each of the attributes to total value. For example, the impact of air pollution on property values could be determined by use of a Hedonic model to separate influences of location, size, landscaping, and other attributes as well as pollution on the total value of a parcel of land.

Contingent valuation is a direct approach for estimating environmental values. An experiment is designed where people are asked how much they are willing to pay to prevent environmental damage to, say, a scenic vista. Alternatively, they may be asked how much they would have to be paid in order to accept a specified amount of environmental damage to the vista. These alternative approaches to contingent valuation are known as willingness to pay and willingness to accept. The contingent valuation method is flexible and thus can be applied to a wide variety of environmental valuation problems. Because the responses are hypothetical, however, the method has sometimes been criticized as unreliable. A third valuation approach is the travel cost method. Here the amounts of time and distance that people travel to reach a resource are used to infer the value of that resource to the user. This technique has been especially useful for the valuation of recreation experiences where people must frequently travel to enjoy natural beauty in the outdoors.

Cost-benefit analysis is standard economic theory and practice, but nevertheless it has critics. Economist Daniel Swartzman has categorized the various criticisms as methodological, political, or ethical.[21] The complaints about methods focus on data and techniques for valuation. The political concerns focus mostly on the potential misuse of the cost-benefit analysis for political ends. The ethical complaints are to some the most perplexing. These focus on the fact that analysts assign exact values to things that are inherently difficult to value and then balance them on the cold scales of economic rationality. Even valuing something so special as human life becomes a clinical exercise. Said economist Dr. Paul Portney, then with Resources for the Future, "The real problem with environmental cost-benefit analysis is not putting value on human life."[22] This matter-of-fact attitude toward the value of human life and environmental resources has reputedly given cost-benefit analysis a horrible reputation on Capitol Hill.[23] During the Reagan administration, White House economists attempted to analyze national antipollution regulations in a cost-benefit framework. The grisly business of trying to express human life in monetary terms so offended the sensibilities of the political establishment that the White House soon distanced itself from the effort.

Objections to cost-benefit analysis sometimes result from a misunderstanding of its intent. Critics frequently hurl stones at their own inaccurate impressions rather than at valid concerns. Philosopher Mark Sagoff has objected to cost-benefit analysis on the grounds that it usurps legitimacy from the political process and tends to bar all parties from discussion of the conflict save those who have an immediate stake, usually business and government.[24] Such comments ignore the fact that cost-benefit analysis itself is not a political process, but only one bit of information that informs political decisions. Economists do not intentionally hide important information from the public, but neither is it their function to see that all relevant information is provided. This is the obligation of elected representatives and the function of a free press. Sagoff has described a role for economists that is grander than the role they have described for themselves, and then criticizes them for not fulfilling the role he has assigned.

The reader of "The Tragedy of the Commons" must be impressed with the wide range of social and legal issues Garrett Hardin discusses but must likewise take note of internal inconsistencies in the piece. Professor Hardin at one time calls for the establishment of legal remedies which, he says, need not be socially "just," and then, only a few pages later, complains that current laws dealing with property rights are "unjust." Which position regarding justice, one might ask, is correct for society? Similarly, Hardin wrote against things associated with capitalism—Adam Smith, self-seeking motives, and freedom of individual choice—while simultaneously calling for expansion and stricter enforcement of laws related to private property. Indeed, Hardin called for more private property, the very foundation of the free enterprise system, while condemning the philosophy of free enterprise itself.

Hardin also seemed to have misinterpreted the social goal attributed to Bentham: "the greatest good for the greatest number." He interpreted the statement to mean "the greatest good *and* the greatest number," which clearly is not what Bentham meant. Bentham had no wish to maximize the total size of the world's population. Bentham's goal is concerned with maximizing only one thing—the "good" of society—and then seeing to it that this "greatest good" is equitably distributed among as much of the world's population as possible. Bentham merely wanted to see that as much of the Earth's population was as well off as possible, not that the world was filled with people.

The common property nature of environmental resources was an important topic raised by "The Tragedy of the Commons" that remains important today. Canadian bio-mathematician Colin Clark discussed the works of both Hardin and Gordon and the continuing relevance of the common property issue to environmental thought:

> The tragedy of the commons constitutes perhaps the most powerful bias against sustainable development. As population and technology expand, the implications of our inability to solve the problems spread from local to global scales. Government institutions capable of dealing with common property problems may exist at local and national levels, but they are often weak and subject to political influence. At the international level, no institutions having any powers of enforcement exist at all and we must rely on the cooperation and goodwill of each individual nation to deal with these problems.[25]

"The Tragedy of the Commons" today remains one of the best-known pieces in the environmental literature. It has become a classic because of Garrett Hardin's ability to convey the fact that the common property nature of environmental resources is a principal cause of their exploitation. Hardin and his wife, Jane, belonged to the Hemlock Society, and on September 14, 2003, shortly after their sixty-second wedding anniversary, they committed a double suicide at their Santa Barbara home. Garrett Hardin lived and acted as best as he could in accord with his favorite saying of the Buddha: "I teach only two things: the cause of human sorrow and the way to become free of it."[26]

12

Barry Commoner and *The Closing Circle*

By the end of the 1960s, environmentalism had become firmly established as a focal point of public attention. Congress had enacted several important ecologically minded pieces of legislation, including the Clean Air Act of 1963, the Wilderness Act of 1964, and the Endangered Species Preservation Act of 1966.[1] A catastrophic event—the January 1969 oil spill in the ocean near Santa Barbara, California—even seemed to underscore the necessity of legislative action. That year Richard Nixon assumed the presidency and his first state-of-the-union address, to the surprise of many, dealt largely with the problems of the environment. Later, in 1969, he signed into law the United States' most important environmental legislation to date, the National Environmental Policy Act, and on January 1, 1970, the Environmental Protection Agency was created.

Aside from government actions and environmental catastrophes, the most significant public event in those early years of the modern environmental era was the first Earth Week celebration held in April 1970. Earth Week's principal activities were planned for Earth Day on April 22, a day set aside for environmental cleanup and for mass demonstrations in support of the environment. Largely a campus-based activity, Earth Week attracted widespread media attention, further heightening public awareness regarding environmental quality. There were speeches and written words from businessmen, academicians, elected officials, and others, each in their own way trying to explain the environmental crisis and to fix blame for what many were coming to view as a public issue of major proportions.

One person who paid careful attention to the many explanations of environmental degradation was Barry Commoner, a professor of biology at Washington University in St. Louis, the same institution, incidentally, where Harold Barnett was employed. Earth Week and the accompanying outbursts of preaching and prognostication troubled

Commoner, who himself had been a speaker on four different college campuses on that first Earth Day.[2] What had surprised him most were the numerous, confident explanations of the causes of and cures for the crisis. The many theories seemed to him like expressions of personal bias rather than objective knowledge and offered no thoughtful analysis of the problem.

In response, Commoner set out to explore and thus clarify the nature of the environmental crisis. As he said, "Earth Week convinced me of the urgency of a deeper public understanding of the environmental crisis and its possible cures."[3] The result of his investigation was *The Closing Circle: Nature, Man and Technology.* The interesting metaphor in the title of the book—"the closing circle"—referred to Commoner's vision of the ecosphere as "the home that life has built for itself on the planet's outer surface."[4] He likened the ecosphere to an endless cycle, a closed circle, where humans *had* interacted in balance with their environment. But now, and for some time, the circle had been broken because of humans' self-alienation and destructive actions. Commoner's aim was to explore the possibilities for closing the circle by once again returning humans to equilibrium with nature.

Barry Commoner brought considerable knowledge and academic credentials to the task of writing *The Closing Circle.* Born in New York in 1917 to Russian immigrant parents, he received a degree in zoology with honors from Columbia University in 1937 and in 1941 a Ph.D. in biology from Harvard University.[5] During World War II, he served in the U.S. Navy and ended his stint in the armed services with an assignment to the staff of the Senate Military Affairs Committee. He joined the faculty of Washington University as an associate professor of biology in 1947 and spent most of his academic career there. Fellow professors there recall Commoner as an energetic scientist with a complex and wide-ranging intellect. Over the years he rose through the ranks to the position of University Professor of Environmental Science. Commoner has been awarded at least eleven honorary degrees by various universities and has served on the boards of directors of numerous public, environmental, and antiwar organizations. Among many other awards for his scholarly achievements are being named a fellow of the American Association for the Advancement of Science, the American Chemical Association, and the American Association of

Plant Physiology. In 1981, he moved to Queens College in New York, where he established the Center for Biology of Natural Systems.

Barry Commoner is generally regarded as a "founding father" of modern environmentalism. Indeed, *Time* magazine printed his picture on its cover, referring to him as the "Paul Revere of ecology."[6] This recognition of Commoner's leadership in the environmental movement was due to his public visibility and willingness to speak out on matters of politics and the environment. He was, in fact, one of the first scientists to openly recognize the importance of political involvement to the resolution of environmental problems.[7] During the 1970s, Barry Commoner, like some other environmentalists, saw environmental degradation essentially as a social problem that was best solved by means of "politically leftward" solutions.[8] In 1980, he even ran for president as a third-party candidate on the left-wing Citizens Party ticket.[9]

While at Washington University, Commoner directed scientific research on several timely issues. Nitrogen cycling, carcinogens in the environment, energy shortages and agriculture, and modern technology and the environment are examples of subjects he addressed. His expert knowledge concerning the biology and chemistry of Earth processes is clearly evident in the pages of *The Closing Circle*. There, at times, he embarked on detailed yet lucid explanations of environmental topics such as the formation of life on Earth or the composition of photochemical smog in California. The strength of *The Closing Circle*, however, was not in its technical explanation of the Earth's biophysical processes, but in its attempt to link those processes to human social, economic, and political systems. It was this attempt to establish the relationship between the natural world and human systems that helped Commoner provide a fresh view of the environmental crisis.

Following the example of *Silent Spring*, a substantial portion of *The Closing Circle* was pre-published in *The New Yorker* magazine. Portions of the thirteen chapters were also previously published as parts of other books or government documents. This perhaps indicated that Professor Commoner had for some time been contemplating and writing about the environmental crisis. Unfortunately, however, the joining together of previously written chapters also caused the flow of the book to suffer. As for documentation of source materials, there were twenty-one pages of endnotes containing more than 160 separate citations.

The book's opening chapter expresses Barry Commoner's concern over the seriousness of the environmental crisis: "Suddenly we have discovered what we should have known long before: . . . that the ecosphere is being driven toward collapse."[10] He then set forth the questions he hoped to answer in the book:

> Our assaults on the ecosystem are so powerful, so numerous, so finely interconnected, that although the damage they do is clear, it is very difficult to discover how it was done. By which weapon, by whose hand? Are we driving the ecosphere to destruction simply by our growing numbers? By our greedy accumulation of wealth? Or [is] the magnificent technology . . . that surrounds us at fault? This book is concerned with these questions.[11]

Thus, *The Closing Circle* begins more or less in the style of a mystery novel. The crime—environmental degradation—is described, and the potential culprits are individually identified: excess population, increasing affluence, and modern technology. Barry Commoner as judge and jury will try each one of the accused using *The Closing Circle* as his trial venue.

In the second chapter, Dr. Commoner plays upon the book's title by explaining ecology as the study of the circular interrelationships and processes linking each living thing to its physical and chemical environment. After exploring complex examples of these ecological relations, he provides four summarizing "laws of ecology." Each law is captioned by a catchy and somewhat humorous title that captures the essence of some ecological truth. To many, these axioms were the most quotable, and thus most memorable, part of *The Closing Circle*:

> *The First Law of Ecology: Everything is Connected to Everything Else.* Because all components within an ecosystem are, by definition, interconnected, then any perturbation, however small, will have effects in another part of the ecosystem.
> *The Second Law of Ecology: Everything Must Go Somewhere.* This is simply a restatement of the law of conservation of matter. Every bit of waste and every bit of pollution must, inescapably, be

deposited somewhere. The problem, of course, is in the accumulation of unnatural, harmful substances in places they do not belong.

The Third Law of Ecology: Nature Knows Best. Simply stated, this law holds that major human-initiated changes in an ecosystem are almost always detrimental to that ecosystem. This, thought Commoner, was likely to be the most controversial of his four laws because of the strong, abiding faith that the current generation had in technology.

The Fourth Law of Ecology: There Is No Such Thing as a Free Lunch. This law, Commoner confessed, he had borrowed from economics. It states that every gain made from exploitation of the environment results in some cost to someone, somewhere.

The next four chapters, "Nuclear Fire," "Los Angeles Air," "Illinois Earth," and "Lake Erie Water," focus on the role of science in detecting the specific mechanisms that cause environmental degradation. Each chapter illustrates how scientists have traced an environmental problem to its technological sources. Examined are the threats posed when calcium irradiated by nuclear testing is picked up in the food chain, when toxic nitrogen dioxide is present in photochemical smog in Los Angeles, when excess nitrogen fertilizer from midwestern farms enters the water supply, and when poorly treated waste is dumped into the Great Lakes.

These chapters provide interesting insights into the technical mechanisms that cause damage to the ecosphere. More important, however, they explain the means by which scientists attempt to find correct answers to these ecological riddles. The key, Commoner says, is something other than an open and unbiased mind:

The reason why the scientific enterprise has a well-deserved reputation for unearthing the truth about natural phenomena is not the "objectivity" of its practitioners, but the fact that they abide by a rule long established in science—open discussion and publication. For science gets at the truth not so much by avoiding mistakes or personal bias as by displaying them to the public —where they can be corrected.[12]

The next four chapters—"Man in the Ecosphere," "Population and Affluence," "The Technological Flaw," and "The Social Issue"—contain the intellectual core of Commoner's thesis. It is here that the author begins to sort though the available evidence and then place blame for the environmental crisis. Here, too, the emphasis of the story shifts from science and ecology to human behavior, an emphasis that is, by and large, maintained throughout the remainder of the book.

The most efficient way to begin searching for the cause of and solution to our environmental woes, believed Commoner, was to examine human activities. Nature alone, he felt, was incapable of causing the kinds of ecological disruptions the world was experiencing. Furthermore, the professor was certain that the cause of the problem was to be found in the way that humans exploited the Earth in their search for livelihood and material gain. In his words, "I believe that the crisis is not the outcome of a natural catastrophe or of the misdirected force of human biological activities. The fault lies with human society —with the ways in which society has elected to win, distribute, and use the wealth that has been extracted by human labor from the planet's resources."[13] Quite clearly, then, Barry Commoner characterized the environmental crisis as a sociological rather than purely ecological problem, and one which was related to the economic activities of the world's population.

At this point, Commoner initiated his investigation of the three most likely culprits as he saw them: excess population, increasing affluence, and modern technology. Population control, perhaps even by draconian methods, was of course, what both Paul Ehrlich and Garrett Hardin had advocated. But, according to Commoner, population was not the principal cause of environmental degradation. Indeed, in references only thinly veiled, Commoner lambasted the ideas of both Ehrlich and Hardin. Coercive methods of population control, which both men had suggested, were nothing more than political repression to Commoner's way of thinking.

The U.S. population, Commoner said, had not grown rapidly enough since World War II to account alone for the nation's increasing levels of pollution. As he pointed out, population growth rates had even tended to decline as big families became obsolete in a nonagrarian society. To place his conclusion on firmer ground, Commoner resorted to some numbers. He estimated that pollution in the United States had increased in the range of 200 to 2,000 percent since 1946. Population, in contrast, had increased by only about 40 to 50 percent during the same period.[14] Thus, excess population, he argued, simply could not be the principal cause of the problem.

Next he examined increasing affluence—that is, the increasing per-capita consumption of goods and services—as the cause of the environmental crisis. As a proximate measure of affluence Barry Commoner used per-capita GNP. Since World War II, he calculated that per-capita GNP, like population, had increased by only about 50 percent, not enough, he concluded, to account for the even larger increases in pollution. Barry Commoner then went beyond the aggregate figures to examine patterns in various types of consumption. The level of consumption of basic items such as food, steel, and fabrics had increased only in direct proportion to population increases. He detected more than proportional increases in the use of electricity, fuels, paper products, and electrical appliances, but even there the increases were not enough to account for the rapidly accelerating levels of pollution. Therefore, Commoner concluded, increasing affluence was not our guilty party.

Finally, he examined modern technology, the last suspect and the one, of course, on which Commoner placed the lion's share of blame. He argued that just prior to World War II, Western civilization had passed through a period of about twenty-five years of rich scientific discovery. In the years after the war had come a sustained period of technological innovation stemming directly from the earlier scientific revolution. Americans had come to view this new technology as a "self-sufficient, autonomous juggernaut, relatively immune to human fallibility."[15] Technology, we believed, would conquer all.

Commoner put forth examples of the types of technologies that had caused modern environmental problems: pesticides, synthetic plastics, mercury contamination, and nuclear explosives. The problem with each technology arose, he said, because it had been developed under short-sighted definitions of success and failure. The product was deemed entirely successful if it merely performed some specific task; it was never asked also to succeed on the grounds of environmental compatibility. Thus, the problem with modern technology was the technologists' narrow conception of their responsibility to society. Barry Commoner said that the tendency for technologists to adopt a narrow view of their work was due to an unfortunate characteristic of the scientific profession. And that characteristic he called reductionism, the tendency to fragment fields of learning into ever-smaller subdivisions until they operated in virtual ignorance of one another and also of the human population their work affected. One of the few academics Commoner thought had given serious consideration to a holistic approach to science was René Dubos of Rockefeller University.

Barry Commoner went so far as to assign numerical weights to the contributions of his three causal factors—population, affluence, and technology—to the overall post–World War II pollution problem. Population increases, he said, accounted for about 12 to 20 percent of the pollution problem, affluence for about 1 to 5 percent, and new technologies for about 95 percent. The numbers are both interesting and troublesome, partly because their total exceeds 100 percent, but also because the procedures by which they were developed are not explained in the text. Perhaps they are regression coefficients from a statistical analysis, but this is impossible to discern from the text.

During his discussion of the causes of environmental degradation, Barry Commoner also raised, as had Kenneth Boulding and Paul Ehrlich, the second law of thermodynamics and its relevance to the future existence of humankind. Once again it was explained that as humans produce economic goods, the ensuing entropy—that is, the continual dissipation of energy that necessarily attends such production—will ultimately and inexorably place a limit on civilization. Thus, for many environmentalists the second law of thermodynamics became all the more firmly established as proof of the inevitable end of civilization.

The next chapter, "The Question of Survival," is to a degree redundant with earlier portions of the book, in that it repeats Commoner's dire predictions for the world unless the environmental crisis is resolved and, also, it revisits the issue of population control. With regard to the future of the Earth, he had these strong words: "My own judgment, based on the evidence now at hand, is that the present course of environmental degradation . . . represents a challenge . . . so serious that . . . it will destroy the capability of the environment to support a reasonably civilized human society."[16]

With regard to population control, Barry Commoner once again expresses utter disdain for Paul Ehrlich's ideas and then proposes a seemingly more positive way of dealing with the situation. Noting that birth rates tend to decline as societies become affluent, Commoner suggests, in the tradition of John Stuart Mill, that prosperous nations such as the United States should help poorer nations improve their economic conditions: "one can adopt the view that population growth in the developing nations of the world ought to be brought into balance by the same means that have already succeeded elsewhere—improvement of living conditions. . . . It is this view with which I wish to associate myself."[17]

The next to last chapter is titled "The Economic Meaning of Ecology" and its inclusion comes as something of a surprise given Commoner's background in biology. But his search for an answer to the environmental crisis had brought him to this point. His investigation had carried him on an odyssey from ecology, through the physical sciences, past engineering technology and demography, and now to economics. Reductionism may have been a problem for some scientists, but not for Barry Commoner.

The professor's discourse on the economic meaning of ecology is complex and tedious but perhaps from necessity because here he is striving to answer what is *the* most crucial question: can any existing economic system effectively mitigate environmental pollution? Commoner explores the concept of economic externalities before finally focusing on both capitalist and socialist economic systems. In his analysis he concludes that both systems are guilty of polluting the environment; neither has a clean record, so to speak. The work of economist Marshall I. Goldman,[18] which examined pollution in the Soviet Union, was an important source of Commoner's information. In his discussion of the ability of capitalism to control pollution, Commoner leaned heavily upon the writings of two economists, Robert L. Heilbroner and K. W. Kapp, who had both concluded that the free-market system had no possibility for success. The problem, agreed Commoner, was that any attempt to internalize the cost of externalities would simply raise costs to companies, which would then be forced to cut wages in order to maintain profits. The result would be an intensification of the division between management and labor, and an increase in the level of poverty. Also, the inability of capitalism to achieve a steady state would render it forever exploitive of natural resources. Commoner's analysis of socialism was less detailed, but he did see some advantage to its centralized state planning which, he believed, could provide an efficient means of eliminating environmental pollution. In the final analysis he called for change in all economic systems, especially capitalism, but his direction was vague:

> Hence an economic system which is fundamentally based on private transactions rather than social ones is no longer appropriate and increasingly ineffective in managing [the ecosphere]. The system is therefore in need of change. These considerations apply to all industrialized nations; all of them need to reorganize their economies upon ecologically sound lines.[19]

The final chapter titled, aptly, "The Closing Circle," once again takes the opportunity to knock Garrett Hardin's ideas on population control, referring to them as "faintly masked . . . barbarism." More important, though, the brief chapter restates the importance of finding an end to the environmental crisis: "Human beings have broken out of the circle of life, driven not by biological need, but by the social organization which has been devised to 'conquer' nature. . . . The end result is the environmental crisis, a crisis of survival. Once more, to survive, we must close the circle. We must learn how to nurture the wealth that we borrow from it." Surprisingly, however, the very last words of the book present an enormous question mark as to how "the circle" could be "closed": "That we must act is now clear. The question we face is how?"[20]

At the time of its release, *The Closing Circle* was the most comprehensive work yet published in terms of its view of the environmental crisis and the possible causes of it. And this was not by chance, but by the author's design. Rather than beginning his investigation with a solution already in mind and then defending his choice, Commoner established possible hypotheses and then set about testing them against available data and information. This, of course, is simply the use of the scientific method. Too, the way in which he attempted to apportion partial blame among different agents is more informative, and more realistic, than simplistically laying the blame on a single cause. Some may fault Commoner for his somewhat anticlimactic, no-solution ending to *The Closing Circle,* but perhaps this was done by intent in order to avoid the rash conclusions Commoner thought Hardin and Ehrlich had made.

While Commoner's approach was laudable, his analysis of data to test his hypotheses is, as earlier stated, a bit disconcerting. The methods he used to measure some variables—for example, the 200 to 2,000 percent increase in pollution since World War II—are not clear from the text, and thus the reader must accept the numbers simply on faith. Also, the assignment of weights to the three causes—population, affluence, and technology—is something of a mystery. We are left with the feeling that Commoner's final results are compelling but not absolutely convincing. One criterion that scientists often use to determine whether or not a scientific manuscript is suitable for publication is whether the study can be replicated from the information given and, thus, produce the same result. From what we are provided in *The Closing Circle,* replication would be difficult.

Barry Commoner's recognition that the cause of environmental problems was rooted in systems of economic livelihood carried him onto foreign ground, so to speak, but this he knew. In *The Closing Circle,* he expressed concern over his unfamiliarity with the study of economics, yet at the same time he felt compelled to venture there. From the work of Marshall Goldman, Commoner examined what remains to this day a classic study of pollution in the former USSR. However, when Commoner spoke in favor of state planning as a remedy, he ignored the advice that Goldman had given: "If the study of environmental disruption in the Soviet Union demonstrates anything, it shows that not private enterprise but industrialization is the primary cause of environmental disruption. This suggests that state ownership of all productive resources is no cure-all."[21]

Also, environmental economists dispute Commoner's notion that, because of its profit motive, capitalism is primarily responsible for the environmental crisis. As we have seen, it is unlikely that capitalism, or any other system for that matter, can eliminate pollution. But by accounting for the rights of and costs to polluted parties, and by enforcing those rights, they argue that we can achieve a socially acceptable level of pollution under capitalism. And achieving a "socially acceptable" level of pollution would be, by definition, equivalent to eliminating the crisis. Commoner was almost certainly correct in his opinion that all political/economic systems had mishandled the environmental crisis. Yet this seems a question of execution rather than intent.

The second law of thermodynamics raised by Barry Commoner is an issue which focuses more on the rate of industrialization than on pollution per se. Entropy occurs, we are told, even in natural biological systems, but there the rates of conversion are very low. Within an industrialized society, the rate of energy dissipation is thought to be too high, thus considerably hastening the end of civilization— pollution or no pollution. The question with regard to industrialization is, how much sooner will the world end? No one seems to have the answer. As one writer has asked, "is it one billion [years] or forty-five billion?"[22]

The dispute between Barry Commoner and Paul Ehrlich over the principal cause of environmental problems was for a time one of the most intense personal feuds of the modern environmental movement.[23] This was not the first such dispute for Ehrlich. As chapter 8 describes, he had also engaged in similar acrimonious debates with economist Julian Simon.

The crux of the Commoner-Ehrlich dispute lay in their differing views regarding the causes of environmental degradation. Ehrlich had insisted in *The Population Bomb* that increasing world population was at the heart of the current environmental crisis. Rapid population growth was furthermore exacerbated by its tendency to concentrate in urban areas, thus placing focused pressure on limited natural resources. The situation was so threatening, according to Ehrlich, that almost any preventive measure was worth taking, no matter what the social cost. He had suggested incentives, penalties, and even compulsion not to have children as remedies. Furthermore, Ehrlich felt that the United States as a world leader was obliged to force other countries to accept programs to limit population growth. He had even proposed the use of military power to accomplish that goal. In contrast, Commoner's major thesis was that modern technology, not human population was the root cause of environmental problems. He believed that national policy should be more concerned with the improvement of engineering efficiencies and the control of pollution than with enforced control of population. Indeed, he found Ehrlich's suggestions for heavy-handed population control totally unacceptable.

Commoner and Ehrlich, by the mid-1970s, came to agree that affluence, population, and technology each played a role in environmental degradation. However, they were unable to agree upon appropriate policy options. Environmental writer Timothy O' Riordan argues that the Commoner-Ehrlich debate, rather than enlightening people, did a great disservice by dangerously misleading the public and creating confusion in the minds of policymakers. Often, the Commoner-Ehrlich dispute is cast more as a battle between two supreme egos for popular recognition than as a serious attempt to resolve environmental problems.[24]

After *The Closing Circle,* Barry Commoner went on to author numerous other books and publications on the environment. Today he lives in Brooklyn, New York, where he is director emeritus of the Center for Biological Studies at Queens College, City University of New York in Flushing.

13

Herman Daly and the Steady-State Economy

For more than thirty years, economics professor Herman E. Daly has advocated the steady-state economy as a solution to environmental and natural resource problems. As a result of his efforts, the steady-state theory has generated one of the most rapidly growing and academically diverse schools of environmental thought. Daly's intellectual contributions regarding the steady-state economy have indeed been important. However, the foundations of the theory predate Daly's writings by more than a century. In *Principles of Political Economy* (1848) economist-philosopher John Stuart Mill first presented a vision of the steady, or as he said, "stationary," state economy. Following are his words excerpted from a six-page chapter on the subject:

> It must always have been seen by political economists, that increase in wealth is not boundless; that at the end lies the stationary state. . . . I cannot [however] regard the stationary state with the unaffected aversion so generally manifested towards it by political economists of the old school. I am inclined to believe that it would be, on the whole, a very considerable improvement over our present condition . . . the best state for human nature is that in which . . . no one is poor [and] . . . no one desires to be richer . . . what is economically needed is a better distribution [of wealth] . . . of which one means is a stricter restraint on population . . . this better distribution . . . attained by the . . . prudence and frugality of individuals, and of a system of legislation favoring equality of fortunes. Society would exhibit affluent workers, no enormous fortunes, [and] . . . leisure. I sincerely hope, for the sake of posterity, that [society] will be content to be stationary long before necessity compels them to it. It is scarcely necessary to remark that a stationary condition . . . implies no stationary state of human improvement. There would be . . . all

kinds of mental culture, and moral and social progress . . . [and]
much room for improving the Art of Living . . . when minds
cease to be engrossed by the art of getting on.[1]

Mill's description of the stationary state economy was admittedly
brief and dealt with the topic only conceptually. His curt treatment,
however, belies the fact that the topic had a long history of concern.
Since the time of Adam Smith the classicists had feared that society, in
its attempt to increase profits and wealth, would eventually find itself destitute, having economically exhausted the planet's natural resources. This impoverished condition was referred to as the stationary
state because society, once there, would have achieved a permanent
though undesirable state of human affairs.

The classical economists before Mill had, quite naturally, viewed
the stationary state with fear. Recall that Malthus painted a grim picture of a world filled with human misery. Mill's optimistic view of the
situation thus stood in stark contrast to that of the older classicists. To
him, attainment of the stationary economic state was a goal worthy of
pursuit because society could voluntarily determine the equilibrium
conditions of that state. Mill's stationary state would permit no fortunes. Yet in exchange for the deprivation of great personal wealth,
society would receive sufficient material comfort and ample leisure
time for intellectually lofty pursuits. In order to attain this Nirvana, society would have to reduce population growth. Wealth would also have
to be distributed more evenly among the existing population. These
goals, in turn, would be achieved through voluntary self-restraint from
needless consumption of precious resources. In addition, Mill suggested that laws might be needed to ensure equal monetary incomes.
Mill's future world, thus, was not one in which humanity was a victim
of its own hedonism. Instead, humankind would control its destiny by
means of moderation in population growth, consumption, and economic equality.

Sadly for Mill, his vision of the voluntary stationary state never
attracted serious attention during his own time nor in the century that
followed. Perhaps because it seemed like fanciful dreaming, or perhaps
because neoclassical economists developed alternative theories which
eclipsed that of the stationary state, Mill's idea all but died. Died, that

is, until the writings of then–Louisiana State University professor Herman E. Daly gave it new life.

In 1971, as part of a distinguished lecture series at the University of Alabama, Daly first published on the stationary state. In 1973, he revised and republished the same essay under the title "The Steady-State Economy: Toward a Political Economy of Biophysical Equilibrium and Moral Growth." This time, Daly's article appeared in a volume containing papers by other environmental luminaries such as Kenneth Boulding, Paul Ehrlich, Garrett Hardin, and Nicolas Georgescu-Roegen. This was certainly select company and just the sort which could best showcase the budding academic talents of Daly, who was then just in his early thirties.

Daly's essay began quickly with a condemnation of "growthmania," a condition afflicting the modern world, which called for ever-expanding levels of GNP.[2] This was not a problem only in the United States. He said it could be found in the Soviet Union, Cuba, Spain, and the rest of the world as well. The ill effects of growthmania included congested living space, industrial pollution, and human stress. The greatest problem, however, was that this obsession with growth had caused a disequilibrium between humans and natural ecosystems.

Maximization of GNP was at its core an inappropriate social goal, averred Daly. First, it accounted only for the benefits and not for the costs of producing national product. Said he, "The marginal benefit is measured by the market value of extra goods and services—i.e., the increment in GNP itself in value units. But what statistical series measures the cost? Answer: *none!* That is growthmania; literally not counting the costs of growth."[3] Second, he said, GNP wrongly regards some environmental costs as benefits. For example, expenditures for pollution control equipment used to protect humans from the by-products of industrial production are added to GNP as a social benefit. GNP also fails to deduct for the depletion of natural resources such as soil, water, and minerals. And finally, GNP accounting cannot determine the distribution of wealth between the "haves" and "have-nots" of society; likely the rich are getting richer while the poor are becoming poorer.

To Herman Daly, society's obsession with the maximization of GNP stemmed not so much from ignorance as from political expediency. The implication was that wealthy individuals, corporations, and government bureaucrats—to their own advantage—supported the prevailing paradigm. Daly argued that for the sake of humanity and the environment a new paradigm was needed. And his proposed solution came straight from J. S. Mill. Said Herman Daly, "What will the new paradigm be? I submit that it must be very similar to an idea from classical economics that never attained the status of a paradigm, except for a brief chapter in John Stuart Mill's *Principles of Political Economy*. This idea is that of the steady-state economy."[4]

Daly defined his version of the steady-state economy as a social system that maintained constant stocks of both human population and physical wealth, the latter of which was more evenly distributed among the population. Also, the rate of throughput (i.e., the rate of resource consumption) was held constant at a level just sufficient to maintain some minimal but comfortable standard of living. The idea of constant stocks he attributed to Mill, while the desire to minimize throughput was a newer notion attributed to Kenneth Boulding.

Daly argued that the steady state was necessary to protect against the physical extinction of natural resources. His rationale for the steady state thus turned aside the more complex economic arguments of the classical economists. They had said that the push for economic growth and profits would ultimately cause an economic scarcity of resources. That is, at some point the cost to society of obtaining resources would contribute to radically declining per-capita consumption. Daly explicitly denied the relevance of such arguments, saying that physical scarcity alone was the justification for immediate movement to the steady state: "The world is finite, the ecosystem is a steady-state. The steady-state is therefore a physical necessity."[5]

Herman Daly advocated "social institutions" as the principal mechanism for attaining the steady-state economy. What he meant by social institutions was not clear in his essay, but one can surmise that he was referring to societal regulation of individual choice. With regard to maintenance of constant populations he recommended the issuance of marketable licenses and certificates to prospective parents (one certificate = one child). Parents who exceeded their assigned limit would be "subject to punishment," although the type of punishment was not specified.[6] The moral basis for such a system would be that all were treated equally; there would be no favoritism.

Constant physical wealth, like population, would be maintained by quotas. Depletion quotas would be set for perhaps three hundred of the world's most important natural resources. Rights to these resource quotas, once established, would be auctioned to private firms, individuals, and public enterprises. "The social decision that determines the aggregate rate of depletion through depletion quotas can be regarded as the correction of the failure of the market to bring an end to over-exploitation," said Daly.[7] Though he never explicitly dismissed pollution taxes or similar schemes for internalizing pollution externalities, neither did Daly voice strong support for them, probably because they smacked too strongly of mainstream economic thinking. Nevertheless, they could serve in the short run: "Pollution taxes are a mere palliative, treating only the symptoms of the disease."[8]

Control of wealth distribution would be conceptually simple: "set maximum and minimum limits on wealth and income."[9] Although this appeared to be an attack on private property, Daly assured the reader that this was not the case. With a bit of intellectual gymnastics, he argued that the taking of private wealth from individuals, curiously, would protect the institution of private property. Citing Mill, Daly supported the notion that wealth should belong only to those who had earned it through ingenuity or sweat, otherwise it should be taken away and redistributed.[10] Thus, under Herman Daly's steady-state economy, vast inherited fortunes would become a thing of the past.

To Daly, the steady state was not a merely a dream but rather a distinct possibility. In order to achieve it, however, humanity would have to look toward, as he said, "moral growth." Humankind would have to replace traditional self-interest with brotherhood and love for this and future generations. Ethics would have to come before economics. As models for this moral growth, Daly suggested the possibility of "ethical socialism." He also cited the "land ethic" of Aldo Leopold as an admirable moral foundation for the steady-state.[11] In closing, Daly said that the ecological movement of the 1960s and 1970s was merely a fad, but as the fad passed it was essential that the movement toward environmental improvement be continued. In order to facilitate this continuation, a new unifying social paradigm was needed, and John Stuart Mill's stationary state, to Daly, offered just such a paradigm.

By 1977, Herman Daly had expanded the ideas in his original essay into a book titled *Steady-State Economics*. The book dealt in greater depth with the steady-state economy and the economic growth debate. In 1991, the second edition of *Steady-State Economics* was published. And even though twenty years had passed since his original essay, Daly's central message remained unchanged. He continued to advance the steady state as the necessary and desirable world future. He still distrusted laissez-faire economics as a means of achieving the steady state. Daly, however, did mention that the recent dismal performance of planned national economies—perhaps like that of the former USSR—"does not inspire optimism."[12] Borrowing a phrase from Garrett Hardin, Daly maintained that civilization's obsession with economic growth had "no technical solution." Instead, the solution was moral and would require "major changes in values as well as radical, but non-revolutionary, institutional reforms."[13]

Daly's theories, despite two decades in the academic literature, were scarcely acknowledged by mainstream economists. In fact, he said that university economists had "aggressively ignored" his book.[14] In evidence of this, by the time of its second edition *Steady-State Economics* had received not a single review in the mainstream economics journals. Economists' dedicated lack of enthusiasm for Daly's ideas was, perhaps, predictable. After all, they had completely ignored Mill's views on the subject for more than a century. Moreover, Daly's ideas ran counter to some key beliefs of neoclassical economics. The theories advanced by the contrarian economist Daly were not so much infuriating to the neoclassical mind as they were irrelevant.

A brief review of some neoclassical theory will reveal why the notion of the steady-state economy held no fascination for these economists. A tenet of neoclassical economic theory is that a properly functioning market is the most effective provider of goods and services for society. Furthermore, two of the most essential conditions for the proper functioning of the market system are freedom of individual choice and freedom for the market to readily adapt to change. Without these key elements, so the reasoning goes, the market economy could not perform its cornucopian wonders. Within the neoclassical scheme of things, individuals must be free to control productive resources and to use these according to their own wishes. Individual freedom is essential also in consumption choices. Only when people are free to "vote" with their money will the market elect to allocate resources properly so as to produce the correct quantities and types of goods and services. Adaptability, too, is crucial to maintaining the market economy. Resources must be freely mobile so they can be put to their highest use as changing needs dictate. Thus, if workers are needed to produce computers in California rather than steel in Ohio, then the labor force must be free to adjust. So when Herman Daly spoke of limiting personal choice through property confiscation, redistribution, and government intervention—all for the purpose of creating a static economy—this must have sounded to conventional economists like utter nonsense. Indeed, a static economy was the antithesis of the necessarily dynamic free market. To neoclassical economists, Daly's ideas must have seemed like a recipe for disaster.

Despite his rebuff by university economists, Daly did find a receptive audience in the biologists and independent-minded economists located at smaller colleges. One topic from *Steady-State Economics* with special appeal to this group was his strategy for integrating economics and ecology. While not a part of Mill's original theory, Daly's call for this melding of ecology and economics would nevertheless form the cornerstone of an important new movement among environmentalists.

According to Herman Daly, there were two existing schools of thought for integrating economics and ecology: economic imperialism and ecological reductionism.[15] Both schools viewed the human economy as a subsystem within the ecosystem, but each had a different view as to how the economy and the ecosystem should function together. Economic imperialism said that the boundary between the two should be erased and the economic system should become dominant. Humankind would be the measurer of all values within the new system, and all values would be expressed in monetary terms. Daly, however, perceived a flaw in this line of reasoning. Economic imperialism, he said, may be adequate to determine the allocation of natural resources within the human economy, but it was inadequate to determine the proper *size* of those resource flows. Thus, economic imperialism would never properly address the issue of the overall scale of human economic activity.

Ecological reductionism, like economic imperialism, also aimed to obliterate the boundary between economy and ecology. In this instance, however, the ecosystem would become dominant and natural energy flows would determine which production processes were to be favored. Quoting from the noted, now late, ecologist Howard T. Odum, Daly said that ecological imperialism was governed by the "maximum power principle," which states, "Those systems that survive in competition . . . are those that develop more power inflow and use it to meet the needs of survival."[16] But the problem with total reliance on energy flows as the governing force, argued Daly, lay in the randomness of the process. An allocation system with no room for the will of humans would never adequately serve human needs. Thus, Daly deemed ecological reductionism, like economic imperialism, an inadequate model for integrating economics and ecology.

Herman Daly described his alternative to these two schools of thought as "the economy as a quasi-steady-state subsystem of the ecosystem."[17] Under this philosophy, the two systems—economy and ecology—would be maintained as separate entities. The focal point of the interrelationship would be resource throughput; that is, the physical flow of resources from the ecologic system to the economy. It would be necessary to govern the minimum and maximum amounts of throughput. And because of the limits on throughput, society would have to look toward improved technologies as a means of getting more output from a fixed amount of resources.

Daly's ideas regarding the integration of economy and ecology were more conceptual than concrete. He had introduced the notion that resource throughput should be regulated and that social institutions would be charged with this power of regulation. Beyond these very general ideas the specifics were missing. How would society determine the maximum and minimum throughput levels? And what means would regulators employ that would not totally intrude on personal freedoms? Unfortunately, Herman Daly could not provide these answers. Yet the attempt to broach the issue of blending economics with ecology was enough to interest a great many academics.

Herman Daly's search for a model to integrate economics and ecology eventually contributed to the creation of the International Society for Ecological Economics (ISEE). This organization, with its journal

Ecological Economics and members representing forty countries, has risen quickly in recent years to become a force in environmentalism. The mission of the ISEE is "integrating the study of the management of 'nature's household' [ecology] and 'humankind's household' [economics]."[18] Through publications and international meetings, ISEE membership has continued to develop the themes raised by Herman Daly, addressing topics such as the management of economic growth, environmentally based national income accounting systems, fairness to future generations, and protection of environmental resources. Herman Daly, who has served as an officer of ISEE, expressed his views regarding the mission of the organization: "[it] seeks to integrate the two key disciplines of our time [ecology and economics] rather than further subdivide each one into ever more arcane and irrelevant sub-subdisciplines."[19]

A major interest of the ISEE related to the philosophies of Herman Daly and John Stuart Mill is the study of ecologically sustainable economies. The issue of sustainable economies, or sustainable development as it is frequently called, has become a focal point not only for the ISEE, but for much of the world community as well. The notion of sustainable development has, in fact, gained such favor that it has been embraced by some national leaders as a guiding principle for national economic development. The concept gained special attention following the work of the World Commission on Environment and Development, also known as the Brundtland Commission after its chairwoman, Norway's prime minister Gro Harlem Brundtland.

The Brundtland Commission was created in 1983 under the auspices of the United Nations. The charge to the commission was "to propose long-term environmental strategies for achieving sustainable development by the year 2000 and beyond."[20] In 1987, the commission's findings were published as a book entitled *Our Common Future.* (An interesting note: In 1973, advertising executive Erik Dammann, like Brundtland a Norwegian, wrote a book titled *The Future in Our Hands,* which sought to interest a wide range of people in a sustainable and ecologically balanced lifestyle. Quite likely, Dammann's work, with its similarly futuristic title, served as a early model for *Our Common Future.*)

Our Common Future focused on the inequitable distribution of the world's wealth between the more developed and less developed countries of the globe, which are often referred to, respectively, as "the North and the South." The more developed nations are currently enjoying the highest standards of living the world has ever known. In those nations, a high proportion of the population is being taught to read and write, and agricultural production has substantially outpaced population growth. But while the more developed nations are prospering, the less developed nations have been rapidly losing economic ground. There are now more hungry people in those countries than ever before, more people without safe water supplies or adequate fuel for cooking and heating, and an ever-increasing number of illiterates. Said the commission, "The gap between rich and poor nations is widening—not shrinking—and there is little prospect, given present trends and institutional arrangements that this process will be reversed."[21]

While the wealth gap is widening, the environment is being pushed closer to its limits by both the developed and less-developed nations, albeit in different ways. The industrialization and modern technologies of the developed nations have created major environmental problems through resource extraction and pollution. In particular, the commission mentioned the problem of excessive fossil fuel burning and energy consumption, which contributes to the problems of both acid precipitation and global warming, the latter being the enhancement of the so-called greenhouse effect. In addition, chlorofluorocarbons (CFCs) escaping into the atmosphere have contributed to the destruction of the stratospheric ozone layer that normally protects plants and animals against harmful ultraviolet radiation. The less-developed nations contribute to environmental degradation through tropical deforestation, desertification of agricultural lands, explosive population growth, and crushing urban poverty.

The solution to these problems, according to the Brundtland Commission, was for the nations of the world to achieve a state of sustainable development. The commission defined sustainable development as that which "meets the needs of the present without compromising the ability of future generations to meet their own needs."[22] The notion, of course, contained the essential elements of the Mill-Daly philosophy: reduced population growth, moderated resource throughput, and more equitable redistribution of the world's wealth. As had been noted by Mill and Daly, the solution would also require changes in social institutions. There was, however, one notable difference between the commission's recommendations and the Mill-Daly proposal. The commission focused more on the transition to sustainable development than on the resulting final equilibrium state: "sustainable development is not a fixed state of harmony, but rather a process of change in which the exploitation of resources, the direction of investments, the orientation of technological development, and institutional change are made consistent with future as well as present needs."[23] The steady-state theory and sustainable development thus differ to the extent that the transition process relies upon economic growth. The steady state, you will recall, insists upon a complete cessation of economic growth, while sustainable development asks only for society to moderate the increase in economic growth.[24]

Herman Daly, upon reading the Brundtland Commission's report, noted that the concept of sustainable development—despite its growing worldwide popularity—lacked a precise definition. In developing the idea of sustainable development, the commission had ignored crucial issues such as schemes for determining the optimal scale of the economy and methods for the optimal allocation of resources. Even a topic as important as the identification of the best economic system (i.e., centrally planned versus free market) for achieving sustainable development had scarcely been mentioned in *Our Common Future.* Daly suggested that such vagueness was not, perhaps, without merit. It could permit society some flexibility in developing a consensus on how to attain this elusive social goal. Yet in the final analysis his words seemed more a rationale than a reason. He was forced to admit that sustainable development, due to its ambiguity, was "in danger of becoming an empty shibboleth."[25] Ironically, the same could have been said for Daly's steady-state economy. It, too, could have been accused of being unclear on crucial issues. Lacking precise methods and measures of accomplishment, both seemingly offered nothing more than hollow promises.

Because the steady-state economy and sustainable development defy rigorous definition, some would say that they are poor models for shaping environmental policy. Yet others would argue that they have great social value because of the ideals they espouse: (1) harmony between humans and the environment, and (2) economic equality. Both philosophies recognize that the environment and its natural resources are essential for satisfying human needs. Therefore, the environment must be to some extent "used" by people. However, both philosophies recognize that the use of the environment for the improvement of human welfare must be constrained. And limits on resource use are determined by the amount of resources needed to provide a minimum level of material comfort as well as leisure time for intellectual development. Beyond providing this minimum standard of living, the environment is not to be exploited simply to indulge frivolous or redundant consumption. The ethical basis for this restraint is a commitment to the equality of the current and future generations. All present and future members of society must have equal opportunity for material comfort and intellectual development.

Therefore, the steady-state economy and sustainable development are philosophies—similar philosophies in fact—more than precise models for managing the environment. Neither one specifies the exact levels of resource consumption nor even the methods for calculating those levels. To insist that they become precise models, though, is to ignore the great social contribution of moral philosophy. For example, the principal contribution of Rachel Carson's *Silent Spring* is not its attempt to define a precise model for the management of pesticides. Instead, its lasting contribution is the philosophic change it wrought in the public mind regarding the relationship of humans to their environment. Following the publication of *Silent Spring,* public expectations concerning environmental quality were fundamentally changed. And from this change came new laws (e.g., the National Environmental Policy Act) and new institutions (e.g., the Environmental Protection Agency) to implement social change. The effect of *Silent Spring* in bringing change was dramatic. Such drama has obviously not yet been in the cards for either the steady-state economy or sustainable development. There has been interest but no massive social stampede to embrace either. Nevertheless, both have alerted at least a portion of the public to the idea that future environmental change could be desirable. The value of the steady-state economy and sustainable development derives from their role as moral philosophies advocating improvement of both the human condition and the environment.

Herman Daly, in his early writings, had suggested the land ethic of Aldo Leopold as a moral foundation for the steady-state economy. Leopold, a professor of game management and occasional essayist, has been a strong influence on the thinking of many environmentalists in addition to Daly. Indeed, some would insist that he ranks among the most important of all environmental philosophers. Thus, it is only fitting that Herman Daly would invoke his memory.

Environmental philosopher Joseph Des Jardins noted that Leopold's principal essay, "The Land Ethic," was most influential for its expression of "ethical holism"; that is, the view that the well-being of an ecological community is found in the stability and continued productivity of the community itself. Des Jardins also stated that the two main criticisms of the land ethic were (1) its "naturalistic fallacy," which asserts that what is found in nature is what ought to be; and (2) its "environmental fascism," which asserts that the rights of individual members of the community are less important than that of the community as a whole.[26] Despite these criticisms, however, "The Land Ethic" became an inspiration to conservationists during the years following Leopold's death. Its popularity, and that of Leopold's other essays as well, soared during the 1960s because of the upsurge in environmental concern following the publication of *Silent Spring*. Today, Leopold's essays continue to be required reading among environmentalists. It is, thus, not surprising that Herman Daly would have suggested the philosophy of Aldo Leopold as a moral foundation for the steady-state economy. By reviving the steady-state theory of John Stuart Mill, Herman Daly made an important contribution to environmental thought. The steady-state economy, along with the idea of sustainable development, serves as a philosophical model which links care for the environment to equality of the human economic condition.

Herman Daly holds a bachelor's degree from Rice University and a Ph.D. from Vanderbilt University. Much of his early academic career was spent at Louisiana State University, where he attained the title of Alumni Professor of Economics. From 1988 to 1994 he worked for the

World Bank in Washington, DC, as a senior economist in their Environment Department. In 1994, he joined the faculty at the University of Maryland as a senior research scholar in the School of Public Affairs. In 1996 he received Sweden's Honorary Right Livelihood Award, and, also in 1996, the Heineken Prize for Environmental Science awarded by the Royal Netherlands Academy of Arts and Sciences. In 1999, he was awarded Norway's Sophie Prize for contributions in environment and development.

14

The MIT Team and *The Limits to Growth*

In 1972 a team of scholars at the Massachusetts Institute of Technology (MIT) in Cambridge were toiling away on what was to become yet another landmark environmental study. The researchers, like other environmental researchers before them, were interested in sorting out the intertwining ecological and social relationships that had contributed to the environmental crisis. However, their approach was a bit more spectacular; they were building a computer model of the world.

Oddly enough, the origin of the MIT project was not in Cambridge, Massachusetts, but thousands of miles away in Rome, Italy. In April 1968, a group of thirty international educators, scientists, statesmen, and businessmen were convened by Dr. Aurelio Peccei, an Italian industrialist, at the Accademia dei Lincei. Their purpose was to discuss the present and future plight of humankind. And out of this first informal meeting grew an organization called the Club of Rome, whose objective was to foster understanding of the economic, political, natural, and social components that make up the global system.

A subsequent series of meetings culminated in the club's decision to sponsor the Project on the Predicament of Mankind, an ambitious effort to further their purpose of learning more about the global system. The first phase of the project took shape at a two-week conference, this time in Cambridge, where noted MIT professor Jay Forrester was asked to discuss his quantitative approach to global modeling. Forrester had been invited to speak because of his pioneering work in systems dynamics, a technique for modeling industrial and life processes. One club member later recalled Forrester's presentation:

> At that moment Professor Jay Forrester of the Massachusetts Institute of Technology (MIT) stepped in as *deus ex machina,* as in the ancient Greek drama, and announced that his method, then still known as "Industrial Dynamics," could do the job. In a

didactically superb manner he demonstrated . . . that a quantitative model . . . could actually be built. . . . I must admit that . . . Forrester's straightforward approach was particularly appealing.[1]

However, not all of those in attendance were as favorably impressed with Forrester. In particular, a faction representing the social science disciplines (economics, sociology, political science, and psychology) thought the proposed methodology would result in a hopelessly simplistic and unrealistic model. In the end, however, they could provide no alternative modeling technique, so Forrester was offered leadership of the project. He declined the offer despite the club's persistence, saying that he preferred to serve only as an adviser; instead, his assistant, Professor Dennis Meadows, was selected to direct the effort. Meadows was to head an international team of seventeen researchers, most of whom were under thirty years of age. Their charge was to construct a computerized global systems dynamic model, a "world model" it was called, that would identify the factors most likely to limit the growth of human civilization on the planet.

Systems dynamics models such as the one envisioned by the MIT team are more generally referred to as simulation models. The term *simulation* comes from the fact that the models attempt to provide a simile—a representation—of real-life systems. Such systems might include industrial, physical, chemical, or biological processes that are far too complex to be re-created in every detail. Instead, the real system is abstracted in order to capture only its essence. Once the abstracted version of the system has been created, usually on computer, the scientist can then play "what if" games. And this was precisely the goal of the MIT group, to simulate "what if" changes in global resource conditions and then observe, via computer output, the predicted effects on civilization. Simulation modeling is an acceptable method of analysis if a system is too complex to study through more traditional, controlled experimentation.

Three particular features of Professor Forrester's systems dynamics made the method particularly appealing for global resource modeling. First, it had the capability of simulating exponential growth, a characteristic typical of many natural systems. Exponential change need not be always positive; things can decrease as well as increase. Also, under exponential growth, explosive change can occur. Second, the systems dynamics approach could apply both positive and negative feedbacks to any particular growth process. Simple examples of positive and negative feedbacks in relation to, say, human population growth are live births and mortality. Third, Forrester's approach permitted the analytical linking of different processes within a system. For example, population growth could be linked to the demand for consumer goods, which is next linked to industrial production, which affects pollution, which then finally goes full circle back to population through the mortality function. This linking characteristic was crucial in the construction of a global model where processes impinge on one another.

In 1971, the team made a written progress report to the Club of Rome. Some members counseled against its early release because the research seemed incomplete. Nevertheless, in 1972 a book authored by four team members, Donella Meadows, Dennis Meadows, Jørgen Randers, and William Behrens III, appeared under the title *The Limits to Growth*. The slim volume, said the authors, was nothing more than an initial report on their research activities. In addition, they stated that the version of the model they had developed for this phase of the study—WORLD3 written in the DYNAMO simulation language—was only a simplistic approximation of global relationships.

Their parsimonious approach treated the world as if it were a single political entity endowed with five basic factors: population, agricultural production, natural resources, industrial production, and pollution. These five elements were then further divided into about one hundred subcomponents. For example, such subcomponents as land yield, land development costs, marginal productivity of land, and agricultural jobs per hectare comprised the agricultural production module. The method used in the study was to present to the computer model several scenarios of future world resource stocks and populations, then to examine the resulting model projections of the five basic resource factors to the year 2100.

A so-called standard computer run served as the basis of comparison for all the various future scenarios. The standard run assumed no major changes in technology, industrial output, food production, or social relationships. Under this restrictive, status quo scenario, the world's stock of natural resources plummeted in the computer model between 1970 and 2100. Per-capita food consumption, industrial output, pollution, and population at first rose as natural resources were used up. However, just beyond the year 2000, food production and industrial output suddenly declined, triggering a 50 percent reduction in world population beginning in about the year 2030. In effect, increasing population and industrial production in grim Malthusian fashion had severely outstripped limited natural resources, thus crashing human civilization. This was what the world model predicted if our present rates of population growth and resource use simply continued on their present course.

In their attempt to save civilization, the researchers concocted and fed to the world model a few more optimistic alternative future scenarios. One assumed a doubling, through new discoveries, of natural resource stocks. Other scenarios made energy more freely available, improved resource use, increased food yield, and instituted birth control. But the final outcome was sadly always the same. At some point during the twenty-first century, natural resource stocks dropped like a lead sinker followed by a dramatic population decline. Said the team, "The basic behavior mode of the world system is exponential growth of population and capital, followed by collapse. . . . We have not been able to find a set of policies that avoids the collapse."[2]

In exploring solutions to the impending crisis, the authors of *The Limits to Growth* said they had absolutely no faith in technological innovation as a panacea for resource overuse and ultimate system collapse. Indeed, referring to Garrett Hardin's "The Tragedy of the Commons," they identified the present situation as one with "no technical solution." Furthermore, said the authors, even the search for a technical solution could prove disastrous: "we have found that technological optimism is the most dangerous reaction to our findings from the world model. Faith in technology as the ultimate solution to all problems can thus divert our attention from the most fundamental problem—the problem of growth in a finite system—and prevent us from taking effective action to solve it."[3]

The proper solution, according to the MIT team, was to be found in policies limiting two key factors: population growth and capital investment in industrialization. In the first computer simulation of these two policies, the team held population growth constant (deaths equal to births). This, they determined, was not sufficient. Population, by definition, was stabilized. However, the model increased the per-capita consumption of food and services to the point that once again the system collapsed. Next, both population and capital investment were restricted, and this time the computer results at last indicated that world collapse would be avoided. This, then, seemed to be the correct solution according to the model. World civilization, in order to survive, must place limits on both population growth and capital investment in industrial processes. And furthermore, time was of the essence said the authors. Delay of even well-intended policies would have terrible consequences.

In the closing pages of *The Limits to Growth*, the MIT researchers called for a new global direction, which they called an "equilibrium state."[4] In this new world, nations would strive to maintain constant levels of capital plant and population, and also to minimize the rates of birth, death, investment, and depreciation. This concept of a stationary, or steady-state, economy, they acknowledged, was not new. More than a century earlier, John Stuart Mill had suggested it, and more recently, Herman E. Daly had emphasized it. This was a concept, said the MIT team, whose time had come, and indeed it offered the only hope of preventing the collapse of civilization.

The Limits to Growth became an international best seller translated into twenty languages and selling more than four million copies.[5] This success was especially remarkable given that the work was supposedly just a preliminary report on a university research project. The book's notoriety even came to overshadow its parent organization the Club of Rome, which then had to struggle for an identity apart from the study. *The Limits to Growth* soon proved to be as controversial as it was popular, and the controversy split its readers into two camps: those who thought it was a scientific masterwork and those who thought it was fatally flawed. The best evidence of the debate is found in the authors' own words:

That book created a furor. . . . [It] was debated by parliaments and scientific societies. One major oil company sponsored a series of advertisements criticizing it; another set up an annual

168 / CHAPTER 14

prize for the best studies expanding on it. *The Limits to Growth* inspired some high praise, many thoughtful reviews, and a flurry of attacks from the left, the right, and the middle of mainstream economics.[6]

Those who agreed with it cheered the study for introducing computer modeling as a way of divining the future. Environmental activists applauded because it confirmed their feelings about the dismal state of world affairs. Undoubtedly, the most damaging condemnation, however, was contained in a book titled *Models of Doom* from H. S. D. Cole and colleagues at the University of Sussex Science Policy Research Institute. Actually a compendium of fourteen papers, the critique represented the work of academicians from economics, biology, physics, psychology, engineering, mathematics, and statistics. Their papers did offer some faint praise for the ambitious modeling work and also acknowledged the importance of the global issue that had been addressed. But the principal thrust was an attack on almost every aspect of *The Limits to Growth*. The Sussex group challenged not only the model's mathematical construction, but its databases and theoretical underpinnings as well.

Of the many criticisms contained in *Models of Doom,* the most damaging dealt with two key issues: the MIT team's handling of technical change in the model, and the introduction of personal bias into the study. The Sussex scholars said that the consistent doomsday prognostications of the world model occurred solely because the team refused to expand or extend the stock of natural resources through technological innovation. Because stocks were finite within the model, collapse was a foregone conclusion. It was not so much a question of if collapse would occur, but rather when. Natural resource reserves, said the Sussex group, had been treated conceptually as having immutable physical limits. The proper approach would have been to view resource stocks as being subject to increase due to technical improvement driven by economic incentive in the form of price signals emanating from the marketplace. Indeed, Meadows and company were judged as having been much too harsh in their general attack on technology and technological optimists. Said the Sussex group, "Technical change is at the heart of our difference. We believe that, like

Malthus, the MIT group is underestimating the possibilities of continuous technical progress."[7]

The second key point, perhaps more sensitive than the first, addressed the possibility of personal bias on the part of the MIT group. The Sussex researchers noted that at that time in the United States there was a strong societal pessimism regarding the future of the environment. They suggested that perhaps the modelers had inadvertently gotten caught up in that wave of public sentiment, making prejudicial mental models part of supposedly objective computer models. "Malthus with a computer," they called the MIT modelers. And when you put "Malthus-in," they said, you get "Malthus-out."[8]

The Sussex group did not speak with a unified voice on every point in their report. They often displayed as much disagreement among themselves concerning proper study methods as they did with the MIT team. Nevertheless, there was a consensus that computer modeling was an appropriate methodology, but the limits-to-growth approach had been abusive. The study, they said, was a gross oversimplification that had substituted mathematics for knowledge and computation for understanding. Minimizing the scientific value of the study, the Sussex scholars conceded only that "the open public debate surrounding the MIT work is their most important achievement."[9]

In the final pages of *Models of Doom,* the four authors of *The Limits to Growth* rebutted the charges of the Sussex group. Unfortunately, much of the reply was merely a pallid discourse on the systems dynamics methodology interspersed with accusations that the Sussex group was "unfamiliar" with the work, "confused" in their comprehension, and guilty of "misreadings, misunderstandings and misinterpretations." At one point, the MIT team even arrogantly referred to the critique as "the trespass of the Sussex group into the field of systems dynamics."[10]

With regard to the two principal charges concerning the omission of technology and the inclusion of personal bias, the MIT team said that they were nonplussed as to how they could possibly have included future, undiscovered technologies in their model. However, they seemed to show no interest in exploring the idea. Instead, their inclination was to recommend ways of changing the existing sociopolitical order rather than to explore the possibility of adaptation through future technical improvement. As they said, "However, our bias as both modelers and managers is to search for understanding and for better policies based on the constraints of the system as it appears now, and not to rely on developments that may or may not come in the future."[11]

With regard to the charge that the team members were biased Malthusians, they candidly replied in the affirmative: "we are indeed Malthusians." And, owning up to their biases, they concluded by saying, "Every model is thus inevitably influenced by prevailing social values and goals. In short, there is no . . . 'scientific' or 'objective' way to construct a perfect model."[12]

The Limits to Growth had a measurable impact on public opinion regarding natural resource scarcity, much more so than did, for example, Harold Barnett and Chandler Morse's less apocalyptic *Scarcity and Growth*. Indeed, despite later global studies by the Club of Rome, the social impact of the original work has never been equaled. Nor is it likely to be. Even today, more than thirty years after its release, the study still serves as an example. To some, *The Limits to Growth* is an example to be emulated, to others, an example to be avoided.

Several factors could be credited for the study's social impact. For example, the authors' association with MIT, the mystique of a computer model, and the ably written and professionally edited text all contributed enormously to the attractiveness of its contents. But the most important reasons are to be found in the observations of the Sussex scholars. The social mindset of the early 1970s was one of deep concern regarding not just environmental quality, but more important, the necessity of rapid remedial action. And *The Limits to Growth* played to those concerns. Although the volume had been presented as a preliminary report, the predictions and conclusions of the study were made with such force and confidence that they fanned the flames of public anxiety.

One cannot say whether the MIT team was irresponsible in the way they presented their findings. The fact that the study was preliminary and based upon a simple world model would lead one naturally to conclude that they did indeed overstate their initial findings. The essential difference between the Sussex scholars and the MIT team is, however, a matter of technological optimism versus pessimism. Because this difference is a matter of intuition, faith, and opinion, it is impossible to resolve objectively. This, of course, is why the debate over *The Limits to Growth,* and also over Malthusian thinking, still lingers.

The Limits to Growth must be acknowledged for its pioneering use of computers. Never before had computer models been employed on such a grand scale to address environmental and natural resource issues. Recall that, at the time, computer applications were not widespread in most universities. Computer instruction was just making its way into the university curriculum, and current technologies such as personal computers were still more than twelve years away. The situation is, of course, quite different today with respect to the use of computer models in environmental studies. Universities, the government, and the private sector abound with environmental applications. *The Limits to Growth* was unquestionably important in demonstrating to the environmental science community the possibilities for computer applications to similar problems.

The indispensable role that computers now play in environmental studies is due to the development of computer models that have the capability to simulate the effects of environmental change across both time and space. Many of the simulations that computers now perform would be impossible to conduct as traditional experiments. It would have been impossible, for example, to conduct *The Limits to Growth* as a traditional experiment; that is, by holding the levels of natural resources constant and then varying human population and resource consumption. Using computer models, however, simplified facsimiles of real-world conditions can be developed and large-scale experiments can be, in effect, conducted through simulation. The reliability of these simulations is, of course, dependent upon the adequacy of the model. Adequate models, in turn, depend upon having enough equations to sufficiently describe the natural systems, accurate quantitative model parameters developed through smaller-scale experiments, and projections which have been validated by comparison to actual data.

The modern environmental literature is replete with applications of computer models. There is even a technical journal, *Ecological Modeling,* that is concerned with the use of mathematical models and systems analysis for the description of ecosystems and the control of pollution and resource development. Topics for environmental modeling have included, for example, hydrologic systems, air pollution transportation over continental landmasses, forest tree species succession, and population growth.

Computer models have likewise played a key role in contemporary major science programs. In the National Acid Precipitation Assessment Program (NAPAP), for example, computer models were developed to estimate the effects of air pollution on a variety of natural systems. NAPAP was a ten-year, $500 million research program initiated by the Reagan administration to explore the effects of acid rain on human and natural systems. The research was conducted ostensibly to provide information to legislators prior to their passage of the Clean Air Act Amendments of 1990 (the principal piece of legislation governing air quality in the United States). Some critics, however, complained privately that computer modeling had played too large a role in NAPAP.[13] The results of the NAPAP research program, they said, had been influenced too strongly by the results of computer modeling. These critics would have preferred to have seen more empirical studies than computer-driven projections. Reviewing the entire NAPAP effort, however, it is unlikely that these criticisms would hold up under close scrutiny. The NAPAP research effort did, in fact, generate a substantial amount of empirical data to support its computer modeling.

Complaints about the use of computer models as a substitute for empirical science can, however, raise valid concerns. Often, the systems of equations and the statistical parameters underlying computer models are shrouded in secrecy. The complex computer code is usually known only to the scientists and their programmers. Hence, complete understanding by an outsider is virtually impossible. Consequently, much must be accepted on faith. Lacking the details, the reader has but two options: either accept the model output or reject it, and usually there is no firm basis for either position. Thus, while computer modeling of natural resources allows investigations that were never before possible, it has attendant problems.

Despite the problems that may be associated with environmental computer models, there is no slowdown in their development. Indeed, the trend is toward more and larger models. One of the major environmental issues of our day, global warming, relies heavily on computer modeling for scientific predictions. The special computer models used to predict global warming are called general circulation models (GCMS). Perhaps six major GCMS worldwide have been developed, mostly by universities and government agencies. These models require huge supercomputers to manipulate hundreds of differential equations in an attempt to mimic the Earth's climate system. One typical scenario analyzed by several GCMS is the effects on global climate of a doubling of atmospheric carbon dioxide, a principal greenhouse gas. The doubling scenario is used to simulate what will happen to the climate if human activities continue to contribute more carbon dioxide to the atmosphere through deforestation and fossil-fuel consumption. Without exception, the major GCMS predict that the planet will become warmer with a doubling of carbon dioxide. However, their specific temperature predictions vary enormously. Interestingly, the climate predictions of the big computer models are quite similar to those obtained a century ago by Swedish chemist Svante Arrhenius using a slide rule.[14] This makes one wonder: for all the technological advancement, how far have computers really brought us?

Donella Meadows, lead author of *The Limits to Growth*, was professor of environmental studies and MacArthur Fellow at Dartmouth College in New Hampshire. She passed away in 2001 at the age of fifty-nine after a two-week battle with bacterial meningitis. Her former husband, Dennis Meadows, who continued to be her professional collaborator until her death, is professor of systems policy and director of the Institute for Policy and Social Studies at the University of New Hampshire. Jørgen Randers is a policy analyst and president emeritus of the Norwegian School of Management. He lives in Oslo, Norway. Jay Forrester received his master of science degree from MIT in 1945. He stayed on to become director of MIT's Digital Computer Laboratory until he changed his focus to system dynamics and began teaching at MIT's Sloan School of Management. Today Forrester, who developed the original model and advised the MIT group, is professor emeritus and senior lecturer at Sloan. William Behrens is a founding owner of The Green Store and Family Wellness Cooperative in Belfast, Maine. He also has been involved in designing and building solar electric house projects since 1988.

Randers, Meadows, and Meadows published in 1992 for the twentieth anniversary of *The Limits to Growth* a new version of their famous study, titled this time *Beyond the Limits*. The foreword to that book was written by Nobel economics laureate Jan Tinbergen who, interestingly enough, expressed gratitude on behalf of all economists "to these authors for showing us where the present path of human development threatens to exceed the limits."[15]

The book contained a poignant message from the authors about the "grief, loneliness, [and] reluctant responsibility" associated with that Club of Rome project twenty years before.[16] Probably few people can appreciate the terrible personal stress that must have been associated with exposure to such intense public scrutiny. The newer work had a softer tone. A few years had passed, bringing time for reflection. Yet, while the tone may have mellowed, the message had not. The authors still felt, as they had originally, that there are limits to growth for human civilization. Pollution, they noted, has already surpassed rates that are physically sustainable. Without significant reduction in material and energy flows, there will be uncontrollable declines. Yet the declines, they argued, are not inevitable. A sustainable society is still technically and economically feasible. "We think the human race is up to the challenge," they said. "We think that a better world is possible, and the acceptance of physical limits is the first step toward getting there."[17]

15
E. F. Schumacher's *Small Is Beautiful*

In 1973, a German-born, Oxford-educated economist named E. F. "Fritz" Schumacher published a book titled *Small Is Beautiful: Economics as if People Mattered.* For twenty years prior to this publication, Schumacher had been a British civil servant employed as chief economic advisor to the British National Coal Board. Hardly the sort of bureaucratic post, one might think, that would lead him to imaginative thinking and creative writing. But imaginative Fritz Schumacher was indeed. So much so that one observer would remark that Schumacher "was to the British National Coal Board what Albert Einstein was to the Swiss Patent Office."[1]

With the publication of *Small Is Beautiful,* Schumacher became to some an overnight intellectual hero and a cult figure who would inspire the formation of a still-active learned society named in his honor.[2] The book itself would go on to sell nearly three-quarters of a million copies[3] many of which were translated into languages other than English. According to the London *Times Literary Supplement* of October 6, 1995, *Small Is Beautiful* ranks among the one hundred most influential books published since World War II.[4] In 1974, Queen Elizabeth II awarded him the civil distinction Commander of the British Empire (CBE). By 1977 his views had become so popular that President Carter invited him for a half-hour talk in the White House, and the president was photographed holding a copy of *Small Is Beautiful.*[5]

Small Is Beautiful was, for the most part, a collection of essays, lectures, and articles bound together as chapters to form a single book. Some have observed that the collection was, in fact, "carpentered together rather crudely" but with themes that were "argued with remarkable force, well-supported by hard facts and figures."[6] Its central purpose was the examination of the proper manner for organizing and structuring national economies. Fritz Schumacher suggested that the compulsion by modern humans—particularly those living under

Western-style capitalism—toward the "philosophy of materialism," as he termed it, had "built a system . . . that ravishes nature and a type of society that mutilates man."[7] Therefore, in the pages of *Small Is Beautiful*, Schumacher was searching for a new economic system that avoided these environmental and social problems. Said Schumacher,

> There has never been a time, in any society in any part of the world . . . to challenge materialism and plead for a different order of priorities. . . . We shrink back from the truth if we believe that the destructive forces of the modern world can be "brought under control" simply by mobilising more resources— of wealth, education, and research—to fight pollution, to preserve wildlife, to discover new sources of energy, and to arrive at more effective agreements on peaceful coexistence . . . what is most needed today is a revision of the ends which [the] means are meant to serve . . . this implies, above all else, the development of a life-style which accords to material things their proper, legitimate place, which is secondary and not primary.[8]

The fact that Schumacher targeted free-market capitalism as the primary cause of environmental, natural resource, and even social problems may strike some, particularly those with an ecological focus, as an ineffective approach to solving environmental problems. However, Schumacher's reasoning was that the economic systems of nations dictated their production and consumption patterns, which in turn, had substantial impacts upon the Earth's natural systems. Hence, the best way to protect the environment was to change the economic system. Others profiled in this book, such as Paul Ehrlich, Barry Commoner, and Herman Daly, shared this idea that in order to preserve the environment, we must change national economic systems. But Fritz Schumacher provided us with some unique views on the issue.

Small Is Beautiful offered some practical means of bringing about economic and ecological change, but mostly it was an attempt to motivate the soul. It appealed to human emotions by empowering, encouraging, and filling the spirit with the possibilities for social change. *Small Is Beautiful* is, in fact, a deeply political book with strong appeal to the political left. So much so that Kirkpatrick Sale, one-time co-director of the E. F. Schumacher Society, said that it went "beyond the conventional confines of" Marxism.[9] Said Sale,

> *Small Is Beautiful* expressed as a philosophy a set of ideas and impulses that had given rise to the New Left of the sixties . . . and countless millions of others, in America and elsewhere, searching for live alternatives to the dead hand of Western corporate imperialism. It was a philosophy . . . best described as the decentralist tradition of Western society, that of institutions built to human scale . . . run by participatory democracy and fueled by self-sufficient regional economies deeply conscious of the limits of natural resources and the need for ecological harmony.[10]

Small Is Beautiful is divided into four main parts: "The Modern World," "Resources," "The Third World," and "Organisation and Ownership." These parts contain a total of nineteen chapters and an epilogue. It is the epilogue that contains many of Schumacher's concerns regarding the environment, specifically pollution, the rising rate of resource depletion, and population.[11] Much of the body of the text deals with means for organizing the national economy so as to avoid environmental problems and provide a better living situation for humans, i.e., "economics as if people mattered."

Part 1, chapter 4, "Buddhist Economics," is perhaps the most discussed chapter in *Small Is Beautiful*. Schumacher generated the basis of this chapter when he traveled in 1955 to Burma (now the Union of Myanmar) as an economic consultant. While there, he developed the set of principles he called "Buddhist economics," which attempt to reconcile economic production with the need to respect people. A rule for this reconciliation comes from the Buddhist principle of "Right Livelihood."[12] The principle calls for a blending of social and religious values with the benefits of modern technology, and thus, Schumacher felt, provides a way to harmoniously meld the need for material production and consumption with a caring for people.

A key element in caring for the desires of the people was to better understand the purpose of work. The Buddhist point of view, argued Schumacher, takes the functions of work to be at least three: (1) it must give humans a chance to use and develop their faculties, (2) it must enable them to overcome their ego-centeredness by joining them with other people in a common task, and (3) it must bring forth the goods and services needed for human existence.[13] Thus, the labor force, while doing work, would produce goods and services but also would be provided a chance to improve themselves through striving with others toward a common social goal.

The striking features of Buddhist economics, according to Schumacher, were its simplicity and nonviolence. With regard to simplicity said Schumacher, "From an economist's point of view, the marvel of the Buddhist way of life is the utter rationality of its pattern: amazingly small means leading to extraordinarily satisfactory results. To the modern economist, this is difficult to understand . . . [because the economist is] assuming all the time that a man who consumes more is 'better off' than a man who consumes less. A Buddhist economist would consider this approach excessively irrational."[14]

Another key difference between capitalism (which the author referred to, euphemistically, as "modern" economics) and Buddhist economics was in their differing regard for natural resources; that is, the forests, water, air, and minerals that provide inputs to the economic production process. Fritz Schumacher agreed with authorities who stated that Western man, through the free-market economic system, had such low regard for natural resources that he "wastes," and "destroys" living matter, treats "harshly" water and trees, and "does not realise at all that human life is a dependent part of an ecosystem." In contrast, the Buddhist economist "enjoins a reverent and non-violent attitude not only to all sentient beings but also, with great emphasis, to trees."[15]

In concluding this chapter, Schumacher stated that "Buddhist economics could be recommended even to those who believe that economic growth is far more important than any spiritual or religious values. . . . It is a question of finding the right path of development, the Middle Way between materialist heedlessness and traditionalist immobility, in short, of finding Right Livelihood."[16]

"Buddhist Economics" mentions, or at least hints at, three principal components of economic reform which Schumacher then goes on to develop in the remainder of his book: (1) smaller enterprises, (2) intermediate technologies, and (3) socialism as the most desirable

tions, such as the United Nations, that may in the long term weaken the small state.[30]

With regard to his life, E. F. Schumacher, "Fritz" to his friends, was born to a traditional academic family in Bonn, Germany, in 1911. According to his daughter, Barbara Wood, in her biography *E. F. Schumacher: His Life and Thought,* he proved to be a talented student.[31] In 1930, he was chosen to represent Germany as a Rhodes scholar at New College, Oxford. Two years later he made his first trip to the United States, where he resided for a time. In 1934, increasingly anxious about the rise of National Socialism in Germany, he left New York and returned to Germany. In 1936, he left Germany with his wife to settle in the United Kingdom, the country that was to become his home.

Since World War II had already begun and anti-German feelings were running high, Schumacher was relegated to work as a farm laborer. At one point he was taken from his wife and infant son and interned for three months in a detention camp. He later came to consider his time at the camp to have been his real university education, for it was there that the thinker became a doer.

After becoming a British citizen in 1946, he was sent to West Germany as a member of the British Control Commission. In late 1949, Schumacher became an economic advisor to the National Coal Board of Britain. He remained in the agency as chief economic advisor for the next twenty years. To accommodate his growing family, he bought a house with a large garden in Surrey. This proved to be another turning point for him; he became fascinated with gardening, joined the Soil Association, and became an enthusiastic proponent of organic gardening.

During the 1950s, Schumacher studied Buddhism and Taoism and the nonviolent message of Mahatma Gandhi. In 1955, he was offered a United Nations assignment in Burma. The time he spent there was to have a lasting influence on his thinking, as witnessed by his writings on "Buddhist economics." Schumacher returned from Burma convinced that a sustainable form of economics appropriate for the developing world must be found—a middle way between materialism and traditionalism. He spent the rest of his life seeking and advocating that path.

In India in 1961, Schumacher had his first exposure to the grinding poverty of that subcontinent. What was needed to ameliorate it, he urged, was a level of technology more productive and effective than that traditionally employed in rural areas but simpler and less capital intensive than Western technologies. Thus, his concept of intermediate technology took form. With the publication of *Small Is Beautiful* in 1973, E. F. Schumacher's status was transformed. He made several trips to North America, where some viewed his message of intermediate technology and economies of scale as being equally applicable to the Western world as to nonindustrialized areas. Fritz Schumacher enjoyed the celebrity and the attendant intellectual challenges brought on by his book until his death in 1977.

16

Arne Naess and the Deep Ecology Movement

In 1973 Norwegian philosopher Arne Naess wrote a paper titled "The Shallow and the Deep, Long-Range Ecology Movement." This paper, which had originated a year earlier as a lecture in Bucharest, Romania, was destined to have a far-reaching social impact. During the next twenty years, the deep ecology movement would gather a following with the power to influence national politics and seize international news headlines. In the process, it would also become the most controversial branch—to some, "the radical fringe"[1]—of modern environmentalism.

Arne Naess spent most of his career as a professor at the University of Oslo. He began there in 1936 and officially resigned from the faculty in 1969 to pursue his interest in ecological matters. During his academic tenure, Naess focused his attention on semantics, the philosophy of science, and the philosophies of Spinoza and Gandhi. He has written many books and papers (in his words, "too many"[2]) on various topics related to philosophy. On the occasion of his seventieth birthday in 1982, his colleagues published a volume titled *In Skeptical Wonder* to honor Naess' many intellectual contributions to philosophy.[3] He is also recognized as having made a substantial contribution to the system of higher education in Norway by stressing the importance of philosophy and the history of ideas in the education of all university students. In addition to his academic interests, Naess has also been an avid outdoorsman and expert mountaineer who has scaled peaks in the Himalayas.

From the beginning of his career, Arne Naess has generated controversy through his insistence that philosophy should be applied to world problems such as those dealing with the environment. He was motivated, according to his associate David Rothenberg to explore the application of philosophy to ecology as a means of alleviating the impending threat of global "ecocatastrophe." Thus, Arne Naess' interest in ecological philosophy was not simply for wisdom's sake, but for wisdom related to action.[4] Naess not only preached but practiced activism to attain environmental goals. In Norway he once tied himself to the cliffs of a fjord until authorities promised to abandon their plans to build a dam there.[5]

In his 1973 paper Naess began by noting that, with the recent emergence of concern for the environment, ecologists had divided themselves into two separate movements. The first and better known movement he termed *shallow ecology*. Its central objective was to fight against pollution and resource depletion in order to improve the health and affluence of people in developed nations. This was the movement, said Naess, which had thus far been the more influential. Unfortunately, however, with the ascendancy of shallow ecology, the environmental message for society had become "twisted and misused."[6]

Thus, there had arisen another branch of the ecology movement whose purpose was to correct the failings of shallow ecology. This second branch Arne Naess named the *deep ecology movement*. In contrast to the narrow focus of the shallow ecology movement (i.e., reducing pollution and resource scarcity for the benefit of the rich countries), Naess said that deep ecology had a broader mission which consisted of seven characteristics. First, deep ecology rejected the traditional "man-in-the-environment approach" to environmentalism in favor of "the relational, total field image."[7] Thus, deep ecology sought to examine with equal emphasis all interrelationships among organisms in the ecosystem, not just those affecting humanity. The second trait was biological egalitarianism, which maintains that all organisms in an ecosystem should have an equal right to protection and life-space requirements; humans should not be favored above others. Third were the principles of diversity and symbiosis, which encouraged new modes of life and diversity of form. The fourth characteristic of deep ecology was its anti-class posture; no organism, except through evolution, should hold sway over another. Likewise, developed nations should not oppress developing nations. The fifth trait, shared with the shallow ecology movement, was the determination to fight against pollution and resource depletion. But while this was an objective of deep ecology, Naess warned that it should not become the movement's sole focus. Sixth, deep ecology distinguishes between complexity and complication. Complexity is a good and natural characteristic of ecosystems, one to be encouraged and studied by humans. Complication, on the other hand, was the result of society having no plan to achieve a better understanding of complexity and, thus, was undesirable. The seventh and final characteristic of deep ecology was its emphasis on local political autonomy and decentralization. Local self-government was encouraged as the best means of protecting against "influences from afar."[8]

The purpose of Arne Naess' paper was to develop some defining characteristics of deep ecology. However, the precise meaning of these characteristics, as you may have observed, was not especially clear. Naess himself admitted as much, saying, "Many of the formulations in the above seven point survey are rather vague generalizations, only tenable if made more precise in certain directions." Furthermore, he said that these principles had been developed not from science nor by means of logic or deduction. Instead, in a particularly cryptic phrase, he said that they had been "suggested and inspired" by the "ecological knowledge and the life-style of the ecological field-worker."[9] Also, Naess noted that because the characteristics were normative—that is, they prescribed what *ought* to be rather than describing what *was*— they had powerful "political potentials which should not be overlooked and which have little to do with pollution and resource depletion."[10] Finally, he noted that the important contribution of environmentalism would not be the scientifically derived facts and principles of ecology, but the development of a philosophy of ecology, or as he termed it "ecosophy." The value of ecosophy was that it provided a means for making one's normative beliefs a part of accepted "wisdom."[11]

In 1976, just three years after the original essay, came a book by Naess titled *Ecology, Community, and Lifestyle*.[12] This book, written in Norwegian, expanded on the ideas contained in the essay. In 1985, Bill Devall and George Sessions, two followers of Arne Naess, wrote another important book on the topic titled *Deep Ecology*. In 1989, *Ecology, Community, and Lifestyle* was finally translated into English by philosopher David Rothenberg working under the guidance of Arne Naess. *Ecology, Community, and Lifestyle* and *Deep Ecology* remain two of the most authoritative early works on the subject, no doubt because of Arne Naess' involvement in both projects.

Deep Ecology outlined eight basic principles which were to serve as a guide to action for members of the deep ecology movement.[13] These principles, developed incidentally by Naess and Sessions during a camping trip in Death Valley, are summarized as follows:

1. Both human and nonhuman life forms have intrinsic and inherent value independent of their usefulness to humans.
2. Richness and diversity of life have value in themselves.
3. Humans have no right to reduce this richness and diversity except for vital needs.
4. The flourishing of human and nonhuman life requires a substantial decrease in human population.
5. Human interference in the nonhuman world is excessive, and the situation is rapidly worsening.
6. Future economic, technological, and ideological policies must be deeply different from those of the present.
7. The needed ideological change is mainly that of appreciating quality of life rather than economic growth.
8. Those who subscribe to the foregoing points have an obligation to implement the changes.

These principles were, in part, a refinement of the points that Arne Naess had outlined in his original essay twelve years earlier. These latest principles, along with the ideas from that original essay, present a diversity of ideas for changing the relationship of humans to the environment. In this diversity, however, there are two basic themes: biocentrism and self-realization.[14]

Biocentrism is the belief that "all things in the biosphere have an equal right to live and blossom." The key to attaining a biocentric point of view is to realize that "there are no boundaries and everything is interrelated."[15] Biocentrism is often contrasted with the opposing concept of anthropocentrism. The latter is the traditional view of Western culture that the value of all life in nature is derived from its value to humans. The emphasis by deep ecologists on biocentrism would eventually evolve into an emphasis on ecocentrism.[16] Ecocentrism, as discussed in chapter 1, represents a broad ecological concern for the inanimate as well as animate things in nature.

Professor of philosophy and geographer Richard A. Watson criticized the particular brand of biocentrism espoused by Arne Naess and other deep ecologists on the grounds that it was not, in fact, true biocentrism. It is in reality, he said, a strict hands-off-nature approach to dealing with the environment. A true egalitarian biocentric ethic, Watson argued, would place no more restrictions on the behavior of humans than on the behavior of any other animal. However, totally uncontrolled behavior might lead to the destruction of the environment and thus to the extinction of humans. Thus, Watson concluded that human self-interest in survival, not biocentrism, was the best insurance against environmental destruction.[17] Arne Naess, in response to this criticism, said that he did not insist that humanity be set apart from the rest of nature.[18] Instead, deep ecology's biocentrism simply argues that all life on Earth has inherent value—that is, value apart from human assessment—which humans should respect.

Gene Spitler, another critic of biocentrism, questioned whether the adoption of a truly biocentric view was even humanly possible. The difficulty, he said, was that humans cannot place themselves wholly outside an anthropocentric viewpoint. We are restricted, he argued, to our own human interpretations of nature and, thus, we can only consider the natural world within the framework of human desires and needs. At best we can only come up with our human interpretation of a biocentric view that inevitably will be constructed to meet some need or desire of our own. Paul W. Taylor, in response, said that Spitler's view was logically true; whenever we speak of a way of viewing the world, we implicitly assume that humans are doing the viewing.[19] Thus, all expressions of value are those of humans. However, Taylor also said that we must keep in mind the practical significance of biocentrism: that it causes humans to view other life with the same respect they afford themselves. Taylor's point is well taken, but so is Spitler's point that biocentrism is a human construct laden with human values. As such, it could be used as a one-sided rationale for "protecting" environmental resources with methods that lack popular consent.

The purpose of the second theme, self-realization, according to Devall and Sessions, was to "see beyond our narrow contemporary cultural assumptions and values, and the conventional wisdom of our time and place." And the best way to achieve this enlightened state was "by the meditative deep questioning process."[20] Self-realization is, indeed, crucial to the deep ecology of Arne Naess. Naess' goal was that followers of deep ecology would turn away from traditional anthropo-centric Western values and use "self" to define new values. Science, we are told, is not needed for self-realization. Neither are logic, deductive reasoning, specific concepts, nor clarity of meaning. All that is required is meditative thinking, local governmental control (the most local being the "self"), and intuition about what ought to be.

This process of self-realization, said Naess, would result in an ecosophy which would then serve as a personal guide for actions with respect to the environment. (Incidentally, Naess' personal ecological philosophy he called "Ecosophy T" derived primarily from his own "intuitions developed over a long life in nature."[21]) But, in the event that the "self" was not yet ready to develop its own ecosophy, then the deep ecologist could always rely upon the views from the enigmatic one, the "ecological field-worker." The "ecological field-worker," has provided "self" with an ersatz ecosophy in the form of either the previously mentioned seven characteristics or the eight basic principles of deep ecology.

The development of an ecosophy had nothing to do with the gaining and evaluating of knowledge in the traditional sense of acquiring facts and information from authoritative sources. Recall that one does not need science, logic, nor deduction to form an ecosophy. There is, in short, no need to refer to conventional wisdom because the process of self-realization generates its own wisdom. And, lest others doubt the respectability of this self-generated wisdom, the true believer gives to it the title of "ecosophy."

Ecosophy thus charges the individual through his or her own intuition to bring about social change. And this change need not be restricted to environmental matters. Recall that Arne Naess in his first essay said that there were political potentials here "which have little to do with pollution and resource depletion." The possibility thus exists that ecosophy could be used to rationalize the attainment of political goals that have absolutely nothing to do with the environment. In this context, deep ecology delivers what is to some a potentially troubling message. It encourages the elevation of personal opinion over traditional values and the democratic process. Furthermore, it opens the possibility that "the environment" may be nothing more than a vehicle for attaining unrelated political goals.

Additional criticism has been leveled at deep ecology by ecofeminists, the followers of ecofeminism, a movement that emerged in the mid-1970s to explore the connections between women and nature. The term *ecofeminisme* was coined by French writer Françoise d'Eaubonne, who called upon women to lead an ecological revolution to save the planet. According to ecofeminists, Arne Naess' use of *man* in his 1973 paper was more than a semantic or sexist flaw.[22] He, and deep ecologists in general, failed to see a connection between the domination of nature by man and the domination of women by men. Furthermore, the biocentric focus of deep ecology ignores the occurrence of androcentrism (that is, the tendency for society to be man-centered). It is men, not women, who have controlled both science and technology, the two principal destructive agents of the environment. These problems, ecofeminists argue, cannot be resolved by mere changes in language. Instead, women must be given an equal role in the development of science and culture.

During the 1980s, an acrimonious debate also developed between social ecologist Murray Bookchin and the deep ecologists. Social ecology, a branch of environmental philosophy largely associated with Bookchin, holds that environmental degradation results from human domination over nature and also over other humans. Therefore, in order to resolve environmental problems, societies must identify and analyze patterns of domination and oppression within themselves and evaluate these patterns in terms of philosophical accounts of justice. With regard to the social-ecology versus deep-ecology schism, Bookchin has argued that deep ecology is an oppressive and misanthropic philosophy. Deep ecologists have countered that social ecology is anthropocentric and erroneously advocates humans as a higher form of life.[23]

The deep ecology movement, just as Arne Naess intended, stimulated interest in so-called green politics, or eco-politics. Naess was aware that deep ecology had potential to be used for political change. Furthermore, he felt that political activism was essential to deep ecology, that its goals "cannot be reached without a change in politics."[24] It was therefore not only desirable but unavoidable that everyone in the deep ecology movement would engage in political activity.

Arne Naess felt that the supporters of deep ecology would most likely favor nonviolent anarchy to achieve their ecological and political goals. Deep ecology's emphasis on personal ecosophies and local, individual control were more compatible with self-rule than with control by hierarchical governing authorities. However, to advance the interests of deep ecology in an expeditious manner, Naess thought it necessary either to redirect the ecological orientation of existing political parties or to create new "green" parties. With regard to existing parties, Naess said that the best fit for "green" was "red," that is, either communism or socialism. Of the two—communism or socialism—Naess thought that socialism was probably the preferred system. At any rate, deep ecology was certainly more similar in philosophical aims to communism and socialism than to capitalism. Green and red, for example, both stress social responsibility, support equality, oppose hierarchical structures, and fight the excesses of the unrestrained market economy. Said Naess, "It is still clear that some of the most valuable workers for ecological goals come from the socialist camps."[25]

The mutual attraction between deep ecology and what Naess described as "red" politics gives rise to a dualistic view of the Malthusian hypothesis among deep ecologists. David Pepper, an English university lecturer and Marxist, has written about the relationship of deep ecology to the philosophy of Robert Malthus.[26] Pepper contended that the philosophy of deep ecology was supportive of the Malthusian hypothesis, but only in part. The two philosophies agree that population growth and resource scarcity constitute a serious ecological problem. Both argue that population growth must be restrained or world calamity will result. However, Pepper also said that Malthus' use of capitalist economic theory to study the issue of resource scarcity was complete anathema to deep ecologists due to their Marxist-Socialist leanings. Similarly, Naess, in comparing the Malthusian theory to his own ecological thinking, identified the same partial compatibility.[27]

Some would argue, however, that Malthusianism is altogether separate from deep ecology because of the anthropocentrism-biocentrism dichotomy. The theory of Malthus, as well as that of John Stuart Mill and the neoclassicists, has a decidedly anthropocentric point of view. The gravity of natural resource and environmental problems is judged by the impact they have on humans, not by the need to conserve resources or protect the environment for the sake of nonhuman organisms. The biocentric view of deep ecology clearly is a perspective that Malthus never adopted. The possibility of a complete separation of Malthusianism from deep ecology is contested by Gene Spitler's observation that humans cannot adopt a truly biocentric view. All human-articulated expressions of environmental value, in the final analysis, reflect human values.

Since the 1970s, a number of national green political parties have been formed in the developed world with Arne Naess' deep ecology as their foundation. The first of these was established in Great Britain in 1973. This was followed by green parties in Belgium, Australia, France, Italy, Sweden, Switzerland, Austria, Ireland, Luxembourg, the Netherlands, and the former West Germany. The last is recognized as having been the politically strongest of the greens. In 1987, the West German Greens—many of whom were Marxists—captured 8 percent of the West German national vote and an even higher percentage at state and local levels.[28] In the 1980 elections in Australia, the Green Party was reported to have played a key role in gaining victory for the Labor Party.[29] Despite the successes of green parties in many parts of the world, the U.S. greens have never had widespread popularity. This has been largely attributed to a lack of public interest in the Green Party political platform coupled with the difficulty for a third party to compete in the U.S. two-party system.

Green politics, where they have been successful, have often been characterized by political showmanship and controversy. When the West German Green Party first entered the Bundestag—the German parliament—they marched into the assembly with dramatic effect bearing a tree limb withered by acid rain. At times their political rallies have been marked by violence. In 1976, during a protest against a proposed nuclear power plant, West German police fired tear gas into a crowd of some 40,000 Green Party protesters who, in turn, tore down fences from around the nuclear site with cables and grappling hooks.[30] Equally violent incidents followed in other German cities, with the final crescendo coming in 1979 when 150,000 Green Party supporters rallied in Bonn, thus constituting the largest political protest in the history of the West German Federal Republic.

Despite the general perception that green parties are dominated by political leftists, the greens themselves regard their own political leanings as "neither left nor right, but forward."[31] In practice, greens have tended to be a coalition of various political interests, including anti-nuclear protesters, feminists, human rights advocates, antiwar protesters, and ecologists. This mixture has often resulted in political confusion and inconsistency, which has not advanced the green political cause. Because of these difficulties, signs of foundering green parties abound. In 1980, Petra Kelly, the outspoken leader of the West German Greens, was forced to stand down due to a rift in her party. By 1990, the German Greens had been nearly eliminated from German politics because of internal party strife.[32] Likewise, the British Greens virtually collapsed as a political party in 1992. Currently, they are said to survive only by adopting the political positions of mainstream British parties.[33] The political failure of green parties is almost certainly related to their alleged misanthropy,[34] which stems from their biocentric philosophy. If green parties, as a fundamental belief, do not place priority on the interests of human beings, then they will predictably have problems securing popular political support. In other words, the great majority of people are still more interested in a chicken in every pot than in the well-being of the chicken.

An irony in the Marxist orientation of the green parties is that countries with communist governments are reputed to have some of the world's worst environmental problems. The Chernobyl nuclear disaster in the former USSR, for example, was one of the worst environmental disasters in history. In addition, Poland, under its former communist regime, was one of the most polluted countries on Earth.[35] In 1987, I visited Krakow and the nearby steel manufacturing town of Nova Huta. The air and water pollution in this section of Poland was worse than anything I had ever seen in a Western industrialized county. On other trips to communist countries such as the former East Germany, Yugoslavia, and Czechoslovakia, I saw similar problems of regional environmental damage.[36] The World Bank estimates that thirty thousand people die every year from industrial pollution in the former Soviet bloc. Furthermore, one-half of those deaths could be avoided by improving air quality in just eighteen cities.[37] Thus, whereas communism may be the ideal political model for the green parties, in practice those governments have tolerated environmental abuses on a scale unseen in Western democracies. A probable explanation for these

large-scale environmental abuses is that because a communist government owns all resources, the nation becomes a massive commons open
to abuse because of unassigned property rights. The totalitarian nature
of Marxist governments also makes them unresponsive to citizen complaints. Such was the situation I found in Poland, where complaints
about environmental abuse fell upon deaf government ears.

Deep ecology has become the philosophical foundation for not
only politically oriented environmentalists, but radical environmentalists as well. The latter are those who eschew the political process
altogether in favor of direct action as a means of resolving environmental problems.[38] Others might say that deep ecology, if not the
foundation of radical environmentalism, is at least consistent with its
objectives.[39] And while those from deep ecology with an affinity for
politics might be called "green-reds," the radical environmentalists
might be dubbed "green-greens."

Author Rik Scarce, in his book *Eco-Warriors*, has traced the international spread during the last twenty years of radical environmentalism. In these people, he said, there is "much to dislike . . . loud, pushy,
morally superior, they tend to answer somewhere between 'everything'
and 'almost everything' when asked what bothers them about society."[40] Radical environmentalists have, indeed, taken seriously the
Naess-Sessions insistence that deep ecologists have an obligation to
implement change. Dozens, perhaps scores (it is difficult to keep accurate count because of their often tribal, anarchic nature), of such
groups have arisen around the world to combat what they regard as
environmental injustices with aggressive, headline-grabbing protests
and sometimes sabotage in defense of ecology (known as "ecotage").

Many radical groups have been formed since the 1970s, each tend-
ing to specialize in a particular environmental cause, ranging from
protection of forests and save-the-whale campaigns to animal liberation and anti-nuclear protests. While most of these groups espouse
nonviolence as a principle, in practice the term has been open to
interpretation. Generally, they seem to mean no violence against humans, but bulldozers, power lines, billboards, even ships are fair game.
Most citizens condemn such destructive tactics because they violate
basic democratic concepts of property rights and majority rule. Free
societies cannot long function if individuals illegally pursue their own

goals. Yet there is a point when democracy must address the humane treatment of animals and all forms of life. The image of a bellowing mother seal guarding the lifeless body of her pup skinned by sealers is enough to inflame the emotions of even the most anthropocentric members of society.

The radical environmental organizations have a more civil counterpart in the form of mainstream conservation and natural resource organizations. The most important of these traditional environmental organizations is the so-called Group of Ten: the Sierra Club, The Wilderness Society, the Audubon Society, the Natural Resources Defense Council, the National Wildlife Federation, the Izaak Walton League, Defenders of Wildlife, the Environmental Defense Fund, the National Parks and Conservation Association, and the Environmental Policy Institute.[41] Like the radical environmentalists, individual groups tend to specialize in particular environmental issues. However, the mainstream groups generally rely on hierarchical structures, bureaucracy, fundraising, lobbying, the political system, and the courts.

Many of the leaders of the radical movement began their environmental careers with mainstream groups. Along the way, however, dissatisfaction, often mutual, caused the radicals to split from the more staid parent organizations. Such was the case with the radical environmental group Earth First! Former Wilderness Society representatives Dave Foreman and Bart Koehler along with three companions formed Earth First! in 1980. The group supposedly modeled itself after the Edward Abbey novel *The Monkey Wrench Gang,* in which four characters went around the Desert Southwest destroying equipment and property to halt encroaching civilization.

Over the years, Earth First! has adopted as its primary cause the protection of U.S. forests and wilderness areas. Its members have chained themselves to heavy equipment, blocked forest roads, and perched in treetops to prevent timber harvesting on federal lands. Among the most controversial of their practices is tree "spiking," which involves driving six- to twelve-inch-long metal spikes into live trees and then cutting off each spike's head. This practice renders the trees useless for milling because the spikes can damage the saw blades and injure mill workers. In one instance, in fact, a West Coast mill worker was injured while sawing a spiked log, although Earth First! later denied responsibility for the action.

In 1990, two Earth First! members were involved in a controversial plot that literally backfired. A pipe bomb exploded under the seat of a station wagon carrying two activists through Oakland, California. The two—a man and a woman—were supposedly headed toward the town of Santa Cruz, where they were to participate in a rally in support of the redwood forests. Both people received extensive injuries but survived the blast. Oakland police and the FBI concluded the bomb had been made by the activists and had simply exploded by accident. The two, however, denied this, saying the bomb had been planted in the vehicle. The Earth First! activists were eventually set free without being convicted.

Greenpeace International is perhaps the best known radical environmental group in the world community. Actually formed in 1969—hence pre–deep ecology—Greenpeace nevertheless came to adopt the philosophy of Arne Naess. The organization is best remembered for its ocean-going vessel, the *Rainbow Warrior,* and for "Zodiacs," those speedy inflatable dinghies that zip circles around hunted whales and offshore oil platforms. Greenpeace was, in fact, one of the first major radical environmental groups, and its members understood early the benefit of actions that captured world news headlines. The group's dedication to nonviolent civil disobedience—they harass but do not harm property nor people—has however caused other radical groups to regard them as a virtual mainstream environmental group. Nevertheless, violence has at times found Greenpeace. In July 1985, the *Rainbow Warrior* was moored in Auckland, New Zealand, preparing to sail for Mururoa Atoll to interrupt French underground nuclear testing. One evening just before midnight, an explosion ripped through the hull of the ship, killing a Greenpeace photographer. The bombs turned out to have been planted by members of the French military. Two of the bombers, French commandos, were eventually convicted, only to be turned over to French authorities after spending just one year in a New Zealand prison.

One story that underscores the compulsion of radical environmentalists is that of Paul Watson and the Sea Shepherds. Watson, a former

Greenpeace director who had been banished from that group for his overzealous activism, set out in 1979 to hunt down an outlaw whaling ship named the *Sierra*. The latter had been responsible for slaughtering 1,676 whales over a three-year period for sale in Japanese markets. In his boat, a trawler rechristened the *Sea Shepherd,* Watson located the *Sierra* off the coast of Portugal and rammed it twice, leaving the ship listing with a six- by eight-foot gash in its side. The *Sea Shepherd* was quickly captured by Portuguese authorities and impounded in the harbor at the town of Leixoes. Four months later, rather than pay a huge fine to reclaim his ship, Watson scuttled it, sending it to the bottom of the harbor, and escaped to London.

The Earth Liberation Front (ELF) and the related Animal Liberation Front (ALF) are perhaps the most notorious of the currently active global, radical environmental organizations. ELF was founded in 1992 in the United Kingdom by disaffected members of Earth First! ELF members use ecotage, primarily vandalism, arson, and theft, to destroy property they believe is being used to injure animals, people, or the environment. In the United States, ELF's first major action was an attack, in 1998, on a Vail, Colorado, ski resort that caused $12 million in damage. Since then they have claimed responsibility for dozens of other destructive actions resulting in $43 million in property damages.

On February 12, 2002, James F. Jarboe, domestic terrorism section chief of the FBI Counterterrorism Division, testified before the U.S. House of Representatives Subcommittee on Forests and Forest Health about environmental terrorism. In his testimony, Mr. Jarboe said,

> During the past several years, special interest extremism, as characterized by the Animal Liberation Front (ALF) and the Earth Liberation Front (ELF), has emerged as a serious terrorist threat. Generally, extremist groups engage in much activity that is protected by constitutional guarantees of free speech and assembly. Law enforcement becomes involved when the volatile talk of these groups transgresses into unlawful action. The FBI estimates that the ALF [and] ELF have committed more than 600 criminal acts in the United States since 1996. . . . Currently, more than 26 FBI field offices have pending investigations associated with ALF/ELF activities. Despite all of our efforts . . . law en-

forcement has a long way to go to adequately address the problem of eco-terrorism. Groups such as the ALF and the ELF present unique challenges. There is little if any hierarchal structure to such entities. Eco-terrorists are unlike traditional criminal enterprises which are often structured and organized.[42]

For all its bombast and bravado, the future of the radical environmental movement is something of a question.[43] Greenpeace, for example, has lost 20 to 30 percent of its membership since 1990 and stands accused of faulty priorities, cozying up to corporations, and selling out the concerns of its members. Rik Scarce has said that the future of radical environmentalism depends upon a series of events.[44] First, radical environmentalism must attract a larger number of followers than it has thus far. This, in turn, will depend upon the movement's ability to better integrate itself into politics. And, lastly, this integration will depend upon the public perception regarding radical environmentalism as a threat to society.

I once heard a historian (I cannot now recall who) say of the ancient Norwegian Viking ships that "they possessed at once both beauty and menace." The beauty, of course, lay in their graceful design, while their menace came from the potential mayhem they brought. With deep ecology Arne Naess, likewise, gave the world both beauty and menace. He provided a beautiful new philosophy of environmentalism. Its adherents are among the most passionate of followers and claim that deep ecology is "a major paradigm shift—a shift in perception, values and lifestyles—as a basis for redirecting the ecologically destructive path of modern industrial societies."[45] The appeal of deep ecology and the source of its power rest in the two central themes of biocentrism and self-realization, and also, curiously, in its lack of clarity as a philosophy. Biocentrism asks humans to regard all life forms with equal respect. This, in turn, offers potential for improved resource conservation and humane treatment of wild species. Self-realization encourages the individual to question the traditional views of society regarding treatment of the environment. This could lead to the development of new, enlightened policies for environmental protection. Likewise, the lack of clarity in the deep ecology philosophy—something that Arne Naess himself acknowledged—permits the individual to explore and define his or her own notions of environmental quality. And this lack of specificity was not pure happenstance. Said David Rothenberg, "No wonder Naess refuses to define his concepts . . . this [lack of] precision is all part of the play."[46]

If there is beauty in deep ecology, there is also potential danger stemming from the call for activism, even if nonviolent, based solely upon personal whim. Such independent-minded activism runs the risk of undermining the legitimate social contract that the people have established with their governments. This is not to say that all forms of activism are to be condemned. There are instances when civil disobedience and even the violation of laws on behalf of an identifiable aggrieved group can lead to social improvements. The nonviolent activism of the U.S. civil rights movement, for example, was eventually supported by a majority of the American public and contributed to the overall betterment of society. However, deep ecology can be interpreted as preaching a different type of activism, one based not upon the perceived needs of a downtrodden group, but rather on the needs of the "self." This raises possibilities for the assertion of "self" over the social welfare by illegitimate means. Once a small group has illegitimately gained power, its members may continue to use this power for personal gain, even at the expense of the environment. Who is to say that self-realized activists, having once gained control of the environment, would not then exploit it in order to advance other personal causes? Indeed, Arne Naess certainly recognized this possibility when he said that ecosophies had political potentials extending far beyond environmental issues.

There can be little question that deep ecology–motivated activism has brought attention to environmental matters. However, many of those who have watched on television Greenpeacers defiantly mounting offshore oil platforms in the North Sea are as frightened by the antics of the activists as they are by the environmental damage the activists are trying to prevent. Ironically, such cowboy activism almost certainly has contributed less to environmental improvement than have efforts that use the traditional political process. Passage of the National Environmental Policy Act, the Clean Water Act, the Endangered Species Act, and other such environmental legislation, although subject to the inefficient give-and-take of the political process, has done more to improve the quality of the environment than have acts of "ecotage." Indeed, it was the federal listing of the spotted owl as an endangered species, not tree spiking, that halted the exploitive logging of U.S. national forests.

But perhaps, one might say, it was deep ecological sentiments that motivated the passage of the Endangered Species Act and also the actions of Audubon Society members to protect the spotted owl. This may well be true. And it is this raising of human consciousness regarding the environment wherein lies the true value of deep ecology.

Arne Naess is professor emeritus at the University of Oslo. He resides in Norway where he heads the Center for Development and the Environment at the University of Oslo. He is assisted in his work by his wife, Kit-Fai Naess.

17

Beyond the Age of the
Environmental Philosophers

This book has examined important contributions to environmental thought written during the 1960s and early 1970s. Many of the key ideas that shaped current attitudes and policies toward the environment first received popular attention during this era. The importance of Rachel Carson's monumental book *Silent Spring* in initiating the modern environmental era cannot be overemphasized. With a mixture of detached professionalism and passionate concern she warned of the dangers that agricultural pesticides posed to the environment and human health. There was, however, a deeper message in *Silent Spring,* one that went beyond the mere warning about pesticides. This deeper message beckoned humanity to fundamentally reexamine its attitude toward the environment. It was a plea for society to cooperate with, rather than dominate, nature. Rachel Carson's words had an immediate impact as the public began to demand changes in the way governments, businesses, and individuals treated the environment. Within a decade, "the environment" rose from relative obscurity to become a major social concern. It also became an issue that political candidates running for office were forced to address.[1]

The era of environmentalism differed from the earlier conservation movement in that it has been far more widespread among the public.[2] Modern environmentalism has been characterized as a "mass movement," meaning that it has received broad public support in response to the perceived mass nature of the threats to the environment.[3] Clearly, *Silent Spring* sounded a clarion call to the public. The environmental philosophers who came after Rachel Carson simply amplified that call.

Because of broad public interest, there have been some meaningful improvements in the way the environment is now managed. Most notably, in 1969 President Richard Nixon signed into law the National Environmental Policy Act (NEPA), arguably the most important piece of environmental legislation passed during the twentieth century.[4] The U.S. Congress had five stated purposes in drafting NEPA: (1) to encourage a harmonious relationship between humans and the environment; (2) to eliminate environmental damage; (3) to stimulate the health and welfare of humanity; (4) to enrich the understanding of ecological systems and natural resources; and (5) to establish the Council on Environmental Quality (CEQ), whose purpose was to make annual reports to the president on the state of the environment.

Another important measure taken in 1970 was the creation of the Environmental Protection Agency (EPA).[5] Today, the EPA is the principal federal agency with responsibility for environmental regulation. Indeed, it is generally regarded as the most powerful regulatory agency in the federal government. The head of the EPA, while lacking full presidential cabinet status, nevertheless reports directly to the president. The agency has a wide-ranging environmental jurisdiction, including the regulation of air pollution, water pollution, drinking water, hazardous waste disposal, pesticides, radiation, and toxic substances. The EPA's special place in the federal bureaucracy affords it a measure of political independence and control in the execution of its regulatory responsibilities. Other legislation, such as the Federal Water Pollution Control Act Amendments and the Endangered Species Act also became law during this era. Thus, Congress and the American people saw to it that the demand for change was answered by new environmental legislation and regulatory efforts. For some people, these changes were not enough,[6] but most saw at least some progress.

During the 1960s, the national interest in the environment was intense, at times bordering on apocalyptic fear.[7] By the mid-1970s, however, that intense public fixation was beginning to fade somewhat.[8] This is not to say that the environment disappeared altogether from public view. As we shall see, this was certainly not the case. However, there was less stridency in the calls for action; the cries from the college campus of "ecology now!" had faded considerably. The heyday of environmentalism had passed, peaking probably between 1967 and 1974.[9] One ironic and rather dramatic illustration of the era's loss of momentum is that Jerry Rubin—the self-styled revolutionary from chapter 2 who had likened money to human excrement—by 1980 had become a Wall Street securities analyst.[10]

Several events and issues helped to subdue the demands for environmental improvement. One factor was the reality that some progress actually was made. Key pieces of federal environmental legislation were passed into law. In addition, Jimmy Carter became president during the latter part of the decade, and there was public confidence in his leadership on environmental matters. This confidence by the electorate contributed, unfortunately, to some public lethargy and lack of urgency regarding environmental matters.[11]

Another factor that led to a decrease in environmental fervor was simply public weariness with environmentalism as a social movement.[12] There was a growing feeling among the U.S. public that, while environmental quality was an important issue, the threats of impending catastrophe had, at times, been exaggerated. Works such as *The Population Bomb* and *The Limits to Growth,* for example, carried threats of ecological disaster that had proven either utterly false or at least unlikely to occur within the time frame the authors had specified. Some of the environmental philosophers defended themselves, admitting that their estimates of the timing of these events may have been inaccurate but, nevertheless, disaster was coming. By the mid-1970s, however, the public was becoming weary of such wildly pessimistic predictions.

A third reason for the decline in environmental interest during the 1970s was the ending of the Vietnam War and, with it, a platform for public protest. One of the great American tragedies, the Vietnam War had for a decade been a major cause for protest on university campuses. Indeed, it was the only public issue during this era that continually drew more public attention than did the environment.[13] Those who remember these times will recall the nightly television news that carried the horror of the war directly into U.S. homes. The government's attempts to continue the war brought protests from college campuses and, eventually, from a majority of the public as well. As college students protested the war, they also took the opportunity to voice their opinions about other social issues, especially the environment. It seemed as though the two—Vietnam and the environment—were inseparable as a subject of campus protest. Thus, with the gradual decrease in U.S. involvement in Vietnam and the final withdrawal of troops in 1975, the principal reason for public protest was now gone, and with it environmental issues likewise became less visible to the public.

Another reason for the shifting environmental emphasis during the 1970s was that the movement was forced to take a backseat to what the public perceived as more pressing national issues. Specifically, by the mid-1970s the U.S. economy had begun a downturn, which unquestionably detracted from the earlier preoccupation with the environment.[14] Recall from chapter 2 that a prosperous economy had facilitated the increase in environmental concern, and changing economic conditions helped to bring the era to a close as well. During most of the 1960s, inflation, as measured by the consumer price index (CPI), had averaged only slightly more than 1 percent per year.[15] By contemporary standards, this was very low and had only a minimal negative effect on purchasing power. By 1970, however, the CPI was increasing at annual rates of about 6 percent, and it jumped in 1974 to 11 percent. Escalating rates of inflation rapidly eroded the personal income of all Americans. At least part of the inflation was due to the 1973 oil embargo initiated by the Organization of Petroleum Exporting Countries (OPEC) against countries that had sided with Israel in its war with Egypt. OPEC-imposed limits on oil shipments caused a tripling of U.S. oil prices.[16]

Another national economic problem was unemployment. In the 1960s, the unemployment rate had hovered around a modest 3 percent. This low level of unemployment was largely attributable to the large number of young men who were conscripted to serve in the Vietnam War and were thus removed from the unemployment rolls. The war also generated domestic employment. By 1975, following the end of U.S. military involvement in Southeast Asia, unemployment rates shot up to nearly 7 percent. This was bad news for the country and for the thousands who were contemplating their career opportunities. The public always responds quickly to pocketbook issues, so with inflation and unemployment both headed in the wrong direction, Americans' interest in the environment was placed on hold.

The latter half of the 1970s, during the presidential administration of Jimmy Carter, saw a lull in environmental activism and interest. By the 1980s, however, there was some renewal in public interest in the environment. Yet, this second phase of the modern environmental movement was distinctly different from the movement of the 1960s and 1970s. The once-strident demands had become more subdued; there was less sense of urgency.

The renewal of environmental interest in the 1980s was principally due to three factors. First, the economy took a turn for the better, allowing the public once again to turn its attention to matters such as the environment. Rates of inflation, which had raged during the Carter administration, were finally brought under control during the Reagan administration. The Federal Reserve Bank lowered money lending rates to member banks, which in turn, precipitated a decline in inflation. The CPI, which had risen to 12 percent during the 1979–1981 period, plummeted to just 2 percent by 1986. Likewise, unemployment, which had been around 7 percent in 1975, improved to less than 5 percent as the 1980s progressed.

A second reason for the renewal of environmental interest in the 1980s was the policies of the Reagan and the first Bush administrations. Earlier Democratic and even Republican presidential administrations had responded to environmental objectives with some degree of favor.[17] In contrast, Ronald Reagan began a pervasive and determined commitment to reverse the environmental gains made during the last two decades. During his two terms in office, Reagan made several key decisions regarding environmental and natural resource matters which prompted strong opposition in Congress, public outrage, and even legal challenges by environmental and conservation groups, whose membership soared during this period.[18] He attempted to make deep cuts in the EPA's budget that would have rendered the agency much less effective in enforcing environmental regulations. In another particularly brazen move, Reagan sharply reduced the staffing, funding, and powers of the CEQ, thus depriving the nation of an important source of environmental policy initiatives.[19]

President Reagan's appointments of James Watt as secretary of the interior and Anne Gorsuch (later Burford) as head of the EPA were regarded by environmentalists as particularly egregious. Both Watt and Gorsuch were openly opposed to the conservation, preservation, and regulation ideologies of the environmental establishment and, because of resulting public indignation, both were eventually forced to step down.[20] One environmental issue in particular that bedeviled both the Reagan and first Bush administrations was the management of the nation's national forests by the U.S. Forest Service. Under pressure from both Reagan and Bush, the Forest Service had accelerated the clear-cutting of old-growth forests in the Pacific Northwest to unsustainable levels in order to appease commercial timber interests.[21] Public outrage over this action, and particularly its effect on the endangered northern spotted owl, ultimately led to the removal of Forest Service Chief Dale Robertson—a career civil servant—by President Bill Clinton.[22] George Bush entered office with promises that he, in contrast to Reagan, would be an environmental president. However, Bush, too, eventually failed in the eyes of many to keep this pledge. The effect of these and other Reagan-Bush policies was to rekindle environmental concern with the American public.

One anti-environmental legacy of the Reagan years, the so-called Sagebrush Rebellion,[23] continued to have a policy impact even into the 1990s. This rebellion was, in fact, a vigorous assault on the federal ownership of national forests, national parks, and other public lands. Reagan eagerly supported the idea of selling public lands to business interests, and eventually made this part of his administration's policy. However, the lack of a ready market for large parcels of arid land, located mostly in the West, finally altered the direction of the Sagebrush Rebellion. Its new aim became to allow immediate and unfettered access to these public lands by timber, mining, and agricultural interests.

The special interest group pressure to open federal lands for private exploitation is known as the wise use movement. The specific goals of this movement, among other things, are to cut down all federal old-growth forests, eliminate the protection to wildlife afforded by the Endangered Species Act, open all public lands to mining and oil drilling, and provide civil penalties against anyone who challenges the economic development of public lands. Most of the groups affiliated with the wise use movement carry names that sound patriotic and environmentally responsible: Alliance for America, America the Beautiful, American Council on Health and Food, American Forest Resource

Alliance. However, some say that the objective of these industry-backed organizations is to exploit the environment and public resources for profit.[24]

The third reason for the renewed interest in the environment during the 1980s was the emergence of environmental issues that were interregional and even global in nature. Whereas most past environmental concerns had been local in scope, these new issues transcended even national boundaries. The first such concern was "acid rain," known more correctly as acid deposition.[25] By the early 1980s, Europeans had become convinced that damage to forests and infrastructure was occurring due to airborne pollutants and precipitation that had a lower than neutral (i.e., acidic) pH. This acidic deposition was thought to result from the chemical by-products of industrial pollutants and fossil fuel combustion. By the early 1980s, the United States and Canada were debating similar transboundary acid rain problems as well. The situations in Europe and North America received a great deal of news coverage that stimulated public interest. Also, the world scientific community became involved in the investigation of acid rain on a scale never before seen for an environmental issue. In the United States, for example, concern over acid rain brought about the National Acid Precipitation Assessment Program (NAPAP), one of the largest non-military science programs ever initiated by the U.S. government. The NAPAP investigations eventually contributed to the passage of more stringent air quality regulations known as the Clean Air Act Amendments of 1990.

The threat of global warming is another global environmental issue that has had an impact on the public.[26] As early as the 1950s, scientists had warned that increased levels of atmospheric carbon dioxide and other so-called greenhouse gases posed a potential danger to the global climate. Such gases have a tendency to absorb heat, and because of this, help to make the Earth inhabitable. However, increases in the atmospheric concentrations of these gases—which come mostly from excessive fossil fuel combustion and the burning of tropical forests—could elevate the Earth's temperature to perilous levels. By the late 1980s, it seemed as though the predictions of climate change were at last coming true. Average annual world temperatures had begun a steady increase, sea levels were on the rise, and computer models of the atmosphere were predicting ever-worsening global conditions. Like acid rain, the issue of global warming has made international headlines and stimulated public interest, leading in turn to scientific involvement. The principal program created to investigate global climate change was a UN-sponsored group of about four hundred international scientists known as the Intergovernmental Panel on Climate Change (IPCC). This represented the largest cooperative international scientific effort to date on behalf of the environment. The IPCC predicted that with their projected levels of global warming, "ecosystems could be significantly altered and the integrity of man-made structures and facilities reduced."[27] Although much of the scientific community now supports the global warming hypothesis, the future timing and seriousness of global warming–induced impacts remains an issue of uncertainty. According to the World Resources Institute, "Considerable uncertainty about the scale, timing, and regional distribution of global warming remains and will continue to plague forecasts, perhaps for two more decades.[28]

A third global environmental issue that caught the attention of the public beginning in the 1980s was concern over the possible depletion of the stratospheric ozone layer. In the stratosphere, a portion of the atmosphere which extends from eleven to sixteen miles above the Earth's surface, exists a beneficial layer of ozone that shields humans and other life forms from dangerous incoming ultraviolet (UV) radiation.[29] Without this protective ozone layer, it is thought that UV radiation would cause increased incidence of DNA damage, skin cancer, human immune system and eye disorders, as well as damage to plant and aquatic life. By 1985, scientists had begun to observe that the ozone layer over Antarctica was being destroyed through reactions with human-made chemicals, most notably CFCs. Once widely used as refrigerants and aerosol propellants, CFCs were now seen as a potential threat. As a result, their use has been either banned or greatly reduced in much of Europe and North America. Yet, despite scientific evidence that ozone layer depletion represents a potentially serious problem, some critics continue to dismiss it as an exaggeration or even a complete hoax.

A fourth environmental issue that generated a great deal of interest in the 1980s was tropical deforestation and the associated loss of biodiversity.[30] Forests worldwide are disappearing at the rate of twenty-five to fifty million acres per year. The problem is especially severe in the humid tropics of Africa, Asia, and South America. Deforestation on these developing continents is serious because of the dependence those people have on forests for essential goods such as fuelwood and food. Tropical deforestation is important to the rest of the world because of the global environmental functions provided by those forests. As noted earlier, the global warming problem is in part due to the release of carbon dioxide during the burning of these tropical forests. In addition, tropical forests, because they are home to perhaps half of the world's plant and animal species, are important for maintaining biodiversity. There is already some fear that declining migratory songbird populations in the United States may be due to loss of tropical forest habitat.

Tropical deforestation is due mainly to the spread of slash-and-burn agriculture in developing nations as well as fuelwood harvesting and commercial logging. However, behind these symptoms lie deeper causes centered on fundamental national economic problems such as excessive population growth, unemployment, lack of assigned property rights, lack of capital for improved agricultural technologies, misguided government land development policies, unequal wealth distribution, and customs of the native peoples. These problems have, fortunately, not gone unnoticed. Various government agencies and international organizations, such as the UN Food and Agriculture Organization and the World Bank, have provided financial assistance to aid in reforestation and improved fuelwood burning technologies. However, substantial barriers remain before the joint problems of tropical deforestation and biodiversity loss are resolved.

Because of these events, by the close of the twentieth century "the environment" was reestablished as a public concern. Environmental values now appeared fixed in the American mind.[31] As in the past, however, the economy and national defense have always had the potential to diminish the prominence of environmental quality on the public policy agenda. And such a diminution has certainly occurred in the post–9/11 world.

On September 11, 2001, the World Trade Towers in New York City and the Pentagon Building near Washington, DC, were targeted and struck with commercial airliners flown by Islamic terrorists.[32] Another airplane also intended as a flying bomb crashed in Pennsylvania as the passengers apparently wrested control from the terrorist hijackers. The impact of these shocking events on the United States and U.S. politics was almost without precedent. The nation had to undergo an abrupt reordering of national priorities in order to deal with the threats to its citizens, property, and freedom. Likewise, the state of the national economy under George W. Bush's presidential administration has also suffered as unemployment rates increased from 4 percent to 6 percent during his first four years in office.[33] Rising gasoline prices have been another issue. Without doubt, the environment has slipped in political importance relative to more pressing concerns.

The lack of support by the U.S. Congress and President George W. Bush for the Kyoto Protocol on global warming, the most far-reaching international treaty on the environment ever written, is evidence of the current lack of enthusiasm in the United States for improvement in environmental quality. The Kyoto Protocol was drafted in 1997 by 159 countries that are members of the 1992 UN Framework Convention on Climate Change. Then it took almost four more years of negotiations to complete the protocol's implementation rules and then nearly three more years to get the treaty ratified. The Kyoto Protocol was finally ratified and took effect on February 16, 2005. The main provisions of the Kyoto Protocol are as follows:[34]

- *Gases:* The protocol seeks to control emissions of six heat-trapping gases: carbon dioxide, methane, nitrous oxide, hydrofluorocarbons, perfluorocarbons, and sulfur hexafluoride.
- *Targets:* It assigns numerical targets for reducing or limiting emissions, compared with a 1990 benchmark, to thirty-five industrialized countries from among the 140 nations that ratified the pact.
- *Trading:* The protocol allows emissions trading among the thirty-five countries. Industrial plants that fall below their output ceilings can sell the resulting "credits" to those who exceed their allowances.
- *Joint implementation:* It allows a nation to earn credits for developing emissions-reduction projects in other countries that have signed the protocol.

- *Clean development mechanism:* It allows a country to offset protocol obligations by conducting emissions-reduction projects in
  developing countries that are parties to Kyoto but are not obliged
  by the treaty to cut their emissions.

The United States and Australia were the only two world industrial
powers that, by the time of implementation, had failed to ratify the
Kyoto treaty. With regard to the U.S. position, the Clinton administration had signed the protocol in 1997; however, the U.S. Senate then
failed to ratify it as required by law. The Senate cited potential damage
to the U.S. economy and also insisted that the treaty include emissions
reductions by developing nations that currently are exempted. Likewise, President Bush denounced the protocol in 2001, saying that com-
pliance would cost millions of jobs in the United States and that developing nations such as China and India should be required to reduce
their emissions.

So, forty years after the publication of *Silent Spring* and the advent
of the modern environmental era, how is environmentalism faring? Is
the environmental movement still robust, hardy, and capable of effect-
ing change? Interestingly, this was the subject of an article titled "The
Death of Environmentalism" written by two environmentalists, Michael Shellenberger and Ted Nordhaus.[35] As their title suggests, the
authors feel that the modern environmental movement has now lost
much of its momentum and political clout. They argue that environmental organizations have invested hundreds of millions of dollars
into combating issues such as global warming, with strikingly little to
show for their efforts. They write that the environmental community's
internal bickering and own self-interest has contributed to what they
see as the movement's ineffectiveness.

Shellenberger and Nordhaus also argue that environmentalists have
too narrowly defined the nature of environmental problems. For example, while global warming is clearly an environmental problem,
environmentalists have failed to recognize that poverty and related
social issues contribute to it. A broader vision of just what is "environmental" is needed to revive the movement. Shellenberger and Nordhaus also say it is unlikely there will ever again be a period like the 1960s
and 1970s where epic environmental victories had such a searing social

impact. Nevertheless, despite the cyclical ups and downs of the economy and the threats of terrorism, there is reason to believe that the concerns raised by Rachel Carson and the environmental philosophers are a permanent part of the U.S. political agenda.

The Origins of Modern Environmental Thought has examined a variety of ideas regarding the causes of and solutions to world environmental problems. In addition to Rachel Carson's pioneering work, I examined the contributions of Harold Barnett and Chandler Morse. These economists conducted the first empirical test of the Malthusian hypothesis and concluded that resource scarcity fears were unfounded for the United States but that concerns regarding loss of environmental quality were probably justified. Stewart Udall argued that by studying the history of natural resource conservation we could plan for a better future. Roderick Nash taught us about the worth of wilderness. A. C. Pigou and the neoclassical economists suggested that a well-functioning system of markets was the key to coping with both resource scarcity and environmental problems. They also said that the hidden social costs of pollution damages, known as economic externalities, must be reduced in order to achieve the greatest possible level of human satisfaction.

Kenneth Boulding argued that the laws of physics, through the process of entropy, place limits on the availability of energy resources. This notion of energy entropy presented humanity with the ultimate Malthusian threat. Lynn White jr. argued that Christian beliefs were the root cause of the environmental crisis. In the process, he initiated a dialogue on the relationship between religion and environmental matters. Paul Ehrlich, in *The Population Bomb,* predicted that excess population and pollution would cause worldwide catastrophe within just a few years. He pressed for draconian constraints on individual freedom in order to save society from its own hedonistic tendencies.

Garrett Hardin alerted us to the fact that the common property nature of environmental resources was an important factor governing their exploitation. His classic article, "The Tragedy of the Commons," became one of the most widely read of all environmental works. Barry Commoner examined growth in human population, resource consumption, and modern technology to determine which was most responsible for our environmental problems, concluding that the last was most at fault. However, Commoner was never able to suggest a social solution. Herman Daly revived the long-forgotten writings of John Stuart Mill and called for a voluntary steady-state economy in order to strike an equilibrium between humans and the natural world. He said that society should look toward intellectual achievement rather than material consumption as a means of personal fulfillment. Innovative researchers from MIT used modern technology in the form of computer models to predict the state of the future world. However, when their results indicated disaster, critics said it was merely "Malthus with a computer." When you put "Malthus-in," they said, you get "Malthus-out." Fritz Schumacher suggested that by changing economic systems and consumption patterns, we could improve our stewardship of the environment. Finally, deep ecology philosopher Arne Naess urged people to look inward for self-realization regarding the proper state of the environment. He then charged them to look outward to find ways of implementing social change in order to achieve their vision of this perfect world.

As society faces future environmental challenges, the ideas presented in this book will have continuing relevance. The importance to society of the wisdom offered by these environmental philosophers will increase with the passage of time. Students, professors, legislators, and politicians—all of those who would find solutions to the problems of growing human population, the exhaustion of natural resources, and the degradation of the environment—will continue to draw from these learned works. By virtue of their continuing social value, these contributions must truly be regarded as classical contributions to the environmental literature.

In this book I have encouraged a search for accommodation among differing environmental worldviews for the purpose of resolving environmental problems. I now challenge you, after studying these literary works, to find ways in which these separate theories might accommodate one another. As an example, I close by examining how three of the environmental theories could be complementary.[36] From Malthus and the neo-Malthusians, we derive an unyielding sense of urgency regarding environmental matters. Their hypothesis provides a haunting image of what might be should we fail to take natural resource and environmental matters seriously. Admittedly, since Malthus' own time his theory has generated reaction and even outrage for its implied lack of faith in humanity. Yet, neo-Malthusian thinking continues to exert pressure on society to solve its environmental problems. Malthusian concerns no doubt provide the impetus for much of the modern environmental movement.

The modern neoclassicists, in their role as analytical economists, have traditionally not been concerned with the philosophical and psychological factors governing resource consumption activities. Instead, they have dealt primarily with empirical validation of that behavior in response to prices, costs, and other market-related phenomena. The ethical motivations behind an economic response have been of less concern than the response itself. Indeed, modern mainstream economists generally conclude that the establishment of normative social goals is beyond their role, because there is no objective way for them to establish those goals. With their particular perspective, environmental economists have brought practical skills to environmental matters. With rigor and mathematics, they have been able to suggest specific methods of analysis to determine the economic importance of environmental damage, to examine the tradeoffs required to control losses, and also to suggest specific policy instruments for reducing damages. These mainstream economists will continue to provide analytical information to elected officials who must draft and vote on environmental legislation.

Finally, from the modern steady-state theorists we receive important recommendations for developing closer working relationships between economists and biologists and for establishing better systems for measuring aggregate economic performance. However, the most meaningful legacy of John Stuart Mill is his expression of faith that humanity can control its destiny. Far from being simply economic man—that pale wraith of a creature who follows his adding-machine brain wherever it leads him[37]—Mill's person had a heart and a mind to make intelligent choices that might involve denial of material needs. To many people, Mill's work represents something more than a utopian ideal; it may prove the solution to our environmental problems.

While researching and writing this book, I have frequently returned to *Silent Spring* and the words of Rachel Carson as a source of insight and inspiration. Her final words in that book are fitting for this conclusion as well, because they eloquently express the themes of accommodation, creativity, and imagination that are needed to sustain life and resolve environmental problems:

> Through all these new, imaginative, and creative approaches to the problem of sharing our earth with other creatures there runs a constant theme, the awareness that we are dealing with life— with living populations and with all their pressures and counter pressures, their surges and recessions. Only by taking account of such life forces and by cautiously seeking to guide them into channels favorable to ourselves can we hope to achieve a reasonable accommodation. . . . The control of nature is a phrase conceived in arrogance, born of a Neanderthal age of biology and philosophy, when it was supposed that nature exists for the convenience of man.[38]

Notes

Chapter 1

1. From Harris and Gallup polls conducted during 2000, 2003, and 2004 reported by Public Agenda, http://www.publicagenda.org/issues/pcc.cfm?issue_type= environment (accessed January 24, 2005).

2. Sale, *Green Revolution,* p. 1.

3. Scholars generally agree that the modern environmental era was initiated by the publication of *Silent Spring.* However, various names have been applied to the period of the 1960s and early 1970s when environmentalism became a prominent social issue. For example, de Steiguer (*Age of Environmentalism*) referred to it, as the title of his book states, as "the age of environmentalism." Hays (*Beauty, Health and Permanence,* p. 39) called it "the environmental era." Sale (*Green Revolution,* p. 1) called it "the environmental revolution." Worster (*Nature's Economy,* p. 333) referred to it as "the age of ecology." Sessions (*Deep Ecology for the 21st Century,* p. x) called it "the ecological revolution."

4. Fisher and Peterson, "Environment in Economics," p. 1.

5. Textbooks typically list the principal environmental topics as human population growth, natural resources, and environmental pollution. See, for example, Miller, *Living in the Environment.*

6. Scholars such as Hays, *Beauty, Health and Permanence,* p. 27, and Pepper, *Roots of Modern Environmentalism,* p. 19, have also recognized the importance of the events of the 1960s and 1970s in establishing environmentalism as a modern social cause.

7. Rubin, *Green Crusade,* p. 20.

8. Hays, *Beauty, Health and Permanence,* p. 1.

9. Worster, *Nature's Economy,* p. 350.

10. Sessions, *Deep Ecology for the 21st Century,* p. 159.

11. Sorrell, *St. Francis of Assisi and Nature,* p. 145.

12. Ashton, "Some Statistics of the Industrial Revolution," p. 237.

13. de Steiguer, *Three theories from economics,* p. 552.

14. Ashton, "Some Statistics of the Industrial Revolution," pp. 249–50.

15. Sessions, *Deep Ecology for the 21st Century,* p. 163.

16. Daly, *Toward a Steady State Economy,* p. 12.

17. Thoreau, *Walden, or Life in the Woods,* p. 66.

18. Pepper, *Roots of Modern Environmentalism,* p. 81.

19. Nash, *Rights of Nature,* p. 37.

20. Sessions, *Deep Ecology for the 21st Century,* p. 165.

21. Nash, *Rights of Nature,* p. 37.

22. Sessions, *Deep Ecology for the 21st Century,* p. 164.

23. Ibid., p. 165.

24. Nash, *Rights of Nature,* p. 38.

25. Sessions, *Deep Ecology for the 21st Century,* p. 165, credits Roderick F. Nash with identifying Marsh as the first environmentalist.

26. Nash, *Rights of Nature,* pp. 39, 40.

27. Worster, *Nature's Economy*, p. 269.

28. de Steiguer, "Can Forestry Provide 'the Greatest Good of the Greatest Number?,'" p. 22.

29. Des Jardins, *Environmental Ethics*, p. 45.

30. In his award-winning biography titled *Gifford Pinchot and the Making of Modern Environmentalism*, Char Miller depicts Pinchot as an important conservationist and early environmentalist as well as a champion of human rights. Miller's portrayal is novel and quite different from those of previous authors, who have most often seen Pinchot as a politically skilled yet strictly utilitarian forester.

31. Brabazon, *Albert Schweitzer*, p. 27.

32. Ibid., pp. 242, 255.

33. Quoted in Meine, *Aldo Leopold*, pp. 458–59.

34. Ibid., p. 503.

35. Des Jardins, *Environmental Ethics*, pp. 191, 192.

36. O'Riordan, *Environmentalism*, pp. 1–19, contains an excellent comparison of ecocentrism and anthropocentrism.

37. See, for example, Sessions, "Ecocentrism and the Anthropocentric Detour," in *Deep Ecology for the 21st Century*.

38. O'Riordan, *Environmentalism*, p. 2.

39. Carson, *Silent Spring*, p. 296.

Chapter 2

1. Hays, *Beauty, Health and Permanence*, p. 13.

2. Quoted in Howard, *The Sixties*, p. 2.

3. Pepper, *Roots of Modern Environmentalism*, p. 16; Hays, *Beauty, Health and Permanence*, pp. 13, 3; Pepper, *Roots of Modern Environmentalism*, 17.

4. The economic statistics presented in this chapter were obtained from Bureau of the Census, *Historical Statistics of the United States*.

5. Nelson, *Arsenal of Democracy*, p. ix.

6. Ibid.

7. Ibid.

8. Cooke, *America*, p. 338.

9. Hays, *Beauty, Health and Permanence*, p. 115.

10. Ibid., p. 304.

11. Pepper, *Roots of Modern Environmentalism*, p. 15.

12. Reich, *Greening of America*, p. 4.

13. Ibid., pp. 6–9.

14. Alinsky, *Rules for Radicals*, p. xiv.

Chapter 3

1. Carson, *Silent Spring*, pp. 1–3.

2. Ibid., p. 3.

3. Brooks, *House of Life*, p. 232.

4. Carson, *Silent Spring*, p. 99.

5. Ibid., pp. 99–100.

6. Ibid., p. 100.

7. Ibid., p. 180.

8. Ibid., p. 188.

9. Ibid., p. 277.

10. Brooks, *House of Life*, p. 296.

11. Ibid., pp. 293–94.

12. Ibid., p. 305.

13. Anonymous, "Pesticides."

14. Brooks, *House of Life*, p. 303.

15. Sterling, *Sea and Earth*, p. 36.

16. Ibid., p. 17.

17. Lear, *Rachel Carson: Witness for Nature*, p. 42, contains a beautiful poem about a butterfly, an example of Rachel Carson's writing during her undergraduate years. Lear's book is generally regarded as the definitive Rachel Carson biography.

18. Brooks, *House of Life*, p. 272.

19. Gartner, *Rachel Carson*, pp. 24–25.

20. Brooks, *House of Life*, p. 306.

21. Ibid., p. 311.

22. Lear, *Rachel Carson: Witness for Nature*, p. 481.

23. Ibid., p. 483.

24. Buck, *Understanding Environmental Administration and Law*, p. 105.

25. Miller, *Living in the Environment*, pp. 627, 625.

26. The Rachel Carson quotation, used here with some omissions, is from Brooks, *House of Life*, pp. 327–29.

Chapter 4

1. Barnett and Morse, *Scarcity and Growth*, p. iv.

2. Heilbroner, *Worldly Philosophers*, p. 78.

3. Barnett and Morse, *Scarcity and Growth*, p. 70.

4. Ibid., p. 64.

5. Ibid., p. 8.

6. Ibid., p. 211.

7. Ibid., p. 164.

8. Ibid., p. 7.

9. Ibid., p. 10.

10. Ibid., pp. 247–48.

11. Ibid., p. 250.

12. Ibid., p. 153.

13. Smith, *Scarcity and Growth Reconsidered;* Simpson, Toman, and Ayres, *Scarcity and Growth Revisited*.

14. Fisher, *Resource and Environmental Economics*, p. 113.

15. Moore, "Coming Age of Abundance," pp. 130–31.

16. Barnett and Morse, *Scarcity and Growth*, pp. 258, 253–55.

Chapter 5

1. On p. 175 of *The Quiet Crisis* Udall refers to Rachel Carson's writings on the threat of pesticides. Clearly, Udall was aware of Carson's intellectual contribution regarding pollution and the environment. As noted later in this chapter, Udall was an honorary pallbearer at Miss Carson's funeral.

2. Ibid., p. 106.

3. Quotations from Ibid., pp. 175, 176.

4. The source of this biographical information about Stewart L. Udall was the following website maintained by the University of Arizona Library, http:/dizzy.library .arizona.edu/branches/spc/sludall/biography.htm (accessed August 25, 2004).

5. Udall, *Quiet Crisis*, p. vii.

6. Ibid., pp. vii–viii.

7. Anthropologist Shepherd Krech III, in *The Ecological Indian: Myth and History*, explores the truths and myths about Native Americans and their relationship with nature. While recognizing that Indians possessed vast knowledge of their environment, Krech contends that they were often not the environmental conservationists that Udall and others have depicted them as. Native Americans, according to Krech, altered their environments, occasionally overhunted, and depleted resources. Krech's provocative thesis contrasts with the popular view of prehistoric Native Americans but is regarded as good scholarship and, thus, deserves consideration.

8. Ibid., p. 6.

9. Ibid., p. 12.

10. Ibid., p. 13.

11. Ibid., p. 37.

12. Ibid., p. 64.

13. Ibid., p. 54.

14. Ibid., p. 49.

15. Ibid., p. 79.

16. Ibid., p. 87.

17. Ibid., p. 103.

18. Ibid. p. 106–7.

19. Lear, *Rachel Carson, Witness for Nature*, p. 481.

Chapter 6

1. Glicksman and Coggins, *Modern Public Land Law*, p. 307.

2. 16 U.S.C.A. 1131–1136©.

3. Glicksman and Coggins, *Modern Public Land Law*, p. 307.

4. Fred Nielsen, *Roderick Nash and American Wilderness.* Talking History: Aural History Productions recorded interview with Roderick Nash, 17:45 minutes, 2002S. *http://www.albany.edu/talkinghistory/arch2002jan-june.html* (accessed December 15, 2004).

5. Ibid.

6. Western Literature Association website, *http://www.unomaha.edu/~wla/Rod erickNash.html* (accessed December 15, 2004); Nielsen, *Roderick Nash and American Wilderness.*

7. Quotations from Nielsen, *Roderick Nash and American Wilderness*, pp. 1, 7.

8. Ibid., p. 8.

9. Ibid.

10. Ibid., pp. 14, 22.

11. Ibid., pp. 23–24.

12. Ibid., p. 24.

13. Ibid., p. 43.

14. *Encarta Encyclopedia online,* s.v. "Romanticism (literature)," http:/encarta.msn .com/encyclopedia_761573164/Romanticism_(literature).html (accessed December 21, 2004).

15. Nash, *Wilderness and the American Mind,* p. 45.

16. Ibid., p. 44.

17. Ibid., p. 108.

18. Ibid.

19. Ibid., p. 122.

20. Ibid., p. 138.

21. Ibid.

22. Ibid., p. 145.

23. *Encarta Encyclopedia Online,* s.v. "Turner, Frederick Jackson," http://encarta .msn.com/encyclopedia_761555885/Turner_Frederick_Jackson.html (accessed December 29, 2004).

24. Nash, *Wilderness and the American Mind,* p. 146.

25. Ibid., p. 147.

26. Ibid., p. 162.

27. Ibid., pp. 179–80.

28. Ibid., p. 181.

29. Ibid., pp. 187, 191.

30. Ibid., p. 196.

31. Ibid., p. 197.

32. Ibid., p. 199.

33. Ibid., p. 202.

34. Ibid., p. 207.

35. Glicksman and Coggins, *Modern Public Land Law,* pp. 307–23.

36. These comments and the following biographical information were obtained from a website maintained by the Western Literature Association, *http://www.unomaha .edu/~wla/RoderickNash.html* (accessed January 2, 2005).

Chapter 7

1. Pigou, *Economics of Welfare,* pp. 23–24.

2. Ibid., pp. 31, 32.

3. Ibid., p. 159.

4. Ibid., pp. 160, 160–61.

5. Ibid., p. 168.

6. J. de V. Graaff, "Pigou, Arthur Cecil (1877–1959)."

7. Pigou, *Economics of Welfare,* p. 159.

8. Gordon, "Economic Theory of a Common Property Resource."

9. Coase, "Problem of Social Cost," p. 39.

10. Field, *Environmental Economics,* p. 248.

Chapter 8

1. Silk, "Kenneth E. Boulding."

2. Nasar, "Kenneth Boulding," p. 6B.

3. Boulding, "Economics of the Coming Spaceship Earth," p. 129.

4. Ibid., p. 124.

5. Georgescu-Roegen, "Entropy Law and the Economic Process," p. 39.

6. Ibid., p. 46.

7. Auer, "Does Entropy Production Limit Economic Growth?"

8. Cobb, Halstead, and Rowe, "If the GDP Is Up, Why Is America Down?" p. 68.

9. Repetto et al., *Wasting Assets.*

10. Cobb, Halstead, and Rowe, "If the GDP Is Up, Why Is America Down?" p. 70.

11. D'Arge, Schultz, and Brookshire, "Carbon Dioxide and Intergenerational Choice."

12. Daly, "On Nicholas Georgescu-Roegen's Contributions," p. 154.

Chapter 9

1. White, "Historical Roots of Our Ecologic Crisis," p. 1203.

2. All quotations from White, "Continuing the Conversation," pp. 63–64, 64, 63.

3. White, "Historical Roots of Our Ecologic Crisis," p. 1203.

4. Ibid., pp. 1203, 1204.

5. Ibid., p. 1205, 1206.

6. Ibid., p. 1205.

7. Ibid., p. 1207.

8. All quotations from ibid.

9. Whitney, "Lynn White," p. 153.

10. Hall, "Biographical Memoir," p. 263.

11. White, "Continuing the Conversation," p. 60.

12. Hall, "Biographical Memoir," p. 263.

13. Whitney, "Lynn White," p. 154.

14. White, "Historical Roots of Our Ecologic Crisis," p. 1206.

15. Whitney, "Lynn White," p. 168.

16. White, "Continuing the Conversation," pp. 56, 58.

17. Ibid., p. 58.

18. Ibid., p. 56.

19. Ibid., p. 57.

20. Sirico, "False Gods of Earth Day," p. A12.

21. Lovelock, "Gaia as Seen through the Atmosphere.

22. Pepper, *Eco-Socialism,* p. 37.

23. Merchant, *Radical Ecology,* p. 99.

24. Whitney, "Lynn White," pp. 157–58.

25. Ibid., p. 169.

Chapter 10

1. Ehrlich, *Population Bomb,* p. 15.

2. "Two Apostles of Control."

3. Ehrlich, *Population Bomb,* p. 184.

4. Ibid., pp. 82, 88.

5. Ibid., p. 131.

6. Ibid., p. 140.

7. Ibid., p. 157.

8. Ibid., p. 171.

9. Ibid., p. 182.

10. Ibid., p. 197, 198.

11. Hager, "Professor Leaps," p. D5.

12. Ehrlich, p. 168.

13. Ehrlich, p. 18.

14. Hager, "Professor Leaps."

15. Ehrlich and Ehrlich, *Population, Resources, Environment*, p. 191.

16. Ibid., p. 274.

17. Ibid., p. 290.

18. Ehrlich, Ehrlich, and Holdren, *Ecoscience*, p. 956.

19. Ibid., pp. 747, 792.

20. Ibid., p. 954.

21. Ibid., p. 957.

22. UN Department of Social and Economic Affairs, Population Division, http://esa.un.org/unpp (accessed November 20, 2005).

23. Ibid.; World Resources Institute, About Earth Trends, "a comprehensive online data base that focuses on environmental, social and economic trends that shape our world" http://earthtrends.wri.org (accessed January 28, 2005).

24. Miller, *Living in the Environment*, p. 224.

25. Ibid., pp. 216–23.

26. Miller, *Living in the Environment*, p. 25.

27. McCoy, "When the Boomster Slams the Doomster."

Chapter 11

1. Wild, "Garrett Hardin and Overpopulation," pp. 161, 162.

2. Ibid., p. 168.

3. Hardin, "Tragedy of the Commons," p. 1243.

4. Ibid., p. 1243.

5. Ibid., p. 1244.

6. Ibid.

7. Ibid., p. 1248.

8. Ibid., p. 1245.

9. Ibid., p. 1247.

10. Ibid., p. 1245.

11. Ibid., p. 1247.

12. Ibid.

13. Wilson, "Test of the Tragedy of the Commons," p. 97.

14. Crowe, "Tragedy of the Commons Revisited," p. 54.

15. Gordon, "Economics and the Conservation Question," pp. 120, 113.

16. Crowe, "Tragedy of the Commons Revisited," p. 54.

17. Ibid., p. 62.

18. Kelman, "Cost-Benefit Analysis," p. 143.

19. Pearce and Turner, *Economics of Natural Resources and the Environment*, p. 121.

20. Pearce and Turner, pp. 142–56.

21. Swartzman, "Cost-Benefit Analysis in Environmental Regulation," p. 58.

22. Easterbrook, *Moment on Earth*, p. 327.

23. Ibid.

24. Sagoff, *Economy of the Earth*, pp. 95–96.

25. Clark, "Economic Biases against Sustainable Development," p. 323.

26. Smil, "Garrett James Hardin."

Chapter 12

1. Buck, *Understanding Environmental Administration and Law*, p. 18.

2. Worster, *Nature's Economy*, p. 357.

3. Commoner, *Closing Circle*, p. 10.

4. Ibid., p. 11.

5. Rubin, *Green Crusade*, p. 52.

6. Ibid., pp. 53, 6.

7. Worster, *Nature's Economy*, p. 354.

8. Pepper, *Roots of Modern Environmentalism*, p. 21.

9. Rubin, *Green Crusade*, p. 52.

10. Commoner, *Closing Circle*, p. 12.

11. Ibid.

12. Ibid., p. 86.

13. Ibid., p. 178.

14. Ibid., p. 139.

15. Ibid., p. 179.

16. Ibid., p. 217.

17. Ibid., p. 242.

18. Goldman, "Economics of Environmental and Renewable Resources."

19. Commoner, *Closing Circle*, pp. 287–88.

20. Ibid., pp. 297, 299, 300.

21. Goldman, quoted in Tietenberg, *Environmental and Natural Resource Economics*, p. 40.

22. Georgescu-Roegen, "Entropy Law and the Economic Process," p. 45.

23. Details of the Commoner-Ehrlich feud are presented in O'Riordan, *Environmentalism*, pp. 65–68.

24. Ibid., pp. 67, 66.

Chapter 13

1. Mill, *Principles of Political Economy*, pp. 746–51, quoted with omissions.

2. Daly, "Steady-State Economy," p. 149.

3. Ibid., p. 150.

4. Ibid., p. 152.

5. Ibid., p. 153.

6. Ibid., pp. 157, 159.

7. Ibid., p. 161.

8. Ibid., p. 168.

9. Ibid.

10. Ibid.

11. Ibid., pp. 168, 172.

12. Ibid., p. 248.

13. Daly, *Steady-State Economics*, p. 2.

14. Daly, *Steady-State Economics*, p. xii.

15. Ibid., p. 211.

16. Ibid., p. 216.

17. Ibid., p. 211.

18. Costanza, *Ecological Economics,* p. v.

19. Daly, *Steady-State Economics,* p. xiii.

20. World Commission on Environment and Development, *Our Common Future,* p. ix.

21. Ibid., p. 2.

22. Ibid., p. 8.

23. Ibid., p. 9.

24. Ibid., p. 2.

25. Daly, *Steady-State Economics,* pp. 248, 249.

26. Des Jardins, *Environmental Ethics,* pp. 195, 198.

Chapter 14

1. Pestel, *Beyond the Limits to Growth,* p. 23.

2. Meadows et al., *Limits to Growth,* pp. 142–43.

3. Ibid., p. 154.

4. Ibid., p. 175.

5. Ayres, "Cowboys, Cornucopians and Long-Run Sustainability," p. 190.

6. Meadows, Meadows, and Randers, *Beyond the Limits,* p. xiii.

7. Cole, Jahoda, and Pavitt, *Models of Doom,* p. 10.

8. Ibid., p. 8.

9. Ibid., p. 10.

10. Ibid., pp. 217–40, 220.

11. Ibid., p. 234.

12. Ibid., pp. 227, 235.

13. Easterbrook, *A Moment on Earth,* p. 167.

14. Ibid., p. 281.

15. Meadows, Meadow, and Randers, *Beyond the Limits,* p. xi.

16. Ibid., p. xvii.

17. Ibid., p xvii.

Chapter 15

1. John McClaughry, foreword to the 1989 edition of Schumacher, *Small Is Beautiful,* p. xiii.

2. Ibid.

3. Cover notes to the 1989 edition of *Small Is Beautiful.*

4. *Wikipedia* online encyclopedia, s.v. "E. F. Schumacher," *http://en.wikipedia .org/wiki/E.F._Schumacher (accessed* January 6, 2005).

5. Joseph Pearce, "The Education of E. F. Schumacher," online essay, http://www .godspy.com/issues/The-Education-and-Catholic-Conversion-of-E-F-Schumacher-by-Joseph-Pearce.cfm (accessed January 10, 2005).

6. Comment from the London *Times Literary Supplement* quoted by McClaughry in the foreword to the 1989 edition of *Small Is Beautiful,* p. xiii.

7. Schumacher, *Small Is Beautiful,* p. 313 (page numbers refer to 1989 ed.).

8. Ibid., pp. 314–15.

9. Kirkpatrick Sale, foreword to the 1989 edition of *Small Is Beautiful,* pp. xix, xxi.

10. Ibid., p. xxi.

11. Schumacher, *Small Is Beautiful,* pp. 315–16.

12. Ibid., p. 56.

13. Ibid., p. 58.

14. Ibid., pp. 59–60.

15. Ibid., p. 63.

16. Ibid., p. 66.

17. Ibid., pp. 67, 68.

18. Ibid., pp. 70, 71.

19. Ibid., p. 155.

20. Ibid., pp. 163, 156.

21. Ibid., p. 156.

22. Ibid., pp. 155, 169.

23. Ibid., p. 181.

24. Ibid., p. 190.

25. Ibid., p. 191.

26. Ibid., pp. 195–96.

27. Ibid., pp. 198–99.

28. Ibid., p. 273.

29. Ibid., p. 278.

30. Hobsbawm, "Future of the State."

31. The biographical material presented here comes from the website of the E. F. Schumacher Society (http://www.schumachersociety.org, accessed January 18, 2005), which in turn extracted it from his biography, *E. F. Schumacher: His Life and Thought,* written by his daughter, Barbara Wood.

Chapter 16

1. Rubin, *Green Crusade,* p. 27.

2. Naess, "Identification," p. 256.

3. Gullvag and Wetlesen, *In Skeptical Wonder.*

4. Naess, *Ecology, Community and Lifestyle,* p. 1.

5. Manes, *Green Rage,* p. 125.

6. Naess, "The Shallow and the Deep," p. 95.

7. Ibid.

8. Ibid., p. 98.

9. Ibid.

10. Ibid., p. 99.

11. Ibid.

12. Sessions, preface to *Deep Ecology for the 21st Century.* On p. xiv, Sessions claims *Ecology, Community and Lifestyle* was first published in 1973, the same year as Naess' original article on deep ecology.

13. Devall and Sessions, *Deep Ecology,* p. 70.

14. Ibid., p. 66.

15. Ibid., pp. 67, 68.

16. See, e.g., Sessions, "Ecocentrism and the Anthropocentric Detour," in *Deep Ecology for the 21st Century.*

17. Watson, "Critique of Anti-Anthropocentric Biocentrism."

18. Naess, "In Defence of the Deep Ecology Movement," p. 265.

19. Spitler's argument is discussed in Taylor, "In Defense of Biocentrism," p. 239.

20. Devall and Sessions, *Deep Ecology*, p. 67.

21. Naess, *Ecology, Community and Lifestyle*, pp. 1–2.

22. Merchant, *Radical Ecology*, pp. 184, 104.

23. Des Jardins, *Environmental Ethics*, pp. 248, 241.

24. Naess, *Ecology, Community and Lifestyle*, p. 153.

25. Ibid., pp. 156, 133; quotation on p. 157.

26. Pepper, *Eco-Socialism*, p. 40.

27. Reed and Rothenberg, *Wisdom in the Open Air*, 93–94.

28. Manes, *Green Rage*, pp. 127, 128.

29. Devall and Sessions, *Deep Ecology*, p. 9.

30. Manes, *Green Rage*, pp. 128, 130.

31. Pepper, *Eco-Socialism*, p. 52.

32. Devall and Sessions, *Deep Ecology*, p. 9.

33. Pepper, *Eco-Socialism*, p. 201.

34. Ibid., p. 246.

35. Miller, *Living in the Environment*, p. 18.

36. World Resources Institute, *World Resources, 1992–93*, chapter 5, "Central Europe," discusses the devastating pollution problems and staggering cleanup costs for Czechoslovakia, Poland, and the former East Germany.

37. Newman, *Earthweek*, p. 2C.

38. Manes, *Green Rage*, p. 155.

39. Scarce, *Eco-Warriors*, p. 32.

40. Ibid., p. xv.

41. Ibid., p. 15.

42. The congressional testimony of James Jarboe of the FBI regarding ELF and ALF is found at *http://www.fbi.gov/congress/congress02/jarboe021202.htm* (accessed November 20, 2005).

43. Rubin, *Green Crusade*, p. 28.

44. Scarce, *Eco-Warriors*, p. 259.

45. Sessions, preface to *Deep Ecology for the 21st Century*, p. ix.

46. Rothenberg, *Is It Painful to Think?* p. 191.

Chapter 17

1. Dunlap, DDT, p. 160.

2. Hays, *Beauty, Health and Permanence*, p. 13.

3. Pepper, *Roots of Modern Environmentalism*, p. 16.

4. Buck, *Understanding Environmental Administration and Law*, p. 18.

5. Ibid., p. 23.

6. Pepper, *Roots of Modern Environmentalism*, p. 3.

7. Worster, *Nature's Economy*, p. 353.

8. de Steiguer, "Environmental Movements," p. 212.

9. Pepper, *Roots of Modern Environmentalism*, p. 19.

10. Howard, *The Sixties*, p. 2.

11. Hays, *Beauty, Health and Permanence*, p. 61.

12. Pepper, *Roots of Modern Environmentalism*, p. 15.

13. Dunlap, DDT, p. 197.

14. Pepper, *Roots of Modern Environmentalism*, p. 15.

15. The economic data in this chapter were obtained from U.S. Department of Commerce, *Statistical Abstract of the United States*.

16. Cunningham and Saigo, *Environmental Science*, p. 331.

17. Hays, *Beauty, Health and Permanence*, p. 491.

18. Miller, *Living in the Environment*, p. 46.

19. Hays, *Beauty, Health and Permanence*, pp. 496, 504.

20. Buck, *Understanding Environmental Administration and Law*, p. 25.

21. Hirt, *Conspiracy of Optimism*, p. 297.

22. Dale Robertson's dismissal as chief of the U.S. Forest Service is discussed at the agency's website: http://www.fs.fed.us/aboutus/history/chiefs/robertson.shtml. The website reads, in part, as follows:

> Robertson had to face a public which was wary of anything the Forest Service had to say or proposed to do. Especially troubling was growing controversy about the harvest of old growth (ancient forest) trees in the Pacific Northwest and the protection of several species of animals and plants that fell under the protection of the Endangered Species Act of 1973 . . . Robertson and George Leonard (Associate Chief) were reassigned in November 1993 to the Department of Agriculture by the new Clinton administration for not advancing changes fast enough in the Forest Service.

23. Hays, *Beauty, Health and Permanence*, p. 498.

24. Miller, *Living in the Environment*, p. 702.

25. Ibid., p. 435.

26. Ibid., p. 305.

27. Quoted in Cline, *Economics of Global Warming*, p. 31.

28. World Resources Institute, *World Resources, 1994–95*, p. 203.

29. Miller, *Living in the Environment*, p. 317.

30. Ibid., p. 279.

31. Hays, *Beauty, Health and Permanence*, p. 259.

32. National Commission on Terrorist Attacks upon the United States, *The 9/11 Commission Report* (2004), National Archives and Records Administration, http://www.9-11 commission.gov/ (accessed February 14, 2005).

33. U.S. Department of Labor, Bureau of Labor Statistics, Labor force statistics from the current population survey, http:// www.bls.gov/cps/home.htm (accessed February 15, 2005).

34. Kyoto Protocol to the UN Framework Convention on Climate Change, http://unfcc.int/essential_background/Kyoto_ protocol/items/2830.php (accessed February 16, 2005).

35. Michael Shellenberger and Ted Nordhaus, *The Death of Environmentalism: Global Warming Politics in a Post-Environmental World* (2004), http://www.thebreakthrough.org/images/Death_of_Environmentalism.pdf (accessed February 16, 2005).

36. de Steiguer, "Three Theories from Economics."

37. Heilbroner, *Worldly Philosophers*, p. 37.

38. Carson, *Silent Spring*, p. 297.

Bibliography

Abbey, Edward
  1975   *The monkey wrench gang.* Salt Lake City: Dream Garden Press.
          Alinsky, Saul D.
  1971   *Rules for radicals: A practical primer for realistic radicals.* New York: Random
          House.
Anderson, F. R., A. V. Kneese, P. D. Reed, R. B. Stevenson, and Serge Taylor
  1977   *Environmental improvement through economic incentives.* Baltimore: Re-
          sources for the Future and Johns Hopkins University Press.
Anonymous
  1962   ˙ The gentle storm center. *Life,* Oct. 12, pp. 105–6, 109–10.
  1962   Pesticides: The price for progress. *Time,* Sept. 28, pp. 45–48.
  1970   Ecology's angry lobbyist. *Look,* April 21, pp. 42–44.
  1970   The two apostles of control. *Life,* April 17, pp. 32–33.
  1992–   Commoner, Barry A. In *Men and women in science,* vol. 2. 18th ed. Provi-
  1993   dence, NJ: R.R. Bowker.
Ashton, T. S.
  1962   Some statistics of the industrial revolution. In *Essays in Economic Theory,*
          vol. 3, E. M. Carus-Wilson, ed. New York: St. Martin's Press.
Auer, Peter L.
  1977   Does entropy production limit economic growth? In *Prospects for growth,* K.
          D. Wilson, ed. New York: Praeger Publishing.
Ausubel, Jesse H., David G. Victor, and Iddo K. Wernick
  1995   The environment since 1970. *Consequences* 1(3):2.
Ayres, Robert U.
  1993   Cowboys, cornucopians and long-run sustainability. *Ecological Economics*
          8:189–207.
Ayres, Robert U., and Allen Kneese
  1969   *Production, consumption and externalities.* Washington, DC: Resources for
          the Future. (Reprint from *American Economic Review* 59(3):282–97).
Bajema, Carl Jay
  1991   Garrett James Hardin: Ecologist, educator, ethicist and environmentalist.
          Population and Environment 12(3):193–212.
Barnett, Harold J., and Chandler Morse
  1963   *Scarcity and Growth: The Economics of Natural Resource Availability.* Bal-
          timore: Resources for the Future and Johns Hopkins University Press.
van den Bergh, Jeroen C. J. M., and Jan van den Straaten
  1994   *Toward sustainable development: Concepts, methods, and policy.* Washington,
          DC: Island Press.
Boulding, Kenneth E.
  1973   The economics of the coming spaceship earth. In *Toward a steady state
          economy,* Herman E. Daly, ed. San Francisco: W. H. Freeman and Co.

Brabazon, James
    1975   *Albert Schweitzer: A biography.* New York: G. P. Putnam's Sons.

Brooks, Paul
    1972   *The house of life: Rachel Carson at work.* Boston: Houghton Mifflin.

Buck, Susan J.
    1991   *Understanding environmental administration and law.* Washington, DC: Island Press.

Bureau of the Census
    1975   *Historical statistics of the United States: Colonial times to 1970.* Parts 1 and 2. Washington, DC: Government Printing Office.

Carson, Rachel
    1941   *Under the sea-wind: A naturalist's picture of ocean life.* New York: Simon and Schuster.
    1955   *The edge of the sea.* Boston: Houghton Mifflin.
    1961   *The sea around us.* Rev. ed. New York: Oxford University Press.
    1962   *Silent spring.* Boston: Houghton Mifflin.
    1963   Rachel Carson answers her critics. *Audubon Magazine* 65(5):262–65, 313–15.

Clark, Colin
    1991   Economic biases against sustainable development. In *Ecological economics: The science and management of sustainability,* R. Costanza, ed. New York: Columbia University Press.

Cline, William R.
    1992   *The economics of global warming.* Washington, DC: Institute for International Economics.

Coase, R. H.
    1960   The problem of social cost. *Journal of Law and Economics* 3:1–44.

Cobb, Clifford, Ted Halstead, and Jonathan Rowe
    1995   If the GDP is up, why is America down? *Atlantic Monthly,* October, pp. 59–78.

Cole, H. S. D., C. Freeman, M. Jahoda, and K. L. R. Pavitt
    1973   *Models of doom: Critique of the limits to growth.* New York: Universe Books.

Commoner, Barry A.
    1971   *The closing circle: Nature, man and technology.* New York: Alfred A. Knopf.

Cooke, Alistair
    1976   *America.* New York: Alfred A. Knopf.

Costanza, R.
    1991   *Ecological economics: The science and management of sustainability.* New York: Columbia University Press.

Crowe, Beryl L.
    1969   *The tragedy of the commons revisited.* Science. 166:1103–7. (Reprinted in *Managing the Commons,* Garrett Hardin and John Baden, eds. San Francisco: W. H. Freeman, 1977.)

Cunningham, William P., and Barbara W. Saigo
    1990   *Environmental science: A global concern.* Dubuque, IA: Wm. C. Brown Publishers.

Daly, H. E.
    1973   The steady-state economy: Toward a political economy of biophysical equilibrium and moral growth. In *Toward a steady-state economy,* H. E. Daly, ed. San Francisco: W. H. Freeman.

1991   *Steady-state economics.* 2nd ed. Washington, DC: Island Press.

1995   On Nicholas Georgescu-Roegen's contributions to economics: An obituary essay. *Ecological Economics* 13:149–54.

D'Arge, Ralph C., William D. Schultz, and David S. Brookshire

   1982   Carbon dioxide and intergenerational choice. *American Economic Review* 72(2):251–56.

de Steiguer, J. E.

   1991   Environmental movements. In *The Academic American Encyclopedia.* Danbury, CT: Grolier.

   1994   Can forestry provide "the greatest good of the greatest number?" *Journal of Forestry* (92)9:22–25.

   1995   Three theories from economics about the environment. *BioScience* 45(8): 552–57.

   1997   *The Age of Environmentalism.* New York: McGraw-Hill.

de V. Graaff, J.

   1987   Pigou, Arthur Cecil (1877–1959). In *The New Palgrave: A dictionary of economics,* vol. 3., J. Eatwell, M. Milgate, and P. Newman, eds., pp. 376–79. London: Macmillan.

Des Jardins, Joseph R.

   1993   *Environmental ethics: An introduction to environmental philosophy.* Belmont, CA: Wadsworth Publishing Co.

Devall, Bill, and George Sessions

   1985   *Deep ecology.* Salt Lake City: Peregrine Smith Books.

Dorfman, Robert

   1989   Thomas Malthus and David Ricardo. *Journal of Economic Perspectives* 3(3):153–64.

Dunlap, Thomas R.

   1981   *DDT: Scientists, citizens, and public policy.* Princeton: Princeton University Press.

Easterbrook, Gregg

   1995   *A moment on earth: The coming age of environmental optimism.* New York: Viking.

Ehrlich, Paul R.

   1968   *The population bomb.* New York: Sierra Club and Ballantine Books.

Ehrlich, Paul R., and Anne H. Ehrlich

   1970   *Population, resources, environment: Issues in human ecology.* San Francisco: W. H. Freeman.

Ehrlich, Paul R., Anne H. Ehrlich, and John P. Holdren

   1977   *Ecoscience: Population, resources, environment.* San Francisco: W. H. Freeman.

Field, Barry C.

   1994   *Environmental economics: An introduction.* New York: McGraw-Hill.

Fisher, Anthony C.

   1981   *Resource and environmental economics.* Cambridge: Cambridge University Press.

Fisher, Anthony C., and Frederick M. Peterson

   1976   The environment in economics: A survey. *Journal of Economic Literature* 14:1–33.

Gartner, Carol B.
  1983   *Rachel Carson.* New York: Frederick Ungar Publishing.
Georgescu-Roegen, Nicolas
  1971   *The entropy law and the economic process.* Cambridge, MA: Harvard University Press.
Glicksman, Robert L., and George Cameron Coggins
  1995   *Modern public land law in a nutshell.* St. Paul, MN: West Publishing.
Goldman, Marshall I.
  1985   Economics of environmental and renewable resources in socialist systems. In *Handbook of natural resources in socialist systems,* vol. 2, A. V. Kneese and J. L. Sweeney, eds., pp. 725–45. Amsterdam: North-Holland.
Gordon, H. Scott
  1954   The economic theory of a common property resource: The fishery. *Journal of Political Economy* 62:124–42.
  1958   Economics and the conservation question. *Journal of Law and Economics* 1(1):110–21.
Gullvag, Ingemund, and Jon Wetlesen, eds.
  1982   *In skeptical wonder: Inquiries into the philosophy of Arne Naess on the occasion of his 70th birthday.* Oslo: Universitesforlaget.
Hager, Mary
  1970   Professor leaps from butterflies to birth control. *Washington Post,* Sunday, Feb. 22, p. D5.
Hall, Bert S.
  1989   Biographical memoir: Lynn White, jr. *The American Philosophical Society Year Book, 1988.* Philadelphia: American Philosophical Society.
Hardin, Garrett
  1968   The tragedy of the commons. *Science* 162:1243–48.
  1974   Living on a lifeboat. *BioScience* 24:561–68.
Hays, Samuel P.
  1987   *Beauty, health and permanence: Environmental politics in the U.S., 1955–1985.* Cambridge: Cambridge University Press.
Heilbroner, Robert L.
  1986   *The worldly philosophers.* New York: Simon and Schuster.
Hirt, Paul W.
  1994   *A conspiracy of optimism: Management of the national forests since World War Two.* Lincoln: University of Nebraska Press.
Hobsbawm, E. J.
  1996   The future of the state. *Development and Change* 27:267–78.
Howard, Gerald
  1991   *The sixties.* New York: Paragon House.
Kelman, Steve
  1982   Cost-benefit analysis and environmental, safety, and health regulation: Ethical and philosophical considerations. In *Cost-benefit analysis and environmental regulations: Politics, ethics, and methods,* D. Swartzman, R. A. Liroff, and K. G. Croke, eds. Washington, DC: Conservation Foundation.

Kneese, Allen V., Robert U. Ayres, and Ralph C. D'Arge
  1970 *Economics and the environment: A materials balance approach.* Washington, DC: Resources for the Future.
Krech, Shepherd III
  2000 *The ecological Indian: Myth and history.* New York: W.W. Norton and Co.
Krutilla, J. V.
  1967 Conservation reconsidered. *American Economic Review* 57(4):777–86.
Lear, Linda
  1997 *Rachel Carson: Witness for nature.* New York: Henry Holt and Co.
Leopold, Aldo
  1949 *A sand county almanac, and sketches here and there.* New York: Oxford University Press.
Lines, Clifford
  1990 *Companion to the industrial revolution.* New York: Facts on File.
Lovelock, J. E.
  1972 Gaia as seen through the atmosphere. *Atmospheric Environment* 6:579–80.
Malthus, T. R.
  [1798] An essay on the principle of population as it affects the future improvement
  1965 of society. Reprinted in *First essay on population 1798: Reprints of economic classics.* New York: Augustus M. Kelley.
Manes, Christopher
  1990 *Green rage: Radical environmentalism and the unmaking of civilization.* Boston: Little, Brown.
Marco, Gino J., Robert M. Hollingworth, and William Durham
  1987 *Silent spring revisited.* Washington, DC: American Chemical Society.
Marsh, George Perkins
  [1864] *Man and nature,* ed. David Lowenthal. Cambridge, MA: Belknap Press of
  1965 Harvard University Press.
McCleary, G. F.
  1953 *The Malthusian population theory.* London: Faber and Faber.
McCoy, Charles
  1995 When the boomster slams the doomster, bet on a new wager. *Wall Street Journal,* Monday, June 5, pp. A1, A9.
Meadows, Donella
  1994 Herman Daly's farewell address to the World Bank. *International Society for Ecological Economics Newsletter.* October.
Meadows, Donella H., Dennis L. Meadows, and Jørgen Randers
  1992 *Beyond the limits.* Post Hills, VT: Chelsea Green Publishing.
Meadows, Donella H., Dennis L. Meadows, Jørgen Randers, and William W. Behrens III
  1972 *The limits to growth: A report for the Club of Rome's project on the predicament of mankind.* New York: Universe Books.
Meine, Curt
  1988 *Aldo Leopold: His life and work.* Madison: University of Wisconsin Press.
Merchant, Carolyn
  1992 *Radical ecology: The search for a livable world.* New York: Routledge.

Mesarovic, Mihajlo, and Eduard Pestel
    1974   *Mankind at the turning point: The second report to the Club of Rome.* New York: E. P. Dutton.

Mill, J. S.
    [1848] Principles of political economy with some of their applications to social
    1965   philosophy. In *Reprints of economic classics.* New York: Augustus M. Kelley.

Miller, Char
    2001   *Gifford Pinchot and the making of modern environmentalism.* Washington, DC: Island Press.

Miller, G. Tyler Jr.
    2004   *Living in the environment: Principles, connections, and solutions.* 13th ed. Pacific Grove, CA: Brooks/Cole–Thompson Learning.

Moore, Stephen
    1995   The coming age of abundance. In *The true state of the planet,* ed. Robert Bailey. New York: Free Press.

Nader, Ralph
    1965   *Unsafe at any speed: The designed-in dangers of the American automobile.* New York: Grossman.

Naess, Arne
    1973   The shallow and the deep, long-range ecology movement: A summary. *Inquiry* 16: 95–100.
    1984   In defence of the deep ecology movement. *Environmental Ethics* 6(3):265–70.
    1985   Identification as a source of deep ecological attitudes. In *Deep Ecology,* M. Tobias, ed., pp. 256–70. San Diego: Avant Books.
    1989   *Ecology, community and lifestyle.* Cambridge: Cambridge University Press.

Nasar, Sylvia
    1993   Kenneth Boulding, philosopher, poet, unorthodox economist, 83. *Raleigh News and Observer,* Saturday, March 20, p. 6B.

Nash, Roderick F.
    1967   *Wilderness and the American mind.* New Haven and London: Yale University Press.
    1989   *The rights of nature: A history of environmental ethics.* Madison: University of Wisconsin Press.

Nelson, Donald M.
    1946   *Arsenal of democracy: The story of American war production.* New York: Harcourt, Brace.

Newman, Steve
    1995   Earthweek: A diary of the planet. *Raleigh News and Observer,* October 30, p. 2C.

O'Riordan, Timothy
    1976   *Environmentalism.* London: Pion.

Pearce, David W., and R. Kerry Turner
    1990   *Economics of natural resources and the environment.* Baltimore: Johns Hopkins University Press.

Pepper, David
    1984   *The roots of modern environmentalism.* London: Croom Helm.
    1993   *Eco-socialism: From deep ecology to social justice.* London: Routledge.
Pestel, Eduard
    1989   *Beyond the limits to growth.* New York: Universe Books.
Pigou, A. C.
    1932   *The economics of welfare.* 4th ed. London: Macmillan.
Reed, Peter, and David Rothenberg
    1993   *Wisdom in the open air: The Norwegian roots of deep ecology.* Minneapolis: University of Minnesota Press.
Reich, Charles A.
    1970   *The greening of America.* New York: Random House.
Repetto, Ralph, William Magrath, Michael Wells, Christine Beer, and Fabrizio Rossini
    1989   *Wasting assets: Natural resources in the national income accounts.* Washington, DC: World Resources Institute.
Ricardo, David
    [1817] *On the principles of political economy and taxation.* First American ed. Washington, DC: Joseph Milligan.
    1819
Rothenberg, David
    1993   *Is it painful to think? Conversations with Arne Naess.* Minneapolis: University of Minnesota Press.
Rubin, Charles T.
    1994   *The green crusade: Rethinking the roots of environmentalism.* New York: Free Press.
Ryan, Alan
    1987   Mill, John Stuart. In *The New Palgrave: A dictionary of economics,* vol. 3, John Eatwell, Murray Milgate, and Peter Newman, eds., pp. 466–71. London: Macmillan.
Sagoff, Mark
    1988   *The economy of the earth: Philosophy, law and the environment.* Cambridge: Cambridge University Press.
Sale, Kirkpatrick
    1993   *The green revolution: The environmental movement, 1962–1992.* New York: Hill and Wang.
Scarce, Rik
    1990   *Eco-warriors: Understanding the radical environmental movement.* Chicago: Noble Press.
Schumacher, E. F.
    [1973] *Small is beautiful: Economics as if people mattered.* New York: Harper and Row.
    1989
Sessions, George
    1995   *Deep ecology for the 21st century.* Boston Shambhala Publications.
Silk, Leonard
    1974   Kenneth E. Boulding: The economics of peace and love. In *The Economists,* pp. 191–239. New York: Basic Books.

Simpson, R. David, Michael A. Toman, and Robert U. Ayres, eds.

2005   *Scarcity and growth revisited: Natural resources and the environment in the new millennium.* Washington, DC: Resources for the Future.

Sirico, Robert A.

1994   The false gods of Earth Day. *Wall Street Journal,* April 22, p. A12.

Smil, Vaclav

2004   Garrett James Hardin (Dallas 1915–Santa Barbara 2003). *American Scientist On-line* 92(1):8. http://www.americanscientist.org/template/AssetDetail/assetid/29864?&print=ye s (accessed January 28, 2005).

Smith, Adam

[1789] *An inquiry into the nature and causes of the wealth of nations.* New York:
1937   Random House.

Smith, V. Kerry

1980   The evaluation of natural resource adequacy: Elusive quest or frontier of economic analysis? *Land Economics* 56(3):257–98.

——., ed.

1979   *Scarcity and growth reconsidered.* Baltimore and London: Johns Hopkins University Press and Resources for the Future.

Smith, V. Kerry, and John V. Krutilla

1984   Economic growth, resource availability and environmental quality. *American Economic Review* 74(2):226–30.

Sorrell, Roger D.

1988   *St. Francis of Assisi and nature.* New York: Oxford University Press.

Sterling, Philip

1970   *Sea and earth: The life of Rachel Carson.* New York: Thomas Y. Crowell.

Swartzman, Daniel

1982   Cost-benefit analysis in environmental regulation: Sources of controversy. In *Cost-benefit analysis and environmental regulations: Politics, ethics, and methods,* D. Swartzman, R. A. Liroff, and K. G. Croke, eds., p. 58. Washington, DC: Conservation Foundation.

Taussig, F. W.

1987   Stationary state. In *The New Palgrave: A dictionary of economics,* vol. 4, John Eatwell, Murray Milgate and Peter Newman, eds., pp. 484–85. London: Macmillan.

Taylor, Paul W.

1983   In defense of biocentrism. *Environmental Ethics* 5:237–43.

Thoreau, Henry David

[1854] *Walden, or life in the woods, and on civil disobedience.* New York: New Ameri-
1960   can Library.

Tietenberg, Tom

1988   *Environmental and natural resource economics.* 2nd ed. Glenview, IL: Scott Foresman.

Train, Russell E.

1991   Religion and the environment: Providing leadership for ecological values. *Journal of Forestry* 89(9):12–15.

Udall, Stewart L.

1963   *The quiet crisis.* New York: Holt, Rinehart and Winston.

U.S. Department of Commerce

1994   *Statistical abstract of the United States.* Washington, DC: Government Printing Office.

Watson, Richard A.

1983   A critique of anti-anthropocentric biocentrism. *Environmental Ethics* 5:245–56.

White, Lynn jr.

1967   The historical roots of our ecological crisis. *Science* 155:1203–7.

1973   Continuing the conversation. In *Western man and environmental ethics: Attitudes toward nature and technology.* Reading, MA: Addison-Wesley.

Whitney, Elspeth

1993   Lynn White, ecotheology, and history. *Environmental Ethics* 15:151–69.

Wild, Peter

1979   Garrett Hardin and overpopulation: Lifeboats vs. mountain climbers. In *Pioneer conservationists of western America.* Missoula, MT: Mountain Press.

Wilson, James A.

1977   A test of the tragedy of the commons. In *Managing the commons,* Garrett Hardin and John Baden, eds. San Francisco: W. H. Freeman.

Wood, Barbara

1984   *E. F. Schumacher: His life and thought.* New York: Harper and Row.

World Commission on Environment and Development

1987   *Our common future.* Oxford and New York: Oxford University Press.

World Resources Institute

1992   *World resources, 1992–93: A guide to the global environment.* Oxford and New York: Oxford University Press.

1994   *World resources, 1994–95: A guide to the global environment.* Oxford and New York: Oxford University Press.

Worster, Donald

1994   *Nature's economy: A history of ecological ideas.* 2nd ed. Cambridge: Cambridge University Press.

Index

About the Author

Joseph Edward "Ed" de Steiguer is professor of natural resource economics and policy in the School of Natural Resources at the University of Arizona. He also holds joint academic appointments in the Department of Agricultural and Resource Economics and with the Arid Lands Resource Sciences Graduate Program. Previously, he was employed for twenty years as a research economist and policy analyst with the U.S. Forest Service. He has also held faculty appointments, both in forestry and the social sciences, at Texas A&M University and North Carolina State University, and was an adjunct faculty member at Duke University's Nicolas School of the Environment. de Steiguer has also been professeur associé at L'Ecole Nationale du Génie Rural des Eaux et des Forêt in Nancy, France, where he lectured in forest economics.

Ed holds a bachelor of business administration in economics from Lamar University, a master of forestry from Stephen F. Austin State University and a Ph.D. in forestry from Texas A&M University. He was named, in 2001, a Udall Fellow by the Udall Center for Studies of Public Policy and the Institute for Studies of Planet Earth. He is the author of more than one hundred books and articles dealing with forestry and the environment. Ed's teaching and research interests focus on policies and laws related to planning on the U.S. national forests. His hobbies include playing the guitar, flyfishing, golf, and bicycling. He also enjoys watching thoroughbred horses race.